Bert Bielefeld (Ed.)

Building Technology

Bert Bielefeld (Ed.)

Building
Technology

BIRKHÄUSER
BASEL

Contents

Electro-Planning _163

Lighting Design _231

Appendix _285

Foreword

Design in architecture is a creative process that is characterized by abstract ideas. As soon as the initial considerations and ideas have been determined, structural and technical conditions have to be taken into account. Today's conveniences in the areas of heating, ventilation, water, light, media supply, etc. ensure that the planning of building technology services is not a separate, additional factor, but rather an integral part of the planning process. Due to the high degree of networking between components and the complex systems that provide and control buildings today, it is essential for architects to understand the technology and the associated rationale. The present series *Basics Building Technologies* provides an introduction to the various disciplines and offers the reader an overall overview, which is necessary to fully understand the specific specialist publications.

Basics Room Conditioning focuses on the topics of heat and air with regard to creating an atmosphere of wellbeing for users and residents in buildings. The conditioning of interior spaces extends far beyond the purely technical implementation of heating and ventilation systems. Firstly, the basic requirements of comfort have to be defined. These can vary greatly depending on the function, use, and climatic conditions. The principles in clearly determining needs and requirements at an early stage of project planning will directly effect later technical implementation with the aim of keeping the energy supply as low as possible. Variations of mechanical and natural ventilation are presented and placed within a meaningful context in order to determine the most appropriate system. Temperature control is explained systematically with regard to energy supply and potential energy storage, from the distribution within the building to the transfer in the rooms, and is then placed in relation to the ventilation system.

Basics Water Cycles in buildings deals with the infrastructure of drinking water supply and wastewater disposal and prevention. As an interface between drinking water and sewage, the distribution, consumption, and disposal of water within buildings plays an important role in architectural planning. The layout of water supply and disposal and the technical requirements influence the location of plumbing and kitchen areas in the floor plan. In addition, the avoidance of high levels of water consumption is an important issue in technical building planning. This volume describes the journey through the house along the various positions, each with their specific tasks and requirements in a step-by-step process, enabling readers to fully understand the connections and to integrate this knowledge into their own designs.

Basics Electro-Planning describes the specialist area of domestic technology, which is generally managed by specialist planners. If recently the electrical installation of a building consisted primarily of the supply of electricity and light via cables, sockets, and switches, nowadays complex networked components and intelligent building control systems connect built components such as windows and doors to building automation as well as the provision of light, air, and heat via building technology. The complexity of electrical planning in buildings has increased exponentially, not least due to steadily increasing user and energy-saving requirements. In order to be able to integrate the guiding principles as well as the technical systems and the interface to all other specialist areas in the design from the outset, this publication provides a clear explanation of the connections and describes the full range of installations utilized.

Basics Lighting Design bridges the gap between electrical planning and architectural design processes. As natural and artificial lighting effect the perception of architecture as a whole or in detail, allowing rooms to be used as intended, it is a fundamental design element. Demands on lighting planning are as diverse as the needs of users. Intelligent solutions in design unite design requirements, functions, and technology into a holistic solution in order to reduce the energy requirements of the building and even to partially avoid the necessity for artificial lighting by the clever use of natural lighting. In addition to the physical properties of the lighting and the technical feasibility, *Basics Lighting Planning* provides an introduction and a basic understanding of the work of architects and technical planners in order to be able to integrate lighting as a design element during the design process.

The interplay of the various topics described above provides an overview of the individual themes as well as the networks and connections of the separate disciplines. Thus the series provides an introduction and a basic understanding of the work of architects and professional planners who have to integrate building structure, function, and technology into a single, holistic solution. Despite the complexity of the subject matter, the reader is provided with an efficient and user-friendly reference.

Bert Bielefeld, Editor

Oliver Klein, Jörg Schlenger

Room
Conditioning

Introduction

The temperature of
the human body

While many species are able to adjust their body temperatures to suit their surroundings, humans require an almost constant body temperature of 37 ± 0.8 °C. As the outside temperature fluctuates depending on the climate zone, time of the day and season, the human body attempts to maintain this temperature using an automatic regulation system, in which the surface of the skin gives off more or less heat, according to the ambient temperature and the level of physical activity. For example, if the body temperature rises, sweat glands allow moisture to emerge onto the skin, where it evaporates and gives off heat into the environment. If the body temperature drops, the skin contracts to reduce the area giving off heat, and the hairs on the skin stand up ("goose pimples"). The body also creates additional heat by quivering its muscles (shivering).

Climatic influences
and compensation

However, this temperature regulation system also has its limits, and the human skin can only fulfill this task to a certain extent. Clothing as additional "thermal insulation," the "second skin," and buildings, the "third skin," provide the solution.

In human history, the discovery of fire was surely the most important step for humankind in achieving independence from climatic conditions and the seasons. It was not only the entry into the fossil fuel age, i.e. energy conversion dependent on a continuous supply of energy sources; the "third skin" could then have artificial heat and light – and thus it was also the original form of room conditioning. Today's problems of environmental destruction associated with the use of fossil fuels are well known to us and omnipresent.

Energy-optimized
room conditioning

The term "room conditioning" is understood as the creation of an indoor climate for people to enjoy a feeling of wellbeing, which is above all unaffected by any outside influences by tempering (heating or cooling), lighting and the introduction of sufficient fresh air (ventilation); with suitable technology, this can lead to an ultimately uniform architecture that is unrelated to its location. In extreme cases, these buildings are hermetically sealed with glass facades, fully air-conditioned by the extensive use of high technology, and can be found built to practically the same design in all climatic regions of the world. In addition to disturbing user sensitivities, another disadvantage is the very high energy requirement for heating, cooling and lighting. The fact that 50% of the total energy consumed worldwide is used in buildings shows that other ways must be devised to provide energy-optimized room conditioning.

A building should always be designed to provide comfort using only a small amount of additional energy. First, all available constructional (passive) measures for room conditioning should be exploited, taking into account local conditions, before turning to technical (active) measures.

> Chapter Design principles

The effective combination of passive and active measures in which all the technical components are mutually compatible is always crucial to obtaining an energy-optimized overall concept for room conditioning. The following chapters explain the basic principles and their various interactions, and are intended to enable an individual and balanced room conditioning system to be developed for every building project.

Design principles

COMFORT REQUIREMENTS
Thermal comfort

The term "comfort" describes a feeling of wellbeing, which is influenced by a number of factors. In the field of building services systems, it generally refers to thermal comfort, describing a state in which the body's thermal balance is in equilibrium with the climatic conditions of the surroundings. The user perceives the climatic conditions of the surroundings as neither too hot nor too cold.

Importance of comfort
Thermal comfort is not a luxury; it is an important criterion for being able to use a building fully for its intended purpose. The quality of the space in a building has many different effects on the ability of its occupants to concentrate and work effectively, as well as their state of health (e.g. in offices). If comfort is inadequate in production areas, this may give rise to premature fatigue with the corresponding consequences for safety at work. The reliable provision of an indoor climate appropriate to use is therefore an important quality characteristic of a successful building concept.

Influence factors

Our perception of comfort depends on a number of influence factors, which are shown in Figure 1.

The designers of a building are normally only able to influence physical conditions, some of which are described in detail in the following chapters. However, the clothing and activity of the user clearly affect his or her perception of comfort. Along with the user's ability to adapt and acclimatize, both belong to a group of "intermediate" factors and are influenced by both physical and physiological conditions.

In some cases, other factors may also play an important role in the preliminary building design, the knowledge of which and the conscious creation of a building concept specifically for a defined user group are often indispensable for the design process. For example, older people often find higher temperatures comfortable, which must be taken into account by providing appropriately higher room air temperatures when designing a nursing home for the elderly.

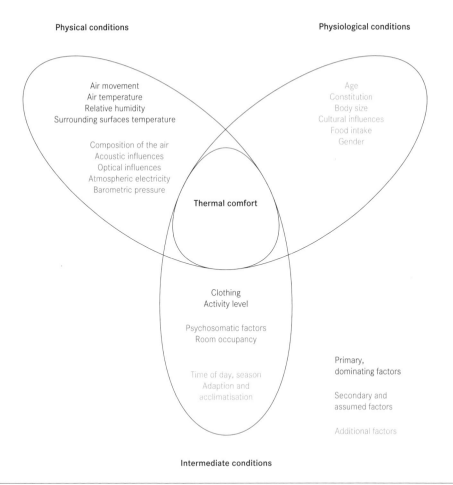

Air movement
Air temperature
Relative humidity
Surrounding surfaces temperature

Composition of the air
Acoustic influences
Optical influences
Atmospheric electricity
Barometric pressure

Age
Constitution
Body size
Cultural influences
Food intake
Gender

Thermal comfort

Clothing
Activity level

Psychosomatic factors
Room occupancy

Time of day, season
Adaption and
acclimatisation

Primary,
dominating factors

Secondary and
assumed factors

Additional factors

Intermediate conditions

Fig. 1: Factors influencing thermal comfort

Physical conditions

After air temperature, the most important physical factor is the av- Air and radiation
erage temperature of the surrounding surfaces. Like any other body, the temperature
human body is also continuously exchanging heat with surrounding surfaces by means of radiation. Depending on the distance and the
temperature difference between two bodies, more or less heat will be

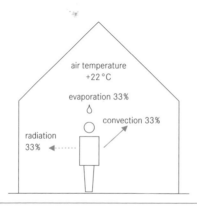

air temperature
+22 °C

evaporation 33%

convection 33%

radiation
33%

Fig. 2: An outline of the way the human body gives off heat

given off or taken up in one or the other direction. This process affects
the body's heat balance.

Slight differences between air and radiation temperatures may still
be perceived as comfortable by the human body. If the difference between
air and radiation temperatures, or even the difference between radiation
temperatures, is too great, this causes discomfort. This is why you feel
uncomfortable standing near a very warm or very cold radiating surface
(e.g. a poorly thermally insulated building component or window), despite
pleasant room air temperatures. > Fig. 3

Operative
temperature
As the human body cannot detect absolute temperatures, only more
or less intense heat loss or gain by the skin, people's temperature
sensitivity depends on the exchange of heat with the air and the surround-

○ **Note:** With little physical activity, normal clothing
and ordinary room temperatures, one third of the heat
the human body loses is through radiation, convection
and evaporation (see Fig. 2).

■ **Tip:** With predominantly sedentary activities, e.g. in
offices or homes, ceilings that are too warm or wall or
window surfaces that are too cold quickly cause discomfort. The temperature difference between surfaces
and room air should not be more than 3 Kelvin (K).
Within certain limits, higher air temperatures can compensate for low surface temperatures and vice versa.

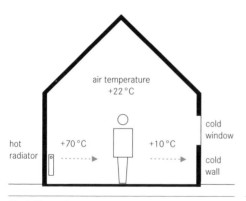

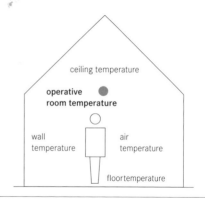

Fig. 3: Discomfort from asymmetrical radiation temperatures

Fig. 4: Factors affecting the operative room temperature

ing surfaces in the room. The combined effect of air and radiation temperatures on the human senses is expressed by the "operative temperature" (or "perceived temperature"), which has become accepted as an authoritative design parameter for assessing comfort. > Fig. 4

The operative room temperature can differ in various parts of the room depending on the distance to the room surfaces. For design purposes, it is calculated as the average air temperature and the average radiation temperature of all room surfaces, and is used to calculate the thermal state of the room.   ○

A further factor affecting our perception of comfort is the relative   Humidity
humidity of the air, because the human body gives off part of the heat through evaporation. Depending on the humidity, a given temperature

○ **Note:** The recommended ranges of operative temperatures vary depending on use and also in international comparisons. For Europe, according to European standard EN 15251, the recommended range for light, sedentary activities is about 20–26 °C. Many other counties have their own regulations, which often differ from this range.

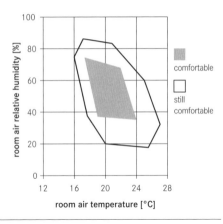

Fig. 5: Influence of room air humidity on the perception
of comfort shown in relation to room temperature
(after Leusden/Freymark)

state with otherwise identical boundary conditions may be perceived as
warm or cold. > Fig. 5

　　In addition to moisture loads (people and plants in the room), another
influence on the relative humidity in the room is the outdoor air humidity (i.e. the climate). Relative humidity also varies with fluctuations in
room air temperature. Thus, warming of cold outdoor air in winter nor-
○ mally results in lower relative humidity indoors.

○ **Note:** A relative humidity of about 50% (± 15%) is
often recommended for most uses (e.g. light sedentary
activities in homes or offices). However, it must taken
into account that very few room conditioning systems
(e.g. full air conditioning systems) allow the user to
have complete control over relative humidity.

Air movement can have a considerable influence on thermal comfort independently of the humidity. Draughts can be caused by air moving at excessive speeds and by eddies (high degree of turbulence in the air flow). The perception of comfort depends on the temperature of the air: the lower the air temperature, the sooner a movement of air is perceived as uncomfortable, while a movement of warm air is tolerated for rather longer. The higher the air temperature, the less strong eddies are a problem.

■

Although the composition of the air at ground level is generally constant, it is nevertheless able to influence the overall perception of comfort. This is because of the widely varying levels of pollution and temperature-dependent moisture content of the air that can occur in particular situations.

○

Air pollutants can arise from outside and inside a building. While the outdoor influences are mainly a function of the building location (road traffic etc.) and the positions and sizes of the ventilation openings, the principal indoor influences can be identified as the emissions of the building (vapors given off from the materials used, other materials in the building or uses of the building), as well as the people present in the building (carbon dioxide content of their exhaled air, water vapor, odors etc.). Eliminating these emissions and/or providing adequate air exchange should enable any specified limits for the various substances in the air to be observed and discomfort – or damage to health – to be avoided.

The carbon dioxide content of the room air is particularly significant. It is added to by the breath of the people in the room and only has to reach a few parts per 1000 before it becomes a problem. Contrary to popular opinion, it is not a lack of oxygen (O_2) but an excess of CO_2 that is the reason for "bad" or "stale" air and provides the need for air changes.

■ **Tip:** For light, sedentary activities in homes or offices ventilated through an adequate number of large air distribution outlets, the limit on the average air velocity is often is often recommended as about 0.2 m/s in conditions of little turbulence (approx. 5%). Local zones of discomfort caused by higher values, e.g. in the direct vicinity of air distribution outlets, must also be considered. More precise information is available, e.g. in European standard EN 15251.

○ **Note:** Dry air consists of 78.1% nitrogen (N_2), 20.93% oxygen (O_2), 0.03% carbon dioxide (CO_2), and 0.94% argon and other noble gases. Furthermore, "normal air" contains a varying proportion of water vapor and pollutants in the form of nitrogen oxide, sulfur dioxide, waste gases, dust, suspended particles and many kinds of micro-organisms.

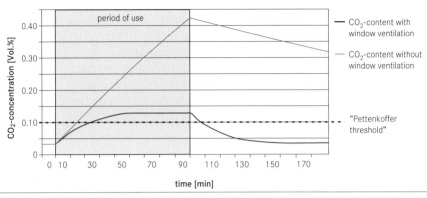

Fig. 6: CO_2 concentration in a classroom (150 m³, 30 people) during and after a period of occupation (90 min.) with and without ventilation through tilted windows (air changes 3/h)

Figure 6 shows the increase in CO_2 during the time of occupation of a classroom.

Other pollutants   If the air we breathe is contaminated with additional pollutants, e.g. from smoking, emissions from the materials used or from manufacturing processes in the workplace, then there is an additional requirement for fresh air. This requirement is determined by the concentration of pollutants, i.e. the room air must be kept within permissible limits by providing an adequate rate of air changes.

○ **Note:** The "Pettenkoffer threshold" established by Munich doctor and hygienist Max von Pettenkoffer says that the CO_2 content of the room air should not exceed 0.10%. This comparatively stringent requirement is used as a comfort criterion for room air quality in most European countries. Adequate means of ventilation must be provided to prevent this value from being exceeded.

○ **Note:** The capacity to adapt has only recently been taken into account in building design. In new regulations, such as European standard EN 15251, the recommended comfort ranges are therefore defined with reference to the coincident outdoor air temperatures. It is expected that other countries will incorporate this new knowledge into their design guidelines.

Tab. 1: Example values of heat given off by people engaged in various levels of activity based on DIN 1946-2

Activity	Total heat given off per person Reference value W
Stationary activities performed while sitting, such as reading or writing	120
Very light physical activities performed while standing or sitting	150
Light physical activities	190
Medium heavy to heavy physical activity	more than 270

Intermediate conditions

When engaged in physical effort, the human body expends more energy and needs to give off heat to the environment. > Tab. 1 Less motion expends less energy and the amount of heat given off does not have to be as great. The user's level of activity therefore has just as much influence on his or her perception of comfort. The lower the activity level, the higher the temperature must be to be perceived as comfortable. Moreover, people engaged in little physical activity (e.g. sitting still at a desk) generally tolerate smaller departures from the "ideal temperature" than those with higher activity levels (sport, physical work etc.).

User activity

Independently of the physical activity, clothing influences the amount of heat given off and therefore the body's heat balance. The less clothing is worn, the greater the amount of heat given off by the human body to the air and the surrounding surfaces. Higher temperatures and warm surfaces (e.g. underfloor heating) are often provided in areas where people go barefoot or naked (e.g. in showers or saunas) to avoid discomfort. However, putting on more clothing reduces the body's sensitivity to fluctuations in the ambient temperature because of the clothing's insulation effect.

Clothing

The human body's ability to become used to a specific climatic conditions (e.g. heating periods) in the short, medium or long term, is described as adaptation or acclimatization. This capacity to adapt can therefore mean that initially uncomfortable conditions are perceived as pleasant or at least less distressing over time.

Adaptation capacity

○

DETERMINING THE REQUIREMENTS

One of the main requirements of a building is to ensure an appropriate, comfortable room climate in terms of the specified criteria throughout the whole year. While these requirements apply to all the various climate zones, the necessary measures will vary from zone to zone.

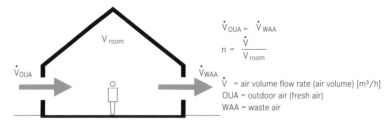

$$\dot{V}_{OUA} = \dot{V}_{WAA}$$

$$n = \frac{\dot{V}}{V_{room}}$$

$\dot{V}$ = air volume flow rate (air volume) [m³/h]
OUA = outdoor air (fresh air)
WAA = waste air

Fig. 7: Air change rate (n)

Ventilation requirement

To ensure the air inside a building is of hygienic quality, the room air must be replaced at specified intervals by conducting away the used air and pollutants and replacing them with fresh air. This is generally accomplished by having opening windows in the external walls, but often by mechanical ventilation systems. > Chapter Ventilation systems How often the whole volume of room air must be replaced with fresh air and within what period, e.g. an hour, is given by the air change rate (n). > Fig. 7

Required minimum air change rate
How frequently the air in the room must be replaced to ensure healthy room air must be considered above all from the point of view of a room's use. The values of air change rate given in specialist literature often differ, and should therefore be taken only as average values for typical room sizes, occupancy densities, and pollution loads. They are particularly useful for preliminary design. > Tab. 2

○ Note: Fresh air is air from an unpolluted, natural environment. In ventilation engineering it is different from outdoor air, which is sucked in from outside the building, where the air may be hot and polluted. The CO_2 concentration and any airborne pollutants are generally found in outdoor air but the quantities are less than in indoor air. The fresh air demand is normally satisfied by introducing outside air; the term "outdoor air" will therefore be used in the rest of this book.

● Example: Consider a living room with an area of 20 m², a clear ceiling height of 2.50 m, and therefore a volume of 50 m³, occupied by one person. According to Table 3 it would be sufficient to replace half of the air in the room with fresh outdoor air in one hour (n = 0.5/h). Table 7 (page 44) shows for how long, for example, a window has to be open. If the room were occupied by two people, it would require an outdoor air flow rate ·V of 50 m3/h and therefore an air change rate of 1.0/h would be required, i.e. the room air must be completely replaced with outdoor air once per hour.

It is better to calculate the required quantity of fresh outdoor air to be introduced into the room per unit of time, the (outdoor air) flow rate $\dot{V}$ (usually expressed in m^3/h) taking into account the expected pollutant load and specific emissions. An air change rate can be calculated from the above flow rate and room volumes, and used as an additional design parameter.

Outside air flow rate

In rooms where the air is not seriously affected by pollutant emissions from building materials or from specific uses, the main factor is the people using the room.

As explained earlier, > Chapter Design principles, Comfort requirements a person's fresh air requirement is met by replacing the room air with air that does not exceed the recommended upper limit for CO_2 concentration. The required outdoor air flow rate depends on the type of use, the anticipated pollutant load of the room, and the number of people in the room. In practice, the values in the table are used. > Tab. 3

●

The air change should, particularly when outdoor temperatures are low, provide only the rate of air changes necessary for hygiene, because an increased supply of outdoor air always results in higher ventilation heat losses. > see below On the other hand, a higher air change rate with high room temperatures can also be used to remove excessive heat.

Different air flow rates

Tempering demand

Tempering demand (heating and cooling energy demand) always arises from a disturbance to the energy balance of a building or room.

Tab. 2: Benchmarks air change rate

Type of room	n in 1/h
Living room	0.6–0.7
Toilets	2–4
Offices	4–8
Canteens	6–8
Bars	4–12
Cinemas	4–8
Lecture theatres	6–8
Committee rooms	6–12
Department stores	4–6

Tab. 3: Recommended minimum outdoor air flow rate on the basis of DIN EN 13779 and DIN 1946-2

Room type	Outdoor air volume flow rate $\dot{V}_{AUL\,min}$	
	related to person in $m^3/(h \times person)$	related to area in $m^3/(h \times m^2)$
Living rooms	25	–
Cinemas, concert halls, museums, reading rooms, sports halls, retail space	20	10–20
Auditoriums, classrooms, seminar rooms and conference rooms	30	15
Individual cell offices	40	4
Open-plan offices	60	6
Bars	30	8

Energy balance
of a room

Room temperatures should remain in a range that is considered comfortable for the room's use. Heat is drawn out of a building by transmission (flow of heat through the building skin because of the temperature differences between indoors and outdoors) and ventilation (exchange of air between indoors and outdoors through uncontrollable leakage points in the building skin and uncontrolled natural or mechanical ventilation). The entry of solar radiation through transparent building components and the heat given off by equipment and persons inside the building brings heat into the building. > Fig. 8

Despite having a building designed for the local climate (e.g. a highly thermally insulated building skin, solar screening etc.), it may still be necessary from time to time, depending on the location of the building, to introduce heat into or remove excessive heat from a building or room artificially (by building services systems), in order to achieve the desired indoor temperature. As this is always linked with an additional energy demand, the objective should be to avoid or keep this additional tempering demand as low as possible by adopting intelligent architecture and building services technology matched to the local climatic conditions.
> Chapter Design principles, Covering the demands

Heating energy
demand

The heat losses of a building or room must therefore be compensated with a corresponding amount of heat from a heating system if the solar and internal gains are insufficient. > Fig. 9 The annual heat energy demand of a building is the sum of the heat losses, taking into account the relevant heat gains, calculated over the year. To be able to assess the thermal quality of a building, it is normally necessary to calculate the annual heat energy demand per square meter of usable space [$kWh/(m^2a)$]. This energy parameter allows buildings to be characterized and classified in energy terms in accordance with national energy standards.

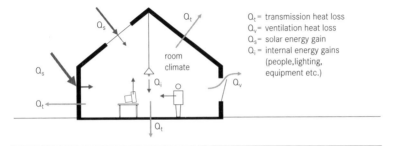

Fig. 8: Factors influencing the heat balance of a building

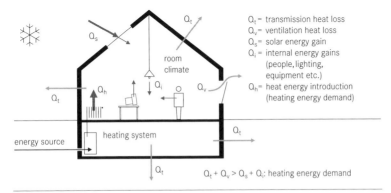

Fig. 9: Components of the heating energy demand

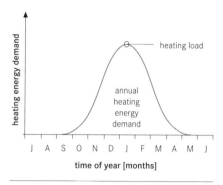

heating energy demand

heating load

annual heating energy demand

J A S O N D J F M A M J

time of year [months]

Fig. 10: Heat load and annual heating energy
demand (Central Europe)

Tab. 4: Standard indoor temperatures for heated rooms (in accordance with DIN EN 12831
Suppl. 1), where the client has not supplied any other values

Building or room type	Operative temperature [°C]
Living and sleeping rooms	+ 20.0
Offices, committee rooms, exhibition rooms, main stairwells, booking halls	+ 20.0
Hotel rooms	+ 20.0
General retail halls and shops	+ 20.0
General classrooms	+ 20.0
Theaters and concert halls	+ 20.0
WCs	+ 20.0
Bath and shower rooms, bathrooms, changing rooms, examination rooms (in general, any use involving undressing)	+ 24.0
Heated auxiliary rooms (corridors, stairwells)	+ 15.0

Heating load   To design the heating system (heat generation and distribution system) it is necessary to determine the heat load, and hence the maximum
required heat output. This value indicates the amount of heat (in W or
kW) that must be supplied to a building on the coldest day of the year to
compensate for heat losses and achieve the required indoor temperatures. > Tab. 4 and Fig. 10

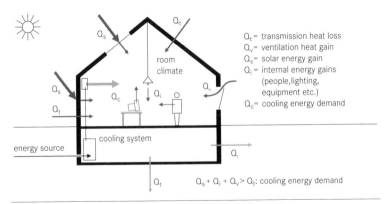

Q_t = transmission heat loss
Q_v = ventilation heat gain
Q_s = solar energy gain
Q_i = internal energy gains
(people, lighting,
equipment etc.)
Q_c = cooling energy demand

$Q_s + Q_i + Q_v > Q_t$: cooling energy demand

Fig. 11: Creation of the cooling energy demand

Cooling energy demand arises when the heat gains (as a result of solar radiation entering the building and internal heat loads) are greater than the heat losses (as a result of ventilation and transmission losses) and the excess heat cannot be effectively stored in thermal storage masses. > Chapter Design principles, Covering the demands Room temperatures rise and active measures, such as building services systems, cannot prevent the room temperatures exceeding the maximum desired values. > Fig. 11 ○

Cooling energy demand

The extremely complex physical interactions of the factors involved makes it difficult to predict the anticipated cooling energy demand precisely. In addition to the external and internal loads, the designer must also take into account the processes of heat take-up and emission of the thermal storage mass of the building construction. Dynamic simulation software is normally required to enable precise analysis of a situation in hourly simulation steps in critical or difficult cases.

Calculation of the cooling energy demand

In normal design situations, therefore, an exact estimate of the cooling energy load is often not made, and a cooling load calculation is performed instead, based on static (constant) conditions. It allows, in particular, an estimate to be made of the maximum cooling load, which

Cooling load

○ **Note:** When outdoor temperatures are high, in addition to the heat gains from the entry of solar radiation and internal heat loads (people, equipment and lighting), the heat gains from ventilation and poorly insulated building components also contribute to the cooling energy demand.

Tab. 5: Examples of internal heat loads

	Output when operating
Computer with monitor	150 W
Laser printer	190 W
Person, sedentary activity	120 W
Lighting	10 W/m² of plan area

can be useful in the design of the system. However, this simplified approach often leads to over-sized systems and is therefore no substitute for a more precise analysis by a heating and ventilation engineer.

For the initial selection of a cooling system in a preliminary building design, it is helpful to be able to estimate the approximate heat load of a room and compare it with the capacities of various cooling systems. ● Table 5 gives some approximate values for common heat loads in an office.

The designer must check the extent to which the demand calculated using a simplified cooling load calculation can also be satisfied from thermal storage masses and ventilation. This usually leads to a more economically efficient size of system.

COVERING THE DEMANDS
Avoidance principle

In order to keep the energy demand of a building as low as possible, in addition to the end energy required for heating, cooling and ventilation, a designer must also take into account user-specific demands (e.g.

● **Example:** The expected cooling load for an individual cell office with a floor area of 10 m2 can be roughly calculated as follows:
According to Table 5, the anticipated internal peak load based on a floor area of 10 m² is 560 W (150+190+120+100) or 56 W/m². However, as loads from devices such as printers or lighting are not constant, these values may be considered a little too high. A reduction of the operating times for printers and lighting to, for example, 50% results in an internal heat load of 41.5 W/m². Solar radiation entering the building through the facade must also be taken into account.

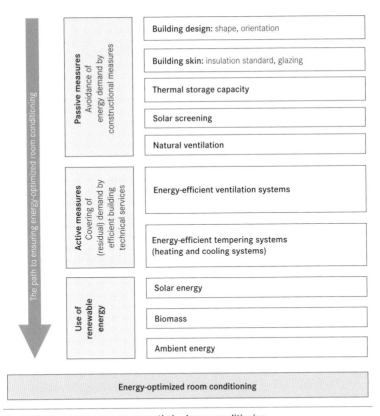

The path to ensuring energy-optimized room conditioning

Passive measures — Avoidance of energy demand by constructional measures
Building design: shape, orientation
Building skin: insulation standard, glazing
Thermal storage capacity
Solar screening
Natural ventilation

Active measures — Covering of (residual) demand by efficient building technical services
Energy-efficient ventilation systems
Energy-efficient tempering systems (heating and cooling systems)

Use of renewable energy
Solar energy
Biomass
Ambient energy

Energy-optimized room conditioning

Fig. 12: Measures to ensure energy-optimized room conditioning

electrical consumers such as computers, machinery etc.). A mixture of different passive and active measures may be used to avoid the energy demand in the first place or provide the necessary amount of energy.
> Fig. 12

Passive measures

Passive measures can be used without significant energy cost to influence heat gains and losses. Certainly, the desired room conditions may not always be achieved, but the effects of the passive measures are in the right direction, and active measures further reduce the demand (i.e. the energy demand). There are various options for passive measures, which depend, to some extent, on the fundamental architectural aspects of a building and should therefore be considered at a very early stage in the planning process.

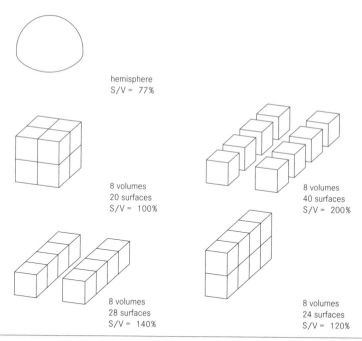

hemisphere
S/V = 77%

8 volumes
20 surfaces
S/V = 100%

8 volumes
40 surfaces
S/V = 200%

8 volumes
28 surfaces
S/V = 140%

8 volumes
24 surfaces
S/V = 120%

Fig. 13: Proportion of surface area for the same volume (not including the area in plan)

Building shape

A building interacts with the outside world through its skin. The dimensions of this heat-transmitting thermal skin also determine the amount of heat transferred. The building shape is therefore a very important design parameter for a building's energy balance. The energetic characteristic for the building cubature is called the S/V ratio, which is the ratio of the area of heat-transmitting building skin to the enclosed building volume. > Fig. 13

The various parameters such as room heights, daylight provision in the depth of the room, or functional requirements are normally determined in the design of a building, which then limits the scope of energy optimization to be gained from the building shape. The final building solution often involves a layout with several independent component objects (separate buildings) and particular layouts in plan (end-linked blocks etc.), which leads to comparatively large surface areas with the corresponding energy effects. Compact shapes and the smallest number of separate buildings offer energetically better solutions.

Alignment and climate zones

Orientation and climatic zoning within a building can make the most of solar gain to the advantage of energy saving and comfort. In a residential building characterized by a high heating energy demand (e.g. in northern Europe), the rooms with the highest temperature requirements (e.g. living rooms) should be oriented with their largest glazed areas facing the sun so as to maximize the benefits of solar gain. Rooms with lower temperatures (e.g. bedrooms) can face away from the sun. A highly thermally loaded room (e.g. a conference room with a high occupancy rate) should be oriented away from the sun if possible, to avoid additional overheating and any cooling loads from the entry of solar radiation. In addition, zones with unallocated uses and low requirements for temperature and comfort (e.g. circulation areas) can also be placed near the main usage areas to act as buffer zones between the indoor and outdoor climates.

Thermal insulation acts as a barrier between the inside and the outside space of a building. The insulation standard is therefore a measure of the thermal quality of the heat-transmitting building skin. In moderate climatic zones where the outdoor temperatures fluctuate only a little during the course of a day or a year, insulation is usually less important, but there are the occasional exceptions. A good standard of insulation is generally considered useful for avoiding heating and cooling energy demands in hot as much as in cold regions. Insulation standard

Transparent components (windows, skylights etc.) are of special importance here because the insulation standard of a window is usually poorer than that of an opaque component. Depending on the window quality and the building location, the advantages of solar gain through large windows may be cancelled out by increased heat loss in winter.

Every material has some ability to store heat and release it again over time. The amount of heat stored and given out over time depends on the material of the components enclosing the room (walls, floor and ceiling). Concrete or masonry blocks, for example, store more heat than wood or gypsum plasterboard. This is expressed as the "thermal mass" of a room or building. > Fig. 14 Thermal storage

Although thermal mass has no direct influence on thermal gains and losses, it is very important to heating and cooling loads and hence the energy demand of a building at any particular time: large thermal masses can store and release more heat from the room air and therefore avoid heating or cooling demand. As a rule, large thermal masses also improve comfort, because surface temperatures rise with increasing air temperatures and take longer to fall with decreasing temperatures.

The solar screening of a building is one of the most important passive measures for room conditioning. The amount of heat entering the Solar screening

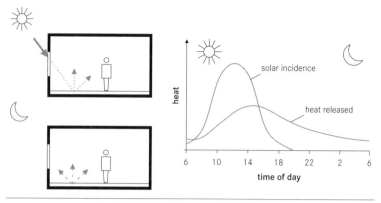

Fig. 14: Principle of thermal storage

building, as already indicated, significantly affects the energy demand. Solar screening must therefore be able to fulfill, as far as possible, the opposing goals of maximizing the amount of solar energy entering the room in cold weather and avoiding overheating in hot weather.

Solar screening may be classified as fixed or flexible. Fixed measures such as window sizes, orientation, shading by other buildings (buildings that are part of the project or nearby buildings, canopies, trees etc.) and the overall total solar energy transmittance of the glass used cannot be varied according to the season or the time of day, which results in disadvantages compared with flexible systems. > Fig. 15

○ **Note:** Further information about the design of windows and solar screening elements can be found in *Basics Facade Apertures* by Roland Krippner and Florian Musso, Birkhäuser Verlag, 2008.

■ **Tip:** Depending on use, solar radiation entering the room can cause critical situations at any time of year. This is often the case, for example, for modern office buildings with high internal loads. In combination with a good insulation standard, even in temperate climates (such as in Germany) these buildings have a heating energy demand on very few days of the year. In such cases, for example with the use of large glazed areas, it is particularly important to check that overheating does not occur in summer.

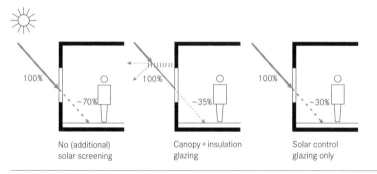

Fig. 15: Effect of fixed solar screening systems in combination with insulation glazing or solar control glazing

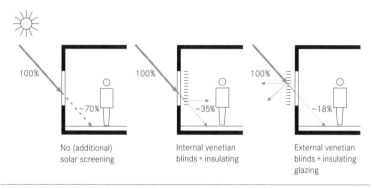

Fig. 16: The effect of solar screening systems in combination with insulating glazing

Flexible measures (Venetian or roller blinds etc.) allow the user short-term influence over how much solar radiation enters the room. In this way the heating energy demand in winter can be reduced as much as possible, while overheating (and the cooling energy demand) is avoided in summer. Flexible systems are therefore preferred to fixed systems. Figure 16 shows the effect of flexible solar screening systems.

Natural ventilation is also considered a passive room conditioning measure. As well as satisfying the outside air demand of a building without using energy for ventilation, it is also possible to conduct warm air out of the building and reduce the cooling loads. The special considerations in the design of natural ventilation concepts and the limits of natural ventilation are described in more detail in the chapter on ventilation systems.

Natural ventilation

Active measures

The energy demand of a building that cannot be fulfilled by passive measures must be covered actively, by introducing energy. The use of active systems may also bring advantages, although perhaps in other areas. Every concept must therefore be considered as a whole, with all its components and energy sources.

Efficiency increases

When considering the provision for the remaining energy demand of a building, it is important that the components used work as efficiently as possible. The designer must ensure that the losses involved in supplying, distributing and transferring energy into the room are as low as possible. There are a multitude of different components available for this, each with its own advantages and disadvantages. However, the components cannot be freely combined with one another. An integrated approach to the design must be used so as not to prevent the development of potential advantages by making poor initial decisions. Figure 17 gives an example of how to increase the efficiency of heating systems.

Energy transfer

The selection of the transfer system particularly depends on "radiation proportion" and "controllability".

A heating or cooling body emits its energy into the room by a combination of radiation and convection (the heat is "carried off" by the air). Radiating heat transfer systems are generally advantageous because of the strong influence of room surface temperatures on the operative room temperatures and therefore on people's perception of comfort in a room.

> Chapter Design principles, Comfort requirements

The speed with which a transfer system is able to react to changes in the controls (e.g. by opening or closing a valve) reflects its "controllability". This property is particularly significant if rooms have varying uses
● or thermal loads.

● **Beispiel:** A conference room is kept at the desired temperature in winter by a heating system. When the conference begins, the room fills with people, all with bodies giving off heat, which means that additional heating is no longer required. In this situation the heating system must be able to reduce its output immediately to avoid overheating and unnecessary energy use.

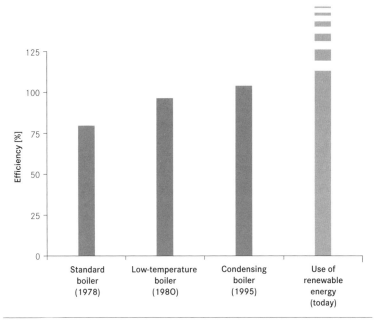

Fig. 17: Increasing the efficiency (expressed as calorific value) of heating systems

Combinations of sluggish radiating surfaces to cover the basic load and quick-reacting air systems for the peaks are therefore often adopted for rooms with frequently changing conditions and high comfort requirements. In these combinations, their disadvantages cancel each other out to produce a powerful, efficient system. Such solutions are associated with relatively high capital costs for their installation. > Chapter Tempering systems, Heat and cold transfer

The transport and distribution of energy from the generator to the transfer station is also important for the overall concept. The first thing to consider is that losses occur every time water or air is transported through pipes or ducts. One part of these losses is due to friction on the inside of the pipes, while another is due to temperature losses, so that the temperature of the medium has often dropped by the time it reaches the transfer station. Pipe lengths should therefore generally be kept as short and as well insulated as possible to minimize these losses.

Distribution

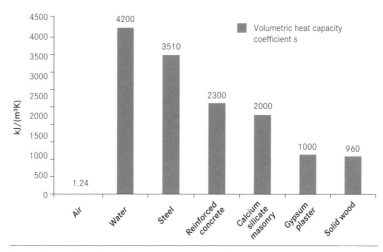

Fig. 18: Comparison of the thermal storage capacity of various substances and materials

The selection of the transport medium is of crucial importance. Water and other liquids can store many more times the amount of heat than air.
> Fig. 18

Selecting the
transport medium When account is taken of the electricity required for the electric fan or pump, this demonstrates that water as a medium for transporting energy is considerably more efficient than air. In terms of the auxiliary energy required for the transport of heat or cold, a water-operated system is preferable to a purely air-operated system. Air-operated systems can be viable, for example, if small heating or cooling loads to be covered are small and a ventilation system has to be used for other reasons.
> Chapter Tempering systems, Heat and cold distribution

Energy supply When deciding on the provision of energy to the building, the question of its source must be considered. In addition to the actual demand (heat, cold, electricity etc.), the decision is influenced above all by availability. With fossil fuels this revolves around the ability to connect to existing services (gas, electricity, district heating etc.); with renewable energy sources the opportunities for their use are important (solar radiation, geothermal, biomass etc.). With some energy sources the ability to store them on site (oil, wood etc.) must be taken into account. > Chapter Tempering systems, Energy supply

As well as the availability of an energy source, the load profile (the changes in energy demand in relation to time) is crucial in the choice of energy source: the demand may vary greatly because of different climatic conditions or uses and the season or time of day. These fluctuations in demand can have a considerable influence on the overall efficiency of a system.

In this context, attention should be paid to the simultaneity of energy supply and requirement and any necessary energy storage measures. A solar energy system for hot service water, for example, works only when there is solar radiation present, i.e. during the day. Domestic hot water demand follows the typical use profile, with the morning and evening peaks being much greater than during the rest of the day. The heat generated during the day must therefore be stored in a buffer, which then makes it available at peak times.

Fossil and renewable energy sources

While fresh air provided by a mechanical ventilation system generally uses electricity as the energy source, there is often a choice of energy sources for generating heat and cold, all of which can be used in a variety of generation systems. Fossil fuels and renewable energy sources are considered separately below.

Fossil fuels (e.g. oil, gas and coal) were created over a long period of time though biological and physical processes below and on the surface of the Earth and therefore cannot be recreated in the short term. The Earth's existing supply cannot be renewed; the stocks are finite. These energy sources are based on carbon, which is released into the atmosphere as CO_2 by combustion and is a significant cause of global warming.

Fossil fuels

In the past, almost all buildings obtained their energy from fossil fuels, and the necessary technology is therefore widely developed and can operate at a high level of efficiency. In spite of these positive developments, the energy supply to buildings is still a major source of global CO_2 emissions, and calls for increased use of renewable energy.

Renewable energy sources are inexhaustible on a human scale and therefore sustainable: they can be exploited without permanently damaging the environment.

Renewable energy sources

O

O **Note:** The term "sustainable" comes from forestry and describes the principle of only cutting down as many trees in one area as will be replaced in the same year. Expressed more generally, the term refers to using a natural system only in ways that preserve its important characteristics over the long term.

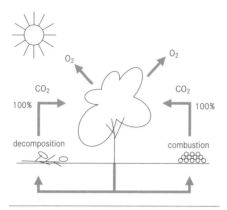

Fig. 19: CO_2-neutral burning of renewable materials

In this sense, solar energy (electricity or heat generation), hydropower, wind, geothermal and bioenergy (biomass such as wood, or biogas such as methane from sewage treatment plants) are considered to be renewable energy sources. Although the burning of biomass and biogas also releases CO_2 into the atmosphere through combustion, this carbon dioxide was taken up in the recent past from the atmosphere as the plants grew and would have been released again by the plants during the natural process of rotting. The burning of biological energy sources is therefore described as CO_2-neutral. > Fig. 19

Thus, it is not the release of CO_2 in general that is critical, but rather the avoidance of CO_2 emissions that would not have occurred and polluted the atmosphere without the combustion process.

The technological systems for using renewable energy in buildings have recently undergone considerable advances, and years of experience have proved them reliable.

Environmental impacts

For a long time, consideration of the energy demand of a building was limited to the demand (e.g. heating energy) arising in the building. To assess the effects on the environment, this way of looking at the situation is not enough, because the equipment losses in the building (e.g. losses in the boiler during the heating of the water and in its transport from the boiler to the radiators) are not taken into account. For another thing, energy is lost en route from the point of its generation to the point

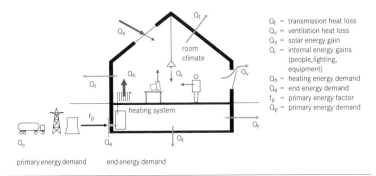

Fig. 20: Extended energy balance covering heating energy demand (used, end and primary energy)

of supply at the building. We therefore now distinguish between the energy use in the building, the end energy demand at the building boundary, and the primary energy demand, which describes the demand on naturally created energy sources. > Fig. 20

The required expenditure for the end energy demand including the pre-chains (material conditions and auxiliary energy) for the extraction, processing, conversion, transport and distribution of an energy source is defined using the primary energy factor. > Tab. 6

Primary energy factors

Electricity is normally produced in several ways, e.g. in coal, hydro-electric or nuclear power stations. A primary energy factor for the "electricity mix" can be calculated from the proportion of fossil fuels, nuclear and renewable energy sources used in the generation of electricity. This factor varies from country to country and can therefore be used to judge the effect of the use of that electricity.

In a similar way to the primary energy factors, CO_2 emission factors can be calculated to estimate the amount of greenhouse gases emitted (in grams) per kWh of end energy used. The unit of measurement for this factor is $[g/kWh_{end}]$. In addition to CO_2 the factor also takes into account the amount of other pollutants emitted and summarizes the resulting greenhouse effect as a "CO_2 equivalent". > Tab. 6 By multiplying this factor by the energy demand of a building, the effect of the energy supplied to the building on global warming can be calculated.

CO_2 emission factors

g/kWh_{end}

Tab. 6: Example of primary energy and CO_2 emission factors in Europe (based on DIN-V-18599

Energy source		Primary energy factor (non-renewable proportion) [kWh_{prim}/kWh_{end}]	CO_2 emission factor (CO_2 equivalent) [g/kWh_{end}]
Fuel	Oil EL	1.1	303
	Gas H	1.1	249
	Liquid gas	1.1	263
	Coal	1.1	439
	Brown coal	1.2	452
	Wood	0.2	42
District heating (at 70%) from power-heat coupling	Fossil fuels	0.7	217
	Renewable fuels	0.0	
District heating from heating plants	Fossil fuels	1.3	408
	Renewable fuels	0.1	
Electricity	General electricity mix	2,0[1]	480
Environmental energy	Solar energy, ambient heat	0.0	

[1] The state of affairs in 2015. Due to the greater power generated by renewable energy, this factor will continue to decline in the future.

Figure 21 gives an example of the effects of the choice of energy source on the primary energy demand and the CO_2 equivalent emissions of a building.

As can be seen in Figure 21, if electricity is used to provide for an end energy demand of 50 kWh per square meter of residential space per year, twice the amount of primary energy is required compared with cov-

○ **Note:** The unit of measurement of the primary energy factor is [kWh_{prim}/kWh_{end}]. The factor indicates how much primary energy in kWh (for example, the quantity of a particular energy source, e.g. coal) is required for the provision of one kWh of end energy (e.g. electricity or heat energy.)

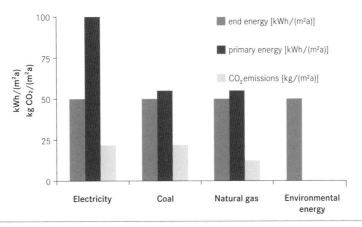

Fig. 21: Example of the primary energy demand and the CO_2 equivalent emissions of a building (end energy demand 50 kWh/(m²a)) with the use of different energy sources

ering the demand using environmental energy. With gas or coal, the primary energy used is only 1.1 times, just 10% more. Environmental energy, on the other hand, is almost primary energy neutral. The same applies to CO_2 emissions.

As far as local circumstances allow, the use of electricity and fossil fuels should therefore be avoided.

Ventilation systems

As can be seen from the discussions of comfort requirements, factors such as air temperature, air velocity, humidity, cleanliness and composition are particularly important in the perception of comfort in a room. These factors are strongly influenced by ventilation, and the particular ventilation system used in the building plays a significant role.

The main task of ventilation is to take odors, water vapor, carbon dioxide and air with a high concentration of pollutants out of a room and, above all, create and maintain a good, uniform thermal environment in a room.

The heating and ventilation industry makes a fundamental distinction between <u>natural (free) ventilation</u> and <u>mechanical ventilation</u>. The boundaries between free and mechanical ventilation (e.g. ventilation systems, heating and ventilation systems, often referred to as HV systems, and air conditioning systems) are fluid and not always clear in speech or in practice. Figure 22 illustrates one possible division for ventilation systems.

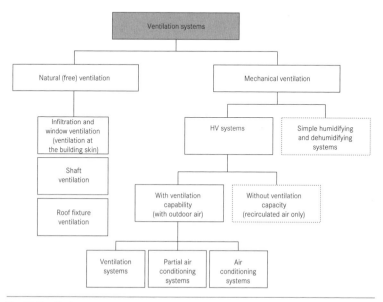

Fig. 22: Ventilation systems

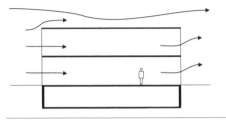

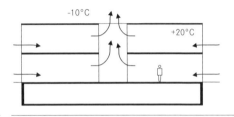

Fig. 23: Ventilation by wind   Fig. 24: Ventilation by thermal buoyancy

NATURAL VENTILATION

With natural (free) ventilation, the movement of the air in a room is caused exclusively by pressure differences at the surface and inside the building. These pressure differences are created by wind > Fig. 23 or temperature differences (thermal buoyancy). > Fig. 24

As shown in Figure 22 natural ventilation can be divided into three categories:

− Infiltration and window ventilation (ventilation at the building skin)
− Shaft ventilation
− Roof ventilation

The required air volume flow depends greatly on the weather, room temperature, and the arrangement and aerodynamic design of the ventilation openings.

Infiltration ventilation

The term "infiltration ventilation" describes the exchange of air that takes place through leaks in the building, mainly through gaps around opening windows and doors. This form of ventilation it is associated with a number of problems.

In conditions of still wind and small temperature differences, the provision of the minimum number of air changes required for hygiene cannot be guaranteed. Moreover, infiltration ventilation cannot normally be influenced by the user, and continuous uncontrolled ventilation results in increased heat loss, which may lead to serious building damage. To avoid this and allow a rate of air change to match the demand, the external skin of an energy-saving building must be as airtight as possible (including the windows), and have no uncontrolled gaps or joints. The outside air demand must also be covered by other means.

Tab. 7: Air change rates using window ventilation

Type of window ventilation	Air changes
Windows, doors closed (infiltration ventilation only)	0 to 0.5/h
One-sided ventilation, windows tilted, no slatted roller blinds	0.8 to 4.0/h
One-sided ventilation, window half-open	5 to 10/h
One-sided ventilation, window fully open[1] (purge ventilation)	9 to 15/h
Cross ventilation (purge ventilation by opposing windows and doors)	to 45/h

[1] Purge ventilation for 4 minutes results in one air change.

Window ventilation

As a rule, windows or other regulated openings (e.g. flaps) provide the natural ventilation of buildings or rooms, and by necessity are either kept open for brief periods (purge ventilation) or kept open over a longer period (permanent ventilation). For most buildings this is the way a room is ventilated to keep it comfortable for most of the year.

In winter and high summer, depending on the climate zone, the high heat losses or heat loads associated with window ventilation create problems and make it suitable for short-term purge ventilation only.

Window types   The air entry and exit openings of sliding and pivot-hung windows are equally large and adjustable, which makes them more suitable for ventilation than tilt windows. > Fig. 25

Air flow behavior   The air flow behavior for window ventilation is different in winter and summer. This difference depends on the temperature difference between indoors and outdoors. > Fig. 26

Cross ventilation   Opening windows in just one wall will only provide one-sided ventilation. Ideally, a building should be ventilated by cross ventilation from windows on opposite sides. In residential buildings, there should be adequate cross ventilation, or at least ventilation across a corner. > Fig. 27

Air change rate   Table 7 gives rough guidance values for air change rates that various window ventilation arrangements may achieve.

The expected rates of air change provided by window or infiltration ventilation fluctuate and depend strongly on the wind speed and building geometry. There are limits to the size of rooms or buildings that can be ventilated naturally. For the one-sided ventilation of a room with a clear ceiling height of up to 4 m, the room depth should be not more than 2.5 times the room height. With cross ventilation this ratio rises to 5. > Fig. 28

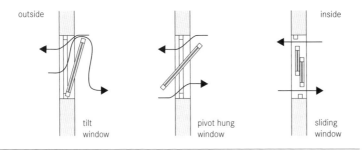

Fig. 25: Window types

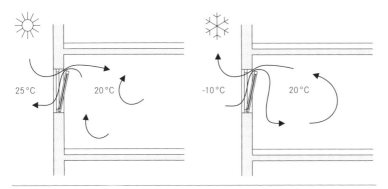

Fig. 26: Air flow behavior for window ventilation (summer and winter)

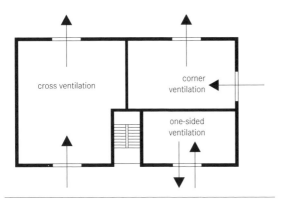

Fig. 27: Air flow shown in plan

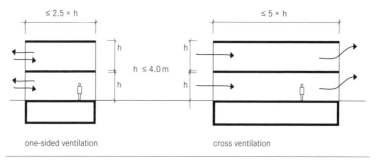

one-sided ventilation   cross ventilation

Fig. 28: Maximum room depths for window ventilation

Table 8 provides an overview of the guidance values for the design of natural ventilation systems.

User behavior   The rate of air change achievable through window ventilation depends greatly on user behavior. It is certainly an advantage for the user to be able to control the air flow into a room directly, but in practice rooms are usually ventilated too much or too little. Controlled air exchange cannot
■ take place by user-controlled window ventilation.

> ■ **Tip:** Atria should be designed so that rooms can be provided with light and air, even in deep buildings. Natural ventilation works in the same way as a chimney: the heated air rises and escapes through openings in the roof. This creates low-pressure zones, which suck waste air out of the adjacent rooms. If the atrium is covered with glass, sufficient vertical exhaust air openings must be provided to prevent hot air building up in summer (see Fig. 29).

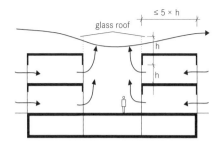

Fig. 29: Atrium ventilation

Tab. 8: Guidance values for room depths and ventilation cross sections (in accordance with German workplace regulations)

System	Clear ceiling height (h)	Room depth maximum	Inlet and outlet air cross-sections in cm^2 per m^2 floor area
One-sided ventilation	up to 4.0 m	2.5 × h	200
Cross ventilation	up to 4.0 m	5.0 × h	120
Cross ventilation with roof fixtures and openings in an external wall or in two opposing outside walls	more than 4.0 m	5.0 × h	80

Shaft ventilation

A further form of natural ventilation is shaft ventilation. It is based on the principle of thermal buoyancy, > Fig. 24, page 43 which involves a drop in temperature between the indoor air and the outdoor air at the top of the shaft, and the suction effect of the wind passing over the top of the shaft. > Fig. 30

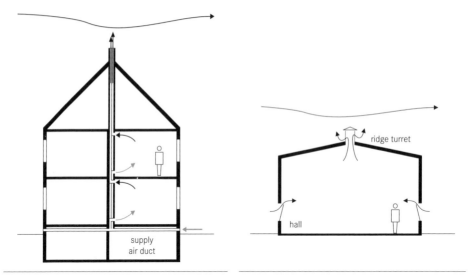

Fig. 30: Shaft ventilation

Fig. 31: Ridge turret ventilation

If these conditions are not present, e.g. in summer when the outdoor and indoor air temperatures may be equal or when there is no wind, this type of ventilation is rendered ineffective without a fan. Shaft ventilation is therefore only suitable for rooms in which there is a primary need for water vapor to be conducted away, such as bathrooms and kitchens. This can be easily accepted in the short term with plastered surfaces, and the shaft effect will resume when there is enough buoyancy again. It is important to ensure that each ventilated room has its own shaft, so that sufficient air can flow through it at all times, and that odors from other rooms can be excluded.

Roof fixture ventilation

Roof fixture ventilation is natural ventilation that occurs through fixtures such as ridge turrets, roof lanterns and similar exhaust air openings in the roofs of buildings. > Fig. 31

This form of ventilation, like shaft ventilation, is primarily based on the principle of thermal buoyancy caused by temperature differences between the air indoors and outdoors. Roof fixture ventilation is mostly used for rooms with ceiling clearances in excess of approximately 4 m, > Tab. 8 i.e. large halls (industrial sheds). Roof ventilation has no associated operating costs but is responsible for high heat losses in winter. ○ Nowadays, mechanical fans with heat recovery are used.

MECHANICAL VENTILATION

Mechanical ventilation systems include <u>simple ventilation systems</u> (e.g. shaft ventilation systems with fans or external wall ventilators) and <u>heating and ventilation (HV) systems</u>, which prepare air in a central mechanical equipment room and supply it to the rooms through air distribution systems (air ducts, shafts). > Fig. 22, page 43

Heating and ventilation systems

Heating and ventilation systems may be <u>with and without ventilation</u>. HV systems without ventilation components are systems that only recirculate air, without adding fresh air. These systems are mainly used in certain industrial manufacturing processes, and are not considered further here.

HV systems that ventilate are intended to renew and filter the room air. They always introduce a certain proportion of outdoor air and have an exhaust or waste air outlet so that the room air can be constantly renewed. If the indoor air is not contaminated with odors or pollutants, part of the exhaust air can be recirculated through a mixing chamber, where it is mixed with outdoor air. The HV systems also treat the air thermodynamically by heating, cooling, humidifying and dehumidifying it. Thus, the systems can be differentiated by their treatment of the supply air:

HV systems with ventilation components

— Ventilation systems with no thermodynamic air treatment capability, or only one (e.g. heating only)
— Partial air conditioning systems with two or three thermodynamic air treatment capabilities (e.g. heating and cooling, or heating, cooling and dehumidifying)
— Air-conditioning systems with all four thermodynamic air treatment capabilities (heating, cooling, humidifying and dehumidifying)

Centralized HV systems always require machinery to process the air and, above a certain size, must be installed in their own rooms (HV equipment rooms). The requirement for outdoor air must first be

Centralized HV systems

○ **Note:** Heat recovery equipment extracts heat energy from the exhaust air and introduces it back into the supply of outdoor air. It saves valuable heating and cooling energy, which otherwise would have been necessary to temper the supply air.

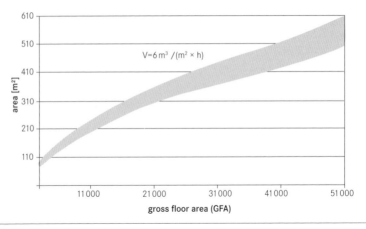

$V=6\,m^3\,/(m^2 \times h)$

gross floor area (GFA)

Fig. 32: Diagram for roughly estimating the space required by RLT Centers in administration buildings in relation to the customary outside air volume flow in open-plan offices (see VDI 2050 Blatt 1).

calculated from the anticipated use, outdoor climate and the desired indoor climate. > Chapter Design principles, Determining the requirements

If the required (outdoor) air volume flow $\dot{V}$ is known > Tab. 3, page 24, then it is possible to determine the amount of space a centralized HV system will require using VDI guideline 2050. > Fig. 32

Distribution

If air conditioning is performed centrally, the air has to be distributed throughout the building through ducts, vertically in shafts and horizontally in the floor zone. The design should make allowance for the space required.

○

Shape and space requirement of ventilation ducts

The shape of a ventilation duct is determined by the flow characteristics and the available space. Circular cross-sections are inexpensive and have good flow characteristics but need more space than rectangular ones, which are therefore used more frequently and are available in

○ **Note:** An alternative to a centralized air-conditioning system is a decentralized ventilation system, which can minimize the space required for shafts and ducts. By using decentralized ventilation units, every room can be supplied directly with the required outdoor air, and the supply air can also be tempered to individual needs by heating or cooling (see Chapter Tempering systems, Heat and cold distribution).

○ **Note:** A ventilation system handling supply and exhaust air requires separate supply and exhaust air ducts. This must be taken into account when allocating space. Supply and exhaust air ducts should not cross one another, and suspended ceilings must be able to accommodate two ducts, one on top of the other, otherwise the ceiling height may be considerably reduced in certain circumstances. Where minimum ceiling heights must be observed this can considerably increase building costs.

a side ratio of 1:1 (square) to a maximum of 1:10 (flat rectangle). Abrupt changes in the direction of the ducts should be avoided in order to minimize the pressure loss and the accompanying air noise. Heavy ducts and ducts with large cross-sections (and hence lower air speeds) also reduce air noise.

In supply air ducts, the air is commonly transported at a velocity of v = 3 – 5 m/s (but in residential buildings at velocities of v = 1.5 m/s and often less). From the above assumptions and the required air volumes, a conservative value for the required cross-section of a duct can be calculated from the following formula:

$$A = \frac{\dot{V}}{v \times 3600}\,[m$$

in which: A: Duct cross-section in m^2; $\dot{V}$: Air volume flow rate (air volume) in m^2 /h; air velocity in the duct in m/s (= 3600 × m/h).

●

Ventilation ducts must be insulated to reduce noise, to minimize heat losses when being used for heating, and to avoid condensation. Approximately 5 cm of insulation is generally used. This must be added to the duct dimensions when considering the space requirements. Added to this is another 5– 10 cm working space around the duct. > Fig. 33

Insulation

○

In addition, the ventilation ducts must incorporate special measures to ensure fire safety and provide sound insulation because ventilation ducts often cross fire compartments and usage zones. Suitable fire safety flaps or sound dampers with larger external dimensions than the ducts themselves must be designed into the system and remain accessible for maintenance.

Fire safety and sound insulation

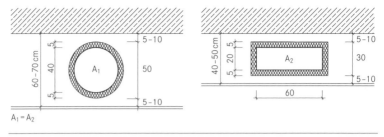

$A_1 = A_2$

Fig. 33: Space requirement for various duct shapes with the same cross-sectional area

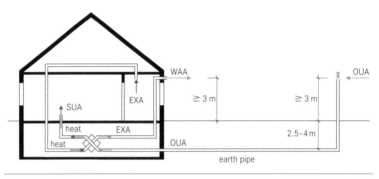

Fig. 34: Supply and exhaust air systems with heat recovery and earth pipe

Waste and outdoor air ducts

Outdoor air intakes and waste air outlets must have protection against the entry of rain, birds and insects, and be at least 3 m above ground level. > Fig. 34 Taking air into the building through an earth pipe approximately 2.5–4 m underground is an effective means of saving energy. The air is precooled in summer and prewarmed in winter by the relatively constant temperature of the soil. > Chapter Tempering systems, Energy supply

Heat recovery

The heat present in the exhaust air can be recovered and used to warm the outside air in a heat exchanger. The streams of exhaust and cold supply air cross one another in the heat exchanger without mixing, so that there is no transfer of pollutants. The efficiency can be up to 90%, depending on the type of heat exchanger. > Fig. 34

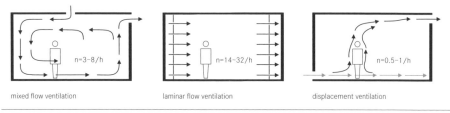

mixed flow ventilation

laminar flow ventilation

displacement ventilation

Fig. 35: Air distribution in the room and achievable air change rates (n)

Air distribution in the room

The method of distributing the conditioned air is crucial to the perception of comfort in a room. There are three basic ways of distributing air in a room: > Fig. 35

— Mixed flow ventilation
— Laminar flow ventilation
— Displacement ventilation

Mixed flow ventilation is the most common means of introducing air into a room. Supply air is blown in at the ceiling or on the walls at a relatively high velocity, and mixes with the still room air.

Mixed flow ventilation

Laminar flow ventilation is a method of ventilating a room used for special purposes. The supply air is introduced over the whole surface of wall or ceiling and removed from the opposite side. Typical uses are operating theaters and clean rooms, where the method of ventilation must ensure that the supply air and room air do not mix in order to create an extremely clean environment.

Laminar flow ventilation

Displacement ventilation is widely accepted as a particularly energy-saving and comfortable form of ventilation. Air some 2–3 K cooler than the room air is introduced into the room close to the floor at a slow velocity (<0.2 m/s). The air is distributed at floor level in the room and forms a pool of fresh air. The sources of heat in the room, such as people or computers, cause the fresh air to rise by convection, and therefore supplies everyone with adequate fresh air. The air change rate can thus be reduced to the minimum required for hygiene (n = 0.5–1.0/h) and the energy demand lowered. Displacement ventilation works independently of the room depth and volume of a building and can therefore be used for very deep buildings and halls with a large air demand and low cooling load (up to about 35 W/m^2), e.g. in theaters, sports halls, or offices.

Displacement ventilation

DECIDING ON THE RIGHT SYSTEM

Every ventilation system has its own series of advantages and disadvantages. > Tab. 9 The principle is to choose a system that can provide the right amount of fresh air to the building or room as efficiently as possible in terms of energy and with a high degree of comfort.

If possible, preference should be given to natural ventilation, as the use of mechanical ventilation is almost always associated with higher building and operating costs. Also to be borne in mind is the great space requirement for the equipment, the air ducts within the building or room to distribute the air, and measures to ensure fire safety and provide sound insulation. On the other hand, there is frequently a higher quality of use with a comfortable indoor climate and the possibility of heat recovery.

Reasons for the use of mechanical ventilation Mechanical ventilation should be installed only if it is necessary for functional (constructional or user-related) reasons, or if overall savings in energy can be expected:

- Windowless or internal rooms require a supply of outdoor air.
- Installation is advised for buildings taller than about 40 m. Wind pressures and convection can cause severe draughts when windows are opened in buildings of this height. This would make

Tab. 9: Characteristics of ventilation systems

	Advantages	Disadvantages
Natural ventilation	No energy required to drive the system or to condition the air	Effectiveness depends on the climatic conditions (wind velocity and temperatures)
	Reduction of space taken up by installations (no air ducts, equipment rooms etc.)	Functioning depends on the building structure and room depths
	Lower initial investment and maintenance costs	High heat losses in winter
	Optimum relationship with outdoor world (with window ventilation)	Heat recovery impossible or very difficult to implement
	High user acceptance	
	julated	High initial investment, operating and maintenance costs
	very possible	Increased space requirement for equipment and air ducts
	all thermodynamic air functions (heating, cooling, and dehumidifying)	Low user acceptance, in particular due to lack of user influence
	e incorporated where the air is	

53

the upper stories almost impossible to use without special constructional measures such as double facades to counter this effect.

— Buildings in locations with strong odor or noise loads or waste gas emissions make its installation worthwhile.

— Very deep rooms in which free ventilation is not sufficient to provide adequate air exchange require mechanical ventilation.
> Fig. 28, p. 46

— In theaters, cinemas and other places of assembly, the absence of windows, or a relatively small window area – linked with high occupancy rates – makes natural ventilation unviable.

— Rooms with a specified indoor air quality in terms of microbial levels, temperature, humidity etc., e.g. operating theaters, museums or special production facilities (microprocessors etc.), make mechanical ventilation necessary.

— Rooms with high thermal loads (e.g. computer centers), where cooling is required, make its installation worthwhile.

— As mentioned above, mechanical ventilation can be an effective means of saving energy. Ventilation systems, in particular those with heat recovery, reduce ventilation heat loss and are an indispensable part of the passive house energy concept.

Tempering systems

The purpose of an active tempering system is to use an energy source as efficiently as possible to provide any additional heat or cold necessary to create a comfortable room climate and introduce it into a room. > Chapter Design principles, Comfort requirements

In general terms, a tempering system might consist of an energy source, a technical system for creating heat or cold, some method of storage if necessary, and a means of distribution and delivery – in combination with user need-related controls and the object to be tempered (building or room). > Fig. 36

All elements of an active tempering system must be fine-tuned to match one another so that the system can cover the demand > Chapter Design principles, Determining the requirements of the building in an efficient manner at all times.

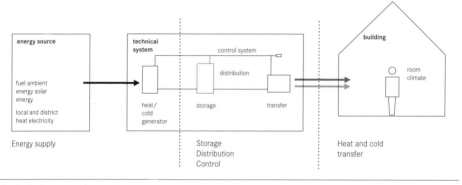

Fig. 36: Active tempering system

○ **Note:** The pipe that carries the water from the heat generator to the transfer system is known as the "feed", and the one carrying the water back, the "return". The temperatures of the water in these pipes are important parameters for the ability to combine generators of heat or cold with transfer systems.

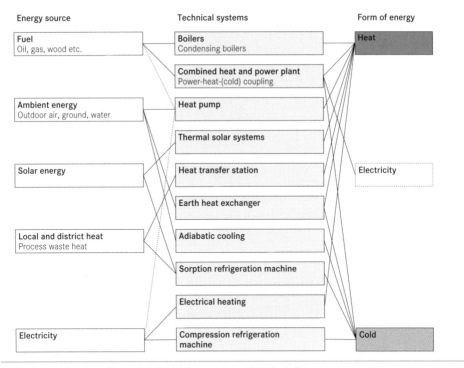

Fig. 37: Energy sources and suitable systems for energy supply (selected)

ENERGY SUPPLY

The supply of heat and cold in the building depends on the energy sources available. Figure 37 shows possible ways of combining various energy sources with selected systems for supplying energy.

Fuels

The use of fossil fuels such as oil, natural gas or coal is mainly concerned with generating heat in room conditioning.

The burning of fossil fuels is criticized because of the environmental effects (primary energy and CO_2 emissions). CO_2-neutral fuels should be used in preference. > Chapter Design principles, Covering the demands

All over the world, heat is supplied to buildings primarily by burning fuels in central heating boilers. The heat released during this process is given up in a heat exchanger into a heat medium, usually water, and distributed in the building (central heating).

Boilers

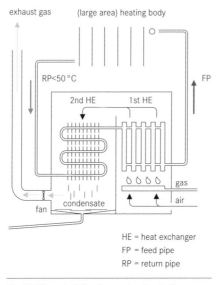

exhaust gas   (large area) heating body

RP<50 °C

FP

2nd HE   1st HE

gas

condensate   air

fan

HE = heat exchanger
FP = feed pipe
RP = return pipe

Fig. 38: The principle of a condensing boiler

The most efficient boiler is called a condensing boiler; this extracts additional heat from the exhaust gas and through this can achieve high efficiencies. Oil and gas are the most common fuels used, but recent years have seen systems that can operate with wood pellets (combustible material made of compressed wood in the shape of small rods) as their fuel. > Fig. 38 Condensing boilers best combined with heating radiators
○ because they require low return water temperatures.

○ **Note:** The low system temperatures of condensing boilers mean they also work well in combination with thermal solar systems. The low exhaust gas temperature requires the chimney for a condensing boiler to be lined with a condensation-resistant inner duct and equipped with a fan because the effect of convection is too weak.

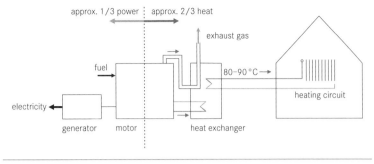

approx. 1/3 power | approx. 2/3 heat

exhaust gas

fuel

80–90 °C →

heating circuit

electricity ◀

generator   motor   heat exchanger

Fig. 39: The principle of the power-heat coupling with CHP

In addition to burning fossil or biological fuels to generate heat, buildings can also be heated by the heat generated as part of other processes. One important example is the use of the heat that arises during the generation of electricity.

Power-heat coupling/ combined heat and power plants

Like heat generation, electricity generation usually relies on combustion processes that produce hot exhaust gases. Two forms of energy are produced from transferring this heat from the combustion process, e.g. in a water-operated system: electricity (power) and heat. These processes are therefore referred to as "power-heat coupling" (PHC). In terms of the amount of fuel used, these processes are very efficient, because most of the energy contained by the fuel can be extracted and used.

The PHC principle can be used equally well in a large heating power station as in a medium-sized plant (e.g. supplying a residential area), or a small one (e.g. supplying a single building). The medium or small electricity and heat plants are called combined heat and power plants (CHP) and supply heat mainly in the form of hot water at temperatures of 80–90 °C. > Fig. 39 The fuels used are most often natural gas and light heating oil, but biogas and biofuels (e.g. rapeseed oil) are also used.

The heat produced by the PHC plants can be used like heat generated from solar energy > see below: Solar energy with the help of sorption refrigeration machines for cooling. These processes are therefore referred to as "power-heat-cold coupling" (PHCC) systems.

Ambient energy

There are various possibilities for using the energy potential of a building's surroundings for cooling or heating. In addition to the temperature level of the outdoor air or the room exhaust air there are the

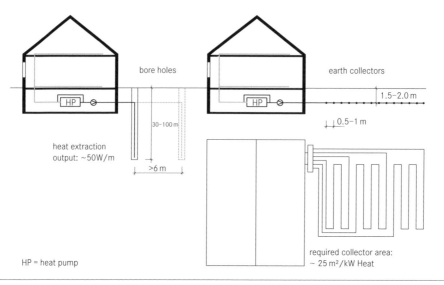

bore holes

earth collectors

1.5–2.0 m

30–100 m

0.5–1 m

heat extraction
output: ~50 W/m

>6 m

required collector area:
~ 25 m²/kW Heat

HP = heat pump

Fig. 40: Example of the use of geothermal heat for heating

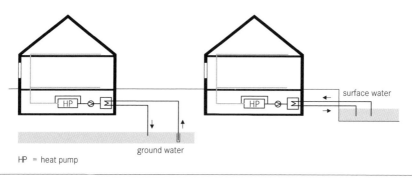

surface water

ground water

HP = heat pump

Fig. 41: Example of the use of groundwater and surface water for heating

relatively constant temperatures at various depths of the soil, the ground-water or nearby bodies of water. > Figs 40 and 41

The energy obtained from these sources can be used in winter for heating and in summer for cooling buildings. To be used for heating, the temperature level usually has to be raised by introducing additional energy.

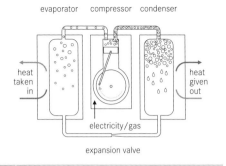

evaporator   compressor   condenser

heat
taken
in

heat
given
out

electricity / gas

expansion valve

Fig. 42: The principle of heat pump/compression refrigeration machines

This is done using heat pumps, which work on the same principle as refrigerators. > Fig. 42 The ambient energy source must be augmented by electricity or gas in order to raise the temperature to the desired level and operate the system efficiently.

Heat pumps

The use of gas offers primary energy advantages compared with electricity. > Chapter Design principles, Covering the demands

■

The use of the heat of the earth ("geothermal energy") is mainly by earth collectors or bore holes in combination with heat pumps. The geothermal heat can also be used simply for preconditioning outdoor air, with the air being fed through an air-earth heat exchanger before it enters the building. In winter the air is prewarmed, and in summer the warm outdoor air is precooled before it enters the building, thus contributing to a reduction of the heating and cooling energy demand. > Fig. 43

Earth heat exchangers

O

■ **Tip:** The higher the temperature of the heat source, or the lower the temperature difference between the heat source and heating circuit, the more efficiently the heat pump works. The use of heat pumps to generate heat is most suitable if the system temperatures are low and the heating surfaces large, such as in underfloor heating.

O **Note:** The additional resistance to flow caused by the air having to pass through the pipes of an earth heat exchanger makes mechanical ventilation plant necessary.

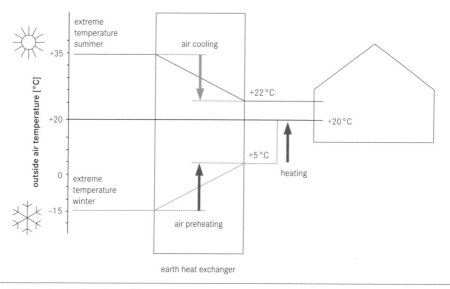

Fig. 43: The principle of an air-earth heat exchanger

Adiabatic cooling   In addition to underground and surface water as sources of natural energy for heating and cooling as described above, water can also be used directly for cooling buildings. Just like the formation of sweat on the human skin, the evaporation of water draws energy out of the air and cools it. This effect can be created directly with buildings and rooms or indirectly by evaporation cooling, also known as adiabatic cooling. With direct adiabatic cooling the supply air is either passed over open water surfaces or plants or, particularly with mechanical ventilation systems, water is sprayed into the air so finely that it does not reach the floor as it drops but remains in the air as water vapor and thus cools the supply air. A disadvantage of this form of adiabatic cooling is that the supply air becomes increasingly humid. > Chapter Design principles, Comfort requirements This makes direct adiabatic cooling most useful in hot, dry climate zones.

By combining the evaporation principle with a heat exchanger, it is possible in mechanical ventilation systems to produce a temperature reduction without increasing the humidity. This is often called indirect adiabatic cooling. It allows the exhaust air from a room to be cooled by evaporation and then expelled from the building through a rotating heat exchanger. The heat exchanger transfers the cold energy highly efficiently into the counter-rotating flow of the supply air. > Fig. 44

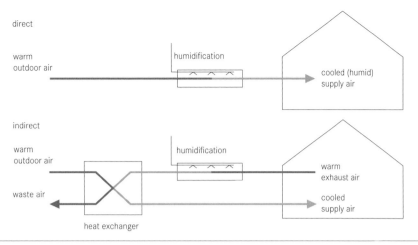

direct

warm
outdoor air

humidification

cooled (humid)
supply air

indirect

warm
outdoor air

humidification

warm
exhaust air

waste air

cooled
supply air

heat exchanger

Fig. 44: The principle of direct and indirect adiabatic cooling in combination with a mechanical ventilation system

Solar energy

Solar energy systems convert sunlight into heat, which is then generally used to provide heat to buildings.

Solar energy as a source of heat primarily for heating and hot water is actively used using suitable collector systems. These systems change the solar radiation into heat and conduct it to the place of use via a heat-transporting medium (water with an antifreeze agent). There are two principal types of system, one using plate collectors, the other vacuum tube collectors. The latter are technically more complicated in construction, and therefore more expensive, but also more efficient.

Thermal solar systems

If the solar energy system provides hot water only, the solar heat energy can be taken directly to the hot water storage tank. Any remaining energy demand for hot water provision is then normally covered by incorporating a more or less conventional boiler. Thermal solar energy systems can also be used as background heating for well-insulated houses. > Fig. 45

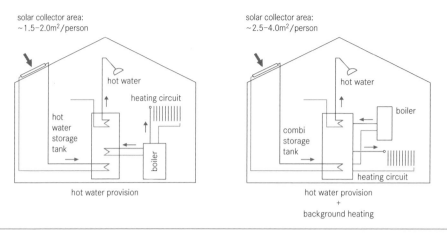

solar collector area:
~1.5–2.0m²/person

hot water

heating circuit

hot water storage tank

boiler

hot water provision

solar collector area:
~2.5–4.0m²/person

hot water

boiler

combi storage tank

heating circuit

hot water provision
+
background heating

Fig. 45: Example of the use of solar energy for generating heat

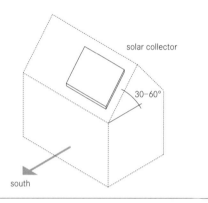

solar collector

30–60°

south

Fig. 46: Suitable alignment of thermal solar energy collectors for background heating and hot water provision (in Germany)

Solar collectors are mainly positioned on roofs. The optimum alignment depends on the local course of the sun and the seasons of use. > Fig. 46 Small departures in orientation and inclination are tolerable and ● reduce the yield by only a small amount.

● **Important:** Thermal solar collectors should not be confused with solar cells! Solar cells are also mainly installed on roofs but only generate electricity. This is either stored in batteries (island solution) and used directly on the premises or, if possible, fed into the public grid and payment is received.

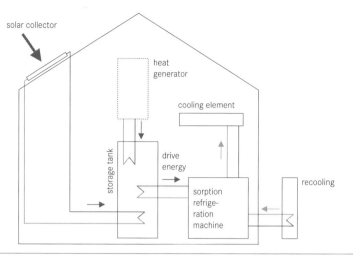

Fig. 47: **Example of the use of solar energy for cooling**

Sorption refrigeration machines work using a similar principle to heat pumps, by compressing and expanding a medium. Instead of electricity or gas providing the auxiliary energy, a source of heat drives the system. The chemical process of sorption generates cold instead of heat. > Fig. 47

Sorption refrigeration machines

Heat as the drive energy makes the use of sorption refrigeration machines advantageous where heat is available at no cost as a process waste (production plants, power-heat coupling plants etc.), or from the environment (thermal solar collectors, hot springs etc.), at a temperature of 80–160 °C. Combining a combined heat and power plant (CHP) with a sorption refrigeration machine for power-heat-cold coupling (PHCC) is perfect with respect to economy of operation, as one system covers the heat and cold energy demand, and can operate throughout the year.

Local and district heat

District heat is generated in central heating or heat-power plants as well as in decentralized combined heat and power plants. The latter solution is called local heat. Local and district heat can be used in remote buildings through an appropriate system of pipes and transfer stations. The generation of heat using the principle of power-heat coupling (CHP) is a low maintenance and environmentally friendly method of providing heat. > Chapter Design principles, Covering the demands

No heat generating equipment is necessary in the building to use local or district heat, nor any components such as heating equipment rooms, waste gas plants or fuel storage facilities. The heat is normally provided to the building in the form of hot water or steam through insulated pipes, and is transferred by a heat transfer station (heat exchanger) into the building's heating or hot water system.

In some cases, superfluous heat from energy-intensive industrial processes (steelmaking, chemical industry etc.) can be fed into buildings through local and district heating networks. As this energy would otherwise be released into the environment, this option also improves the energetic efficiency of the industrial processes.

Electricity

In principle, electricity can also be used to generate heat and cold. However, this option should be avoided, especially if the electricity comes from fossil fuels, because its generation already involves heat, and losses take place every time energy is converted (e.g. from coal to heat to electricity to heat). This can easily be seen from the primary energy factor for electricity for each location. > Chapter Design principles, Covering the demands

Electrical heating systems are used only in exceptional circumstances. One example is bathrooms in existing buildings. Here, the heat demand considered over the year is small and a connection to a central heating system may be technically impossible or not worthwhile on economic grounds. The same applies to the electrical water heating in electrical boilers or immersion heaters.

Electricity is often used as auxiliary energy to drive heat pumps for heat generation. The use of electricity should be kept as low as possible to avoid high costs and a poor primary energy balance for the whole system.

The most common cold generators are compression refrigeration machines. They work on the same principle as a refrigerator and generate cold from electricity, which then can be released to the building through a distribution system. With the use of appropriate energy, this can be a practical means of achieving any desired temperature level.

The waste heat from refrigeration machines can be used if there is a simultaneous need in the building for heat and cold (e.g. for room cooling and hot water provision). This waste heat is often released into the outdoor air so that, in combination with the (normally electrical) energy demand for the compressor, only a small amount of electricity is used.

There is an increased dependency on electricity as an energy source, which adversely affects the primary energy balance. Hence, the use of compression refrigeration machines should be avoided as far as possible.

HEAT AND COLD STORAGE

By storing heat and cold it is possible to decouple use-dependent energy take-up from energy generation. This is necessary, in particular, in order to use solar energy for heating purposes, as the energy received from the sun varies according to the weather and often does not coincide with the times of day energy is required. > Fig. 48 Solar heat can be stored using the thermal storage capacity of the building itself, > Chapter Design principles, Covering the demands but this provides no possibility for users to regulate its use. Solar systems for hot water provision and background heating generally have a hot water storage tank, which may contain enough hot water for several days, but will take up space within the building.

Seasonal storage can be used to store solar heat over a longer period of time. This usually involves water tanks, which can be placed inside or outside the building. This allows heat to be stored in summer and made available in winter.

In principle it is also possible to store cold, e.g. using "ice tanks", which allows the whole system to be optimized in a similar way to heat storage. It is particularly the case with solar energy that the peak solar yield coincides with the greatest cooling demand. > Fig. 48

HEAT AND COLD DISTRIBUTION
Centralized systems

Distribution is the link between the generation of heat or cold and the system for transferring the heat or cold into the room, i.e. heat or cold is mostly generated centrally and carried to the transfer systems in

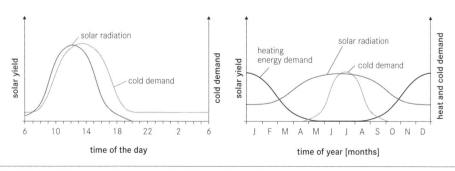

Fig. 48: Solar yield and coincident heat and cold demand (Central Europe)

the rooms by water or air as a transport medium. Water-operated systems are generally more viable with respect to energy content and the required delivery energy, and should be preferred to air-operated systems in most situations. > Chapter Design principles, Covering the demands The most common form of heating system in buildings is hot water-operated central heating. However, there are also design and economic factors in favor of
● using air-operated systems, which are discussed below.

The ductways should be kept as short as possible and be well insulated to minimize energy losses. The insulation also prevents water from condensing during the transport of cold media.

Decentralized systems
Individual heating units generate heat energy directly in the room, where they also release it. There are various types of individual heating units, including stand-alone stoves, gas fires and electric fires. These are special forms of heating systems and are therefore not considered further in this publication.

Decentralized mechanical ventilation systems draw in outdoor air from directly in front of the facade, which dispenses with the need for ventilation equipment rooms and large duct networks. On the other hand, it costs more to maintain a large number of small devices, although this is mitigated by the units being increasingly modularized and simpler to maintain. They are normally also able to heat or cool the air required for ventilation. > Chapter Tempering systems, Heat and cold transfer

Regulation
In addition to insulated pipework, valves and pumps, there must also be a suitable means of regulating the distribution of heat and cold. These controls continuously match the output of heat and cold to the ever-changing demand caused by weather conditions (outdoor temperature,

---

● **Example:** Buildings with a very high standard of thermal insulation, such as passive houses, have no need for a conventional heating system (with heating boiler, distribution and heat transfer by radiators). In spite of the physical disadvantages of air as a heat transfer medium, the required heat can be provided by a ventilation system, along with the minimum number of air changes necessary for hygiene.

○ **Hint:** Radiator panels, which are used primarily for heating large halls, are one exception. They need to be operated at high feed temperatures.

wind, solar radiation), internal heat sources, and changes in room use. It must also be possible for the controls to act automatically in response to indoor and outdoor temperatures and be programmed with respect to time. In residential buildings the most common controls include thermostatic radiator valves, outdoor and room thermostats with suitable sensors, and automatic controls to reduce output at night at set times and in response to temperature changes. For larger buildings or systems, it may be worthwhile to install a building management system (BMS), which controls the heating or cooling in different rooms by means of sensors and a central computer.

HEAT AND COLD TRANSFER

A suitable heat and cold transfer system uses water or air to carry the heat or cold from the generator to the tempered rooms where it is released.

Heat and cold transfer systems can be differentiated by the method of transfer, i.e. the proportions of radiated or convected energy, the feed temperature T_f, the specified capacity and controllability. > Chapter Design principles, Covering the demands

Heat transfer systems

Heat may be transferred in a room by radiator, surface heating, or a ventilation system (air heating system). The construction and arrangement of the heating elements determine the temperature profile in the room, and have considerable influence on comfort. The transfer of heat in the room should be constant over time, and uniform in the horizontal and vertical directions to provide the ideal temperature profile. > Tab. 10, page 72, and Fig. 49

Common heat transfer systems in hot water-operated heating systems include radiators, convectors and surface heating. They are universal in use and can be easily controlled. Radiators and the like should be positioned on external walls and close to glazing to counteract the formation of draughts. > Fig. 50 One particular disadvantage of convectors is the high feed temperature required, which makes their use in combination with solar thermal systems, heat pumps or condensing boilers less viable. _Heating radiators_

Surface heating systems (floors, walls and ceiling heating), in which concealed heating pipes are buried in screeds, plaster or special panels, transfer their heat mainly by radiation into the room and create a comfortable temperature profile. > Fig. 49 The large heated area permits much lower feed temperatures than other heating bodies. _Surface heating_

○

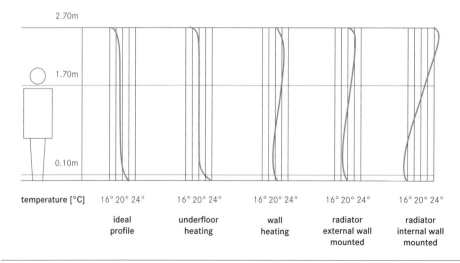

temperature [°C]	16° 20° 24°	16° 20° 24°	16° 20° 24°	16° 20° 24°	16° 20° 24°
	ideal profile	underfloor heating	wall heating	radiator external wall mounted	radiator internal wall mounted

Fig. 49: Room temperature profiles of heat transfer systems

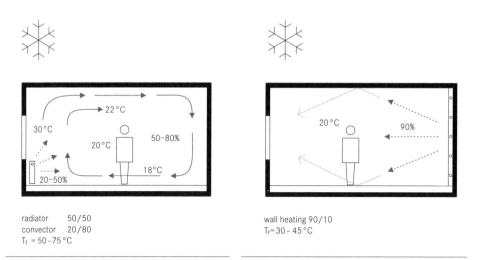

radiator   50/50
convector   20/80
T_f = 50-75 °C

wall heating 90/10
T_f= 30- 45 °C

Fig. 50: Heating bodies (proportions of radiated and convected output and feed temperatures T_f)

Fig. 51: Wall heating (proportions of radiated and convected output and feed temperatures T_f)

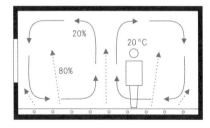

underfloor heating 80/20
$T_f = 30 - 45\,°C$

Fig. 52: Floor heating (proportions of radiated and convected output and feed temperatures T_f)

Surface heating is a suitable system for heat transfer in houses with a particularly low heating energy demand and in combination with low temperature systems, such as condensing boilers, heat pumps and coupled thermal solar energy systems. > Figs 51 and 52

In principle, the heat demand of a building can also be covered by an existing ventilation system. The air can be provided either centrally or locally, mainly through electrically driven heating registers. This is, however, only worthwhile if a ventilation system is already required for other reasons and the building's overall heat energy demand is low (e.g. as a result of very good thermal insulation or high internal heat loads). Table 10 gives a brief overview of the main heat transfer systems.

Air heating

Cold transfer systems

Transfer systems for cold energy, like those for heat energy, can be classified as convection or radiation systems according to their methods of transfer. The advantages and disadvantages arise from the effects on the operative room temperatures, as described in the chapter on Design principles, Comfort requirements. The risk of radiation asymmetry discussed there should be taken into account. In addition, controllability and the required feed temperatures are determining factors in the choice of a suitable cooling system. > Tab. 11, page 75

Tab. 10: Characteristics of heat transfer systems

Heat transfer system	Advantages	Disadvantages	Proportion of output radiated/ convected	T_f [°C]
Radiators	Inexpensive, quick-acting, good controllability	Space required, appearance	50/50	50–75 (90)
Convectors	Space-saving, quick-acting, good controllability	Cleaning, create dust	20/80	50–75 (90)
Floor heating	Pleasant temperature profile, concealed	Cold air drop may occur, varicose veins may develop due to relatively high near floor temperatures, sluggish controls, not suitable for some floor coverings	80/20	30–45
Wall and ceiling heating	Pleasant temperature profile, concealed, heating and cooling possible	Sluggish controls, no furniture or fittings may be placed against heated walls, adequate ceiling height necessary for ceiling heating, people must keep a distance from the heated surfaces	90/10	30–45
Air heating	Combination of ventilation and heating, quick-acting controls	Draughts possible, dust created over 49 °C	0/100	30–49 (70)

As with the transfer of heat energy, cooling systems that exploit the mass of large building components are sluggish to respond to controls. Air-operated systems and systems that do not involve large building components respond quickly to controls and react more rapidly to changes in conditions. Large surface area heat transfer devices tend to have moderate (in the case of cooling: higher) feed temperatures than smaller devices, and are therefore better suited for use in combination with renewable energy sources.

A special point that must be kept in mind with cooling systems is the danger of falling below the dew point: depending on the temperature and humidity of the room air and the surface temperatures of the cooling element surfaces, the moisture contained in the air may condense on the cold surfaces because their temperatures fall below the dew point. The

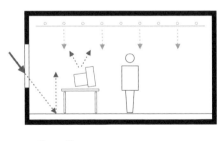

cooling ceiling
T_f = 10-16 °C

Fig. 53: Radiated cooling from a suspended cooling ceiling

condensate formed there must at least be collected; an even better solution is to drain it away. If this is not possible, condensation on cooled surfaces can be dealt with by temporarily increasing the surface temperature of the cooling body, which reduces its cooling capacity.

Cooling ceilings can be found in many office and administration buildings. These transfer systems are suspended from, and may cover, large areas of the ceiling. > Fig. 53

Cooling coils filled with a flowing cold medium are suspended from the ceiling. About half of the cold transfer takes place by radiation, and the system responds well to controls. Feed temperatures are 10-16 °C and it is practically impossible to drain condensate away. To prevent condensation from forming, either high levels of humidity should be avoided or the feed temperature should be raised for a short period. In combination with natural ventilation in particular, these measures can mean the full cooling capacity is not available on warm, humid days.

Cooling ceilings

A solution in widespread use is room cooling by air that has been extracted from the room itself, cooled, and then reintroduced into the room (recirculated air operation). These systems are normally decentralized and respond quickly to controls, which may be separate for each

Recirculated air cooling

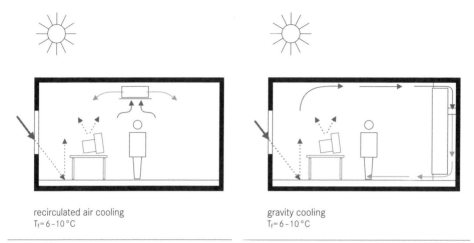

recirculated air cooling
$T_f = 6-10\,°C$

gravity cooling
$T_f = 6-10\,°C$

Fig. 54: Convective cooling by recirculated air units

Fig. 55: The principle of gravity cooling

room. They can also be controlled by the user. Air can be cooled by a cold register directly at the air outlet of a device suspended from the ceiling. The effect is purely convective. Feed temperatures of 6–10 °C are generally required. > Fig. 54

Gravity cooling   Fully recirculated air cooling can also be performed without the need for a fan, using the principle of gravity cooling (or downdraught cooling). The movement of air is due to the fact that cold air is heavier than warm air. The room air is cooled by a cold convector near the ceiling (where the highest room air temperatures are found) and gradually drops down a shaft, accelerating the convection effect, before emerging at the bottom and spreading out across the room as a "pool of cold air." > Fig. 55

Gravity cooling offers the advantage of being completely silent. The cooling capacity in the room varies with temperature difference at the cooler and operates automatically to a certain extent. It can be installed inconspicuously behind a wall lining or a curtain without detrimental effect on its performance, as long as the top and bottom air entry and exit points are there. The problem of condensation can be solved as described in the systems above. A brief overview of the main cold transfer systems can be found in Table 11.

Tab. 11: Characteristics of cold transfer systems

Cold transfer system	Advantages	Disadvantages	Proportion by radiation/ convection	T_f [°C]
Cooled ceilings	Moderate feed temperatures; rapid controllability; radiation effect; individual room control possible	Draining away condensation water is practically impossible	50/50	10–16
Recirculated air cooling	Rapid response to controls; individual room control possible	Purely convective effect; draining away condensation water is practically impossible; fan noise possible	0/100	6–10
Gravity cooling	Rapid response to controls; individual room control possible; completely silent; inconspicuous installation possible	Purely convective effect; draining away condensation water is difficult	0/100	6–10

Hybrid systems

A number of transfer systems are suitable for supplying heat and cold to a room. > Tab.12, page 78

These systems also include air conditioning equipment that provides ventilation as well as heating and cooling a room from a central plant. > Fig. 56 The advantage of an air conditioning system is that it can humidify or dehumidify the room air, which means that practically any desired indoor air conditions can be achieved. > Chapter Ventilation systems, Mechanical ventilation

Air conditioning equipment

One fundamental disadvantage is that air is a poor heat transport medium, because of its low thermal storage capacity. > Chapter Design principles, Covering the demands Increasing the air volume flow to cover a demand for heat or cold energy therefore leads to increased energy use for delivering the air, which could be avoided in a water-operated system. Air conditioning systems often have no facility for allowing individual room control or user influence. This fact and the pronounced effect of air temperature, velocity and degree of turbulence on thermal comfort can result in user complaints and dissatisfaction.

Increased comfort can usually be created with systems that work by radiation, > Chapter Design principles, Comfort requirements for example with thermally activated components. In these systems, pipework coils car-

Thermally activated components

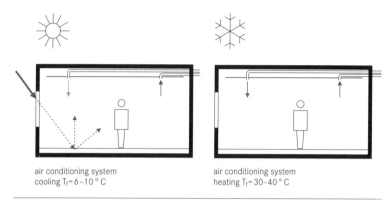

air conditioning system
cooling T_f= 6 - 10 ° C

air conditioning system
heating T_f= 30–40 ° C

Fig. 56: Convective heat and cold transfer by air conditioning systems

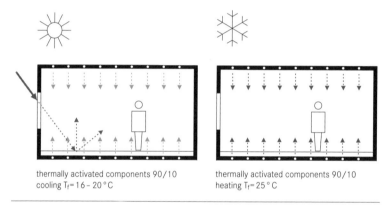

thermally activated components 90/10
cooling T_f= 16 - 20 °C

thermally activated components 90/10
heating T_f= 25 ° C

Fig. 57: Radiated transfer of heat and cold by thermally activated components

rying a heat or cold medium are cast into the core of a concrete slab.
> Fig. 57

The thermal inertia of the concrete mass makes controllability very low. Thermally activated components are therefore mainly used to cover constant loads or to meet a basic level of demand. > Chapter Design principles, Covering the demands

For heating, the feed temperature is 25 °C. The performance of the activated component depends mainly on the temperature difference between the ceiling surface and the room air. This produces a self-

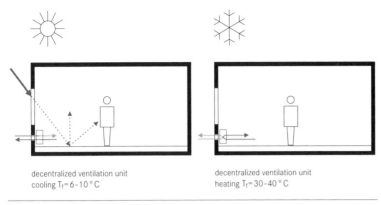

decentralized ventilation unit
cooling T_f = 6–10 °C

decentralized ventilation unit
heating T_f = 30–40 °C

Fig. 58: Convective heat and cold transfer using decentralized ventilation units (here in the facade spandrel wall)

regulating effect as the cooling output increases with rising room air temperature.

The problem of the dew point is similar to cooling ceilings, but the higher feed temperatures of 16–20 °C permit higher humidity without condensation taking place. The moderate feed temperatures for both heating and cooling modes mean that renewable energy sources can be used.

The coolant medium and the thermal mass of the concrete are integrated effectively, resulting in efficient de-energization of the component, for example overnight. Like night ventilation, this reduces > Chapter Design principles, Covering the demands the cooling output demand during the day and achieves a more uniform load profile. > Fig. 14, page 32

The concrete surface must be thermally accessible for activated components to work properly. Thermally activated ceiling systems are incompatible with suspended ceilings. Impact sound insulation also reduces the effectiveness of these systems, as cold transfer on the top surface is limited.

Decentralized ventilation units are built into the facade (e.g. in the spandrel wall), or in the facade area (e.g. in the double floor), and have a direct connection to the outdoor air. > Fig. 58

Decentralized ventilation units

Controllability is very good, but air conditioning units require an increased flow of air to cover higher cooling loads, which means their use

Tab. 12: Characteristics of hybrid systems for heat and cold transfer

Hybrid system	Advantages	Disadvantages	Proportion of output radiated/ convected	T_f [°C] Heating	T_f [°C] Cooling
Air conditioning systems	Rapid response to controls; draining away condensate simple	Purely convective effect; individual room control options poor	0/100	30–40	6–10
Thermally activated components	Moderate feed temperatures; radiation effect; partial self-regulation	Limited capacity; draining away condensation water practically impossible	90/10	25	16–20
Decentralized ventilation units	Rapid response to controls; individual room control easily possible	Draining away condensate difficult; increased maintenance cost	0/100	30–40	6–10

as the only means of heating or cooling is not always a workable option. If decentralized air conditioning units are used to cover higher cooling loads, then some means of draining away the condensate is necessary.

Decentralized systems can work well in combination with activated components, as the systems' advantages complement one another and their disadvantages cancel out.

As with centralized air conditioning systems, decentralized units normally require a feed temperature of 6–10 °C for cooling and 30–40 °C for heating. Table 12 shows the most common hybrid systems for heat and cold transfer. > Appendix, pp 84 and 85

CHOOSING THE RIGHT SYSTEM

Selecting the most suitable tempering system to fit all demands often presents the architect with a difficult task. The various energy sources each require suitable heat and cold generators, but not every generator can be combined with every transfer system. It is often this complex interaction of the individual components and the number of more or less viable possible combinations that renders working closely with a specialist design engineer quite indispensable.

Tab. 13: Criteria in the selection of a tempering system

Technical criteria	Capacity (covering of demand)
	Suitable system temperatures of the components
	Suitability for renewable energy
	Availability of the energy source
	Possibility of heat recovery
	Controllability
Environmental effects	Primary energy demand
	CO_2 emission
User acceptance	Comfort requirements
	User influence
Economy	Initial costs
	Operating costs

There is a series of further criteria relevant to the selection, which go beyond purely technical considerations. These are, primarily, energy efficiency, user acceptance and economic viability, all of which mean that the architect must proceed very carefully with the design.

Table 13 gives an overview of the most important criteria to consider in the choice of a suitable tempering system.

Combination of ventilation and tempering

THE RANGE OF POSSIBLE SOLUTIONS

The proposed ventilation and tempering systems must be positively combinable with one another so that overall concepts for indoor air conditioning systems can be developed that ensure the desired room temperature and required room ventilation.

Low-tech and high-tech   Depending on requirements, there are numerous possible combinations that vary in their degree of technical sophistication. Possible concepts for room conditioning range from the technologically simplest (low-tech) variants with window ventilation and radiators, through to the most complex (high-tech) systems with full air conditioning. > Fig. 59

Even though these systems represent the two extremes and therefore the start and end points of the range of possible solutions, nevertheless, depending on the requirements and the criteria applied, they may still be the most suitable concept for room conditioning, providing a performance to match the demand.

The number of possible combinations of system components precludes any universally applicable arrangements in the sense of a "patented solution" for room conditioning. A more fruitful approach is for the architect or specialist design engineer to evaluate the possible concepts based on the project criteria in order to arrive at a suitable concept.

SELECTION CRITERIA

The combination of components for ventilation and heat and cold transfer can be evaluated according to technical criteria (e.g. renewable energies and heat recovery) and criteria relevant to user acceptance (e.g. comfort and user influence).

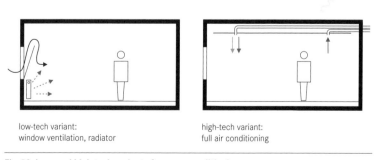

low-tech variant:
window ventilation, radiator

high-tech variant:
full air conditioning

Fig. 59: Low- and high-tech variants for room conditioning

Examples of Concepts

Window ventilation, radiators

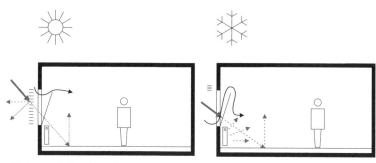

Window ventilation with radiators + solar screening

Suitability	Advantages	Disadvantages
– Residential – Office	– Efficient energy transport by water – User influence and individual room control easily possible – Decoupling of ventilation and tempering	– Unconditioned supply air – No defined air change rate possible – No heat recovery possible – No cooling, humidification or dehumidification possible – Uncomfortable and high heat losses in winter – Noise and dust emissions possible

Window ventilation, underfloor heating

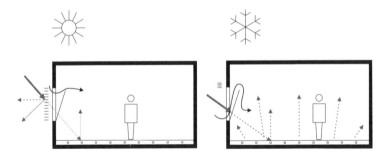

Window ventilation with underfloor heating + solar screening

Suitability	Advantages	Disadvantages
– Residential – Office	– Efficient energy transport by water – Suitable for the use of renewable energy – User influence and individual room control easily possible – Comfortable heat transfer – Decoupling of ventilation and tempering	– Unconditioned supply air – No defined air change rate possible – No heat recovery possible – No cooling, humidification or dehumidification possible – High heat losses in winter – Noise and dust emissions possible – Very sluggish response to controls

Air heating

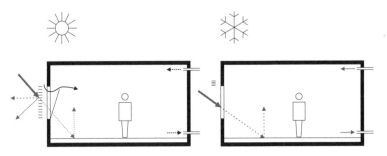

Air heating with optional window ventilation in summer + solar screening

Suitability	Advantages	Disadvantages
– Residential	– No additional heating surfaces required – Defined air change rate possible – Heat recovery possible – Noise and dust emissions can be avoided	– Inefficient energy transport by air – Only efficient with low heat demand – Only convective heat transfer – User influence and individual room control difficult to incorporate – Coupling of ventilation and tempering

Window ventilation, convectors, cooling ceilings

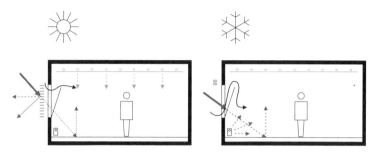

Window ventilation, convectors, cooling ceilings + solar screening

Suitability	Advantages	Disadvantages
– Office – Conference room	– High comfort in summer – Efficient energy transport by water – User influence and individual room control easily possible – Decoupling of ventilation and tempering	– Unconditioned supply air – No defined air change rate possible – No heat recovery possible – No humidification and dehumidification possible – Condensate drainage difficult to incorporate – Discomfort and high heat losses in winter – Noise and dust emissions possible

Window ventilation, onvectors, recirculated air units

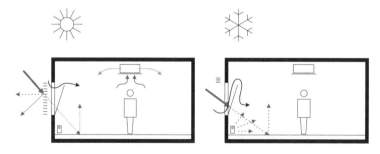

Window ventilation, convectors, recirculated air units + solar screening

Suitability	Advantages	Disadvantages
– Office	– User influence and individual room control easily possible – Decoupling of ventilation and tempering	– Unconditioned supply air – No heat recovery possible – Only convective heat and cold transfer – Possible discomfort and high heat losses in winter – Noise and dust emissions possible

Decentralized ventilation systems, thermally activated components

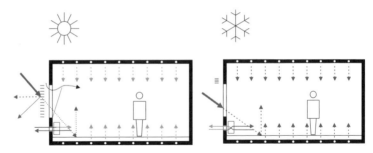

Decentralized ventilation systems, thermally activated components with optional window ventilation in summer + solar screening

Suitability	Advantages	Disadvantages
– Office – Conference room	– Efficient energy transport by water (basic load cover) – Heat and cold transfer partially by radiation – Preconditioned supply air – Defined air change rate possible – Heat recovery possible – User influence and individual room control possible – Decoupling of ventilation and tempering – Noise and dust emissions can be avoided	– Higher installation costs – Condensate drainage difficult to incorporate – No humidification and dehumidification possible – Higher maintenance costs

Air conditioning systems

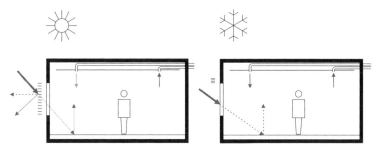

Air conditioning system + solar screening

Suitability	Advantages	Disadvantages
– Residential – Office – Conference room	– Preconditioned supply air – Defined air change rate possible – Heating, cooling, humidification and dehumidification possible – Heat recovery possible – Condensate drainage easy to incorporate – Noise and dust emissions can be avoided	– Inefficient energy transport by air – Only convective heat and cold transfer – User influence and individual room control difficult to incorporate – Coupling of ventilation and tempering

The following table gives an overview of possible combinations of the ventilation and tempering systems presented in this book. This table is neither generally applicable nor exhaustive, but should be used as an example of how the various concepts can be compared and a suitable solution found. The concepts selected as examples are also shown in detail in the appendix to this book.

room conditioning system	venti-lation type		tempering type								characteristics					typical use		
	natural	mechanical	heating bodies	surface heating	air heating	cooling ceiling	recirculated air cooling	air conditioning system	thermally activated components	decentralized ventilation unit	suitable for renewable energy	heat recovery	controllability	comfort	user influence	residential	office	conference room
	X		X								o	–	+	o	+	X	X	
	X			X							+	–	–	+	+	X	(X)	
	(X)	X			X						–	+	+	ç	–	X		
	X		X		X						o	–	+	+	+		X	X
	X		X				X				o	–	+	ç	+		X	X
	(X)	X							X	X	o	+	o	+	+		X	X
		X					X				–	+	+	–	–	(X)	X	X

In conclusion

Buildings generally require individual solutions for room condition-ing. In contrast to other industries, each component has to be checked against the specifically applicable framework conditions and require-ments in detail and a customized solution devised. For this reason, achiev-ing a successful concept usually involves a comparative examination of alternatives. Even having reached a satisfactory solution should not stop other possible combinations from being examined and their advantages and disadvantages evaluated.

Experienced architects and engineers are able to recognize advan-tages and disadvantages more quickly and therefore recommend par-ticular applications. However, it is not possible to master the complexity of this subject without more accurate analysis.

This book therefore seeks to show that the detailed explanations of the individual system components and the examples of combinations are important as an overview. They provide an introduction to the subject of room conditioning in order to be able, later on, to create a fully designed room conditioning concept through calculations and technical drawings. However, it is only through understanding the dependencies, and being aware of the interaction of the specific project parameters with the tech-nical possibilities, that an optimum solution can be found for the project.

Doris Haas-Arndt

Water Cycles

Introduction

Part of the technical services in a modern building is a complex pipe-work system for supplying drinking water and disposing of waste water. This system is a cycle, somewhat similar to the natural water cycle: fresh water is collected, supplied to the building, distributed through a pipe-work system, and heated if required. It is piped to the draw-off points in bathrooms, kitchens and other sanitary rooms. As soon as it leaves the drinking water pipe through the faucet, it becomes waste water and flows through the waste water pipework into the sewers, from where it is cleaned again and finally returned to natural watercourses. Architects must integrate this cycle into the design of their buildings, as without a carefully planned and properly functioning fresh and waste water system, WCs cannot be flushed, washing machines cannot be operated, and no water will emerge from a shower.

The chapters that follow consider the individual positions of water in a building along the water cycle, and describe the functions of the elements connected to this cycle. It should become clear how a drinking water supply system works, how it is designed into a building, and which aspects should be taken into account. There is also an explanation of how waste water is created and conducted into the drainage system, the general problems that arise in the supply and disposal of water, and the options for their solution.

Water supply

Approximately two thirds of the earth's surface is covered with water. Of this, only 0.3% is fresh water and therefore potential drinking water. Drinking water is very high-quality fresh water that is suitable for human consumption.

THE NATURAL WATER CYCLE

The natural water cycle—or hydrologic cycle—is a continuous sequence of evaporation, precipitation, and rainwater draining into bodies of open water or seeping into the ground to accumulate as groundwater. Water vapor rises under the influence of solar radiation or other heating effects to form clouds, and falls as precipitation back onto the earth's surface. Some of the rainwater that seeps away is absorbed by the ground, some evaporates, and some is taken up into plants by capillary action. A proportion reaches the lower soil strata and helps maintain the groundwater table. > Fig. 1

Groundwater   Groundwater is described as precipitation water that is stored on top of an impervious stratum and has a temperature of between 8 and 10 °C all year round. Groundwater is generally microbe-free and is pumped up to the surface from deep wells. It provides about three quarters of our drinking water, and goes through several stages of cleaning and filtering before it is fed into the public supply network.

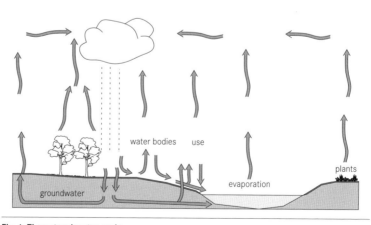

Fig. 1: The natural water cycle

Substantial groundwater extraction and extensive sealing of urban land surfaces have a substantial impact on the natural water cycle. Rainwater falling on impervious areas cannot seep naturally into groundwater, but is conducted directly into bodies of open water or into the drains. The groundwater table is greatly reduced by building developments, deforestation and drainage works. ○

In addition, the extensive extraction of groundwater for agriculture and industry, and the pollutants that these activities introduce, are harmful to the system. Pollutants from sources such as manure, agricultural pesticides, landfill, highway drainage and industrial emissions, which fall as acid rain and seep into the groundwater, are a serious cause for concern and can be removed only by expensive cleaning and filtering. The increasing contamination of water combined with high water usage produces an ecological imbalance, the consequences of which result in high costs.

STANDARDS FOR DRINKING WATER

Drinking water intended for human consumption has to meet certain standards. It must be good to taste, odorless and colorless, and free of pathogens and microbes. Every draw-off point must provide best-quality drinking water at sufficient pressure. Quantities of chemicals added to disinfect the water, and of other possible constituents, must be kept within limits specified for European Union countries by an EU directive and regional drinking water regulations. The water's quality and the limits for the substances it contains are checked regularly in accordance with the applicable national standards for drinking water. These standards for drinking water quality change constantly. Today's level of pollution means they can be met only with great difficulty and at increasing cost. ○

Water with high calcium and magnesium content is described as hard, while water with low calcium and magnesium content is soft. High levels of hardness produce a build-up of mineral deposits in pipe networks; these deposits are known as scale. Considerably more detergent is required for washing clothes in hard water, and the dishwasher may leave

Hardness level

○ **Note:** Surfacings such as asphalt are impervious to water and effectively seal the ground, thus preventing groundwater from being replenished.

○ **Note:** The European Union Council Directive 98/83 (EU Drinking Water Directive) concerns the quality of drinking water for human consumption and obliges all member states to implement it stepwise into their national legislation.

Tab. 1: Water hardness ranges

Hardness range	Hardness in mmol/l	Description
1	< 1.3	soft
2	1.3–2.5	medium hard
3	2.5–3.8	hard
4	> 3.8	very hard

a thin film of lime on the dishes. Water hardness is measured in mmol/l (millimoles per liter). The hardness level depends on the source of the water. > Tab. 1 Water with less than 30 mg/l calcium bicarbonate, on the other hand, does not allow the pipes to form a protective surface layer, with the result that the pipe material is attacked by acids, and corrodes. The effect of water hardness on health is insignificant.

pH An important measure of the "aggressivity" of water is its pH (Latin: *potentia Hydrogenii*). The pH describes the concentration of hydrogen ions in water, or more precisely: the negative logarithm of the hydrogen ion concentration. On this scale, pure water has a pH of 7, i.e. there are 10^{-7} g H ions in one liter of pure water. If the pH drops below 7, the water behaves aggressively like an acid; if the pH is higher, the water behaves as a base (alkali) and more lime is deposited.

THE DEMAND FOR DRINKING WATER

In the 19th century, Germany required about 30 l of drinking water per day per head for consumption and personal hygiene. Today, by contrast, the figure will soon reach 130 l, due to the increasing levels of sanitary convenience, such as flowing water, showers and flushing toilets. This consumption is doubtless very high, but it has already decreased, because a great number of water-saving fittings have been installed in bathrooms and WCs in recent years. However, industry, commerce and agriculture are using increasing amounts of water. The irrigation of agricultural land consumes the largest quantity of drinking water worldwide.

In the industrialized countries, almost all buildings are connected to the public drinking water supply network. Many billion cubic meters of water are removed from the natural water cycle for drinking water supplies every year. Most of this comes from groundwater and bodies of open water, and the rest from sources such as river bank filtration. The term "bodies of open water" refers to rivers or lakes, the water of which is usually contaminated with bacteria and mechanically eroded solids, and can be supplied as drinking water only after a long purification process.

Conurbations and regions where water is scarce have to rely on some of their drinking water being transported from far away. At the same time, the high proportion of impervious surfaces in cities means most of the rainwater flows directly into their drainage systems. As it is particularly difficult to supply the quantities of drinking water required in these areas, it is imperative to reduce drinking water demand.

The daily drinking water demand of domestic households can be divided into different uses. The amount actually consumed is quite a small proportion of the total. Only about 5 l water are drunk or used for cooking, and the rest used for other purposes. Peaks and troughs during the day are compensated for by water storage at waterworks.

The average hot water demand in domestic residential properties is between 30 and 60 l per person per day. It can vary greatly from day to day and with the habits of the users. A bath requires about 120 to 180 l hot water at 40 °C; a 5-minute shower about 40 l at 37 °C. Energy and drinking water can be saved by choosing to have a shower instead of a bath.

SAVING DRINKING WATER

Today there are many sanitary engineering solutions for saving drinking water: flow limiters in shower heads, water-saving faucets and toilets, and domestic appliances (e.g. washing machines and dishwashers) with reduced water consumption. Installing a water meter in each apartment instead of having one central metering point in the basement has a proven water-saving effect, because users can track their consumption directly; they just pay for the water they have used. WC cisterns with stop buttons and a water usage of 4–6 l per flush are now standard. More advanced

Tab. 2: Typical usage of drinking water

Activity	Usage in l/day/person
Drinking and cooking	5
Basic personal hygiene	10
Baths and showers	38
Dishwashing	8
Cleaning	8
Clothes washing	15
Toilet flushing	40
Garden watering	6
Total	**130**

systems such as vacuum toilets use 1.2 l water per flush. Composting toilets of various types use no water at all. > Chapter Drinking water systems in buildings, Sanitary rooms

A precise analysis of drinking water usage demonstrates that water of drinking quality is not always necessary. > Tab. 2 Pure drinking water is necessary only for personal hygiene, washing kitchenware, cooking and drinking. Rainwater-quality water is adequate for toilet flushing, cleaning, or watering the garden. Water consumption can therefore be substantially reduced by using rainwater. Cleaned gray water from showers and hand basins, for example, can also be used for flushing WCs. > Chapter Waste water, Uses of waste water

Merely installing modern water-saving faucets in sanitary rooms can reduce average drinking water demand to about 100 l per person per day. With a few more of the measures mentioned above, it would even be possible to manage on half of normal drinking water consumption with no significant loss of comfort.

Drinking water systems in buildings

The water cycle normally begins in buildings with the supply of cold drinking water through a pipe connected to the public water supply network, unless the plot has its own private supply (well). In larger towns and settlements, the connection to the public drinking water supply is normally at a frost-free depth of between 1.00 and 1.80 m below the sidewalk. Each plot has its own drinking water service pipe, which heads off into the building at right angles to the public supply pipe, as far as the house connection or main stopcock and water metering point. > Fig. 2 In residential properties this pipe has a nominal diameter of about 25 mm (DN 25).

○

In some European countries, the position of the drinking water connection is marked with a colored sign on a nearby house wall for ease of identification and location of the connection point. The lines and numbers on the sign give the distance to the drinking water connection—from the sign—and the direction (to the right, left, in front or behind). The other abbreviations normally describe the type of connection; the accompanying numbers give the nominal internal pipe diameter.

To prevent microbes from flourishing, the drinking water supplied to the building is cold, i.e. between 5 and 15 °C. To obtain hot water, the drinking water must first be heated in the building. Hot water in this context is described as drinking water with a temperature of between 40 and 90 °C. For personal hygiene, a water temperature of 40 to 45 °C is adequate, while washing dishes requires water at 55 to 85 °C to produce hygienic results.
Water temperature

The water supply company creates a pressure within the water supply network to distribute the drinking water. The water pressure of the public supply is usually between 6 and 10 bar, and is brought down to about 5 bar or less by pressure reducers in the building's pipework system. > Chapter Drinking water systems in buildings, Components of a drinking water supply system
Water pressure

○ **Note:** The abbreviation DN, which is used as a label in every pipework drawing, means "diamètre nominal" and defines the nominal internal diameter of a pipe. This must comply with national regulations and depends on the size of the system.

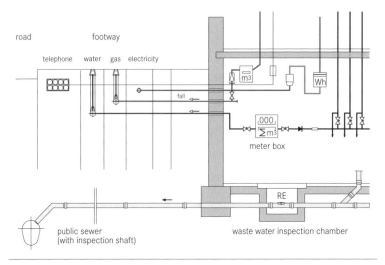

road　　　　　footway

telephone　water　gas　electricity

m3

Wh

fall

,000,
Σm3

meter box

RE

public sewer
(with inspection shaft)

waste water inspection chamber

Fig. 2: Supply and discharge pipes in a building

These values may vary from place to place and should only be taken as a guide. The absolute minimum pressure at the draw-off point should not fall below 0.5 bar, as otherwise the water cannot be distributed properly. Pressure losses in the pipework system may be caused by, for example, a great difference in height between the service pipe and the draw-off point. Loss of pressure can be taken roughly as 1 bar for every 10 m height.

COMPONENTS OF A DRINKING WATER SUPPLY SYSTEM

Drinking water is distributed within a building's supply system through a branched network of horizontal and vertical pipes, which are normally concealed in <u>service ducts</u>, <u>wall lining cavities</u>, floor voids, or wall chases. Other water supply system components include a water meter to record consumption, safety devices, stop valves and draw-off points.

House connection The service pipe to the public water supply and the water meter are part of the supplied service and usually belong to the water supply company. The service pipe takes the shortest route into the building and must not be built over, so that it can easily be located and repaired if necessary. For safety reasons, the pipe duct must pass through the outside wall or foundation of the building at right angles, and the pipe must be enclosed by a protective sleeve.

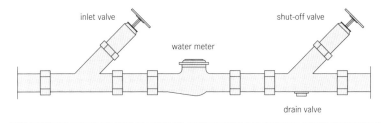

Fig. 3: Drinking water meter in the meter box

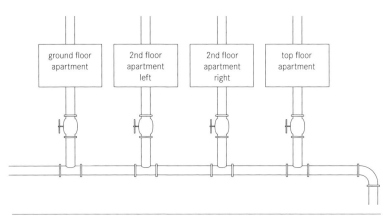

Fig. 4: Subdistribution of the drinking water supply by a distribution manifold

The calibrated water meter is positioned directly between the public water supply stopcock and the stopcock for the building's internal water pipework system. These two shut-off valves allow the meter to be removed without complications. > Fig. 3

Water meter

The architect's design role starts at the water meter. The meter should be housed in a frost-free and readily accessible enclosure, e.g. in a meter box on the road side of the building, so that it can be read easily. If the meter cannot be installed inside the building, it may be housed in a meter chamber outside the building. This may even be specified so as to allow the meter to be read by the water supply company without the building occupant's being present.

If the drinking water distribution system has several risers (which may be required, for example, for supplying water to the different floors of an apartment block), a manifold is also incorporated to feed the individual apartments. > Fig. 4 In addition to the subdivision of the drinking water feed, there are often also heating supply pipes, separate draw-off points (e.g.

Distribution manifold

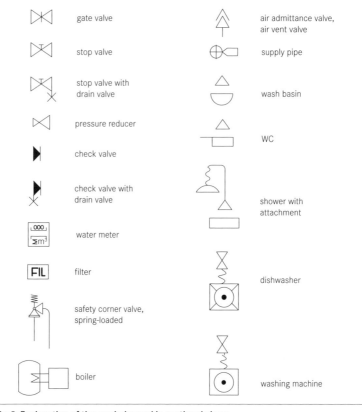

	gate valve		air admittance valve, air vent valve
	stop valve		supply pipe
	stop valve with drain valve		wash basin
	pressure reducer		WC
	check valve		shower with attachment
	check valve with drain valve		
	water meter		dishwasher
	filter		
	safety corner valve, spring-loaded		washing machine
	boiler		

Fig. 5: Explanation of the symbols used in sectional views

outdoors) and, if necessary, separate pipes supplying water for firefighting. Each riser from the manifold is carefully labeled so that it is clear which pipe feeds which premises. Each riser network has its own shut-off valve so that replacement of system components can be carried out independently of the rest of the system.

Layout drawings and symbols

European Standard EN 806 and its national annexes give special graphic symbols for system components and sanitary fixtures for use on design drawings of drinking water systems. They indicate the components to be installed in buildings and their spatial positioning and arrangement. > Fig. 5 These standards may vary from country to country. The system must be drawn in plan and sectional views to fully depict the drinking water system and its associated pipework. Since sanitary appliances in plan are seen from above, some appliances may require different sym-

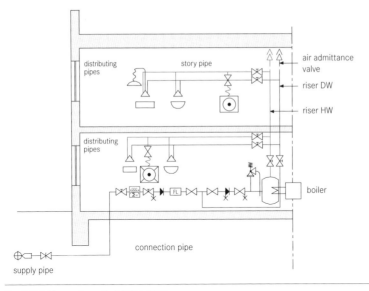

distributing pipes

story pipe

air admittance valve

riser DW

riser HW

distributing pipes

boiler

connection pipe

supply pipe

Fig. 6: Drinking water network in section

bols for plan and sectional views. A key on the drawing is generally helpful to explain the symbols used.

The representation of the system in section should be schematic and contain as much information about the drinking water system as possible. The sequence of the drinking water system symbols used should correspond to the actual arrangement of the sanitary items. Symbols and pipework are drawn as if the supply network and draw-off points were in the same, single plane. > Fig. 6

Representation in section

When drawing the system in plan it is important to identify the rising and falling pipes separately with arrows showing the direction of flow in the pipes. > Fig. 7 You should also show whether a pipe begins, ends or carries through each story. > Fig. 8

Representation in plan

Description of pipework components

Many pipework components in drinking water systems are referred to by special terms that are not used in other supply systems. > Fig. 6 The most important terms are:

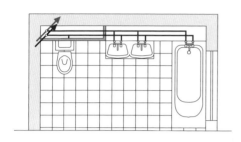

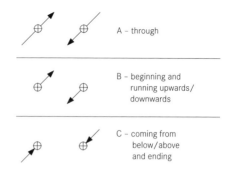

Fig. 7: Pipe network in a bathroom shown in plan

Fig. 8: Representing direction of flow in pipes

- service pipe for the pipe between the public supply and main stopcock in the building
- riser for the pipe which passes vertically through the building, from which the
- pipes supplying the individual stories branch off horizontally
- circulation pipe, which provides continuous hot water at the draw-off points, but is not always required
- distributing pipes are the vertical pipes branching from the horizontal pipes supplying each story to the draw-off points.

The internal diameter of risers in residential buildings is about DN 20, and for pipes supply stories about DN 15, i.e. nominal diameters of 20 and 15 mm respectively.

Circulation pipes   A circulation pipe ensures that hot water is available immediately at draw-off points. This has the advantage that a large amount of cold water does not have to flow through the pipe before the hot water appears, which is frequently the problem with instantaneous water heaters. A disadvantage is the electrical energy continuously consumed by the pump to keep the water circulating in the pipework. A time-switched pump, which only runs when hot water is needed, can mitigate the effect.

Pipe routes
Horizontal pipe routes may pass under a basement ceiling or be placed in the floor construction. Larger buildings often have floor ducts, or position the pipes above suspended ceilings. > Fig. 9 Vertical pipes in basements or equipment rooms may be fixed openly on the walls, > Fig. 10

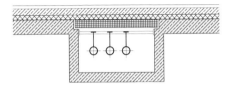

Fig. 9: Pipes installed in a floor duct

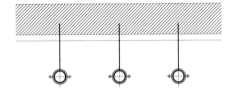

Fig. 10: Pipes attached to a wall

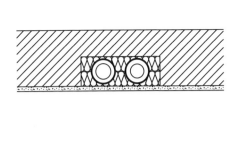

Fig. 11: Pipes fitted in a wall chase

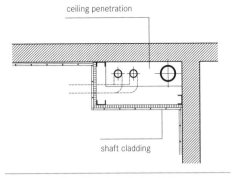

Fig. 12: Pipes fitted in an installation shaft

and in the stories above in installation shafts or, for short lengths, be concealed in half-height false walls. > Chapter Drinking water systems in buildings, Sanitary rooms

In solid wall and floor construction, pipes are fitted into insulated wall chases, if the wall has a large enough cross section and there are no structural engineering reasons to preclude it. > Fig. 11 This method of installation is increasingly being superseded by installation shafts in sanitary rooms because of its complexity and poor sound insulation. > Fig. 12 False walls, in comparison with shafts, just clad the pipes in the wall cavity and generally terminate at half room-height, while an installation shaft can carry pipes through several stories. > Fig. 13

Calculation of pipe sizes

The nominal diameter of the pipes is determined by the number of consumer points connected. > Tab. 3 It is also important to consider the probability of simultaneous draw-off, the material used for the pipes, the pressure loss due to friction, and minimum flow pressure. The system

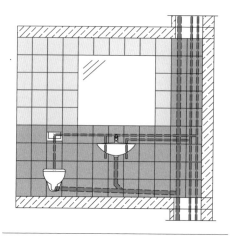

Fig.13: False wall installation and installation shaft

Tab. 3: Diameter of drinking water pipes

Pipe type	Approximate internal diameter
Service pipe	DN 25 to DN 32
Riser	DN 20
1–5 draw-off points	DN 20
5–10 draw-off points	DN 25
10–20 draw-off points	DN 32
20–40 draw-off points	DN 40
Story distribution pipes	DN 15
1 WC cistern	DN 10 to DN 15
1–2 wash basins	DN 15
1 shower	DN 15
1 bath	DN 20 to 25
1 garden hose	DN 20 to 25

must be designed to have a minimum flow pressure in the pipe such that the remotest drinking water draw-off point always has sufficient pressure to operate properly. The pipe friction pressure loss factor is the fall in pressure within a section of pipe divided by its length.

Materials

Modern drinking water pipes that are in the ground outside the building are normally of plastic (polyethylene HD), because metal pipes require additional corrosion protection. A new development is the multilayer metal composite pipe, which combines the advantages of metal (strength) and plastic (corrosion resistance).

Copper, galvanized steel, stainless steel or plastic (polyethylene) are used inside the building as materials for drinking water pipes. Plastic pipes are not rigid and their small cross section and ability to be bent to tight radii allows them to be installed even within a floor construction. Polyethylene pipes are usually designed as a pipe-in-pipe system: the flexible drinking water pipe (PE-X) is surrounded by an additional flexible, external protective pipe (PE-HD), and can be taken out of the protective pipe and replaced if necessary. As well as their high flexibility, plastic pipes have the advantage of resistance to scale and corrosion. When metal pipes are used or when pipework is replaced as part of a refurbishment project, attention should be paid to placing the less noble material after the more noble material (relative to the direction of flow), e.g. copper after steel, as otherwise corrosion could occur.   ○

Safety devices

Most systems incorporate safety measures to maintain the high quality of their drinking water. The quality must not be reduced by the entry of non-potable water, for instance. These devices include safety fittings that prevent back-flow or suction of contaminated water and the mixing of drinking water with water of lesser quality, which may happen, for example, if there is underpressure in the system due to a pipe developing a leak at the same time as a shower head has been left in bathwater. These safety devices prevent the underpressure from sucking bathwater into the drinking water supply.   ○

○ **Note:** Polyethylene HD is also used for buried pipes; PE-X is used mainly for internal pipework with a protective outer covering of PE-HD. HD means high density, PE-X crosslinked polyethylene.

○ **Note:** The maintenance of purity of drinking water in buildings is governed by European Standard EN 1717, "Protection against pollution of potable water in water installations and general requirements of devices to prevent pollution by backflow".

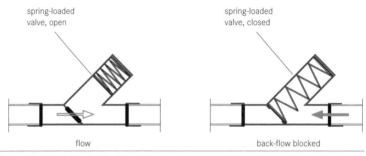

spring-loaded
valve, open

spring-loaded
valve, closed

flow

back-flow blocked

Fig. 14: The principle of a check valve

Check valves

One of the safety devices normally built into a domestic water installation is a check valve placed after the water meter. It is a self-closing, spring-loaded valve that prevents the backflow of drinking water in the pipe. The check valve opens only to allow water through in the correct direction of flow. If the flow stops, it closes again. If the direction of flow reverses, the valves closes with increased pressure. > Fig. 14

Air admittance valve

Check valves are normally installed in combination with an air admittance valve, which acts to compensate any underpressure occurring in the pipework system and prevent back-suction of contaminated water into the drinking water supply. The air admittance valve is positioned at the highest point in every cold or hot water riser. The valve inside the air admittance valve is normally closed. > Fig. 15 In conjunction with the check valve, the air admittance valve opens when underpressure occurs, and the inward flow of air prevents used water from being sucked back into the pipework. > Fig. 16

As there is a risk of water escaping from the air admittance valve when there is overpressure in the pipework, the valve may be connected to a drip collection pipe, which drains any escaping water into the waste water pipework and thus into the sewer. A drip collection pipe is not required if the air admittance valve is positioned above a shower or basin, where any escaping water cannot cause any damage.

Pressure reducer

The water pressure provided by the water supply company may be too high for normal draw-off points and may need to be reduced by a pressure reducer inside the building. The delivery pressure acts on a moving diaphragm, which either opens or closes a connected spring valve, depending on the setting. > Fig. 17 The pressure reducer should be installed in a position where it can be easily maintained.

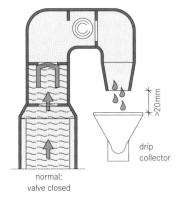

normal:
valve closed

drip
collector

>20mm

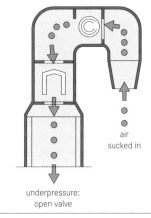

underpressure:
open valve

air
sucked in

Fig. 15: Operation of an air admittance valve with drip collection pipe

Fig. 16: Operation at underpressure of an air admittance valve without a drip collection pipe

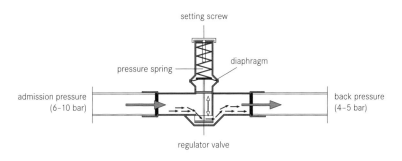

setting screw

pressure spring

diaphragm

admission pressure
(6–10 bar)

back pressure
(4–5 bar)

regulator valve

Fig. 17: Principle of a pressure reducer

A fine filter is built into every drinking water system to ensure that it is free of dirt and rust particles. In most cases it is installed between the water meter and the pressure reducer, so that the latter is not contaminated. Installing a filter is worthwhile only if it is regularly serviced, because a filter insert cannot be expected to remain permanently free of microbes.

Buried drinking water pipes should be placed more than 1 m from any wastewater pipes above them, so as to prevent contamination of the drinking water supply in the event of a leak. If it is not possible to

Tab. 4: Typical insulation thicknesses for cold water pipes

Pipe	Insulation thickness
– In the open in an unheated space – In an installation shaft with no nearby pipes carrying hot water – In a wall chase	4 mm
– In the open in a heated space	9 mm
– In an installation shaft with nearby pipes carrying hot water	13 mm

The insulation thickness is calculated assuming a thermal conductivity of 0.035 W/m²K and must be recalculated for other insulation materials

maintain this safety distance, the drinking water pipe must be laid above the waste water pipe, at a distance of at least 20 cm.

Thermal insulation   Cold drinking water pipes should be prevented from inadvertent heating from nearby hot water or heating pipes by insulating them, or by maintaining a suitable distance to keep them free of microbes. Drinking water pipes should also be insulated when they pass through heated spaces.
> Tab. 4

HOT WATER SYSTEMS

To satisfy the daily demand for hot water, part of the drinking water in a building is heated before being distributed. Hot water supply systems consist of the cold water feed, a boiler, perhaps a hot water storage tank, hot water distribution pipes leading to draw-off points, and in some circumstances circulation pipes, which ensure that hot water is instantly available at the draw-off points.

● **Important:** Cold water pipes should always be fixed below gas pipes, as there is always a risk that condensing water could cause corrosion of the gas pipe and result in a dangerous gas leak.

Tab. 5: Conventional insulation thicknesses for hot water pipes

Nominal pipe diameter	Insulation thickness
– up to DN 20	20 mm
– from DN 22 to DN 35	30 mm
– from DN 40 to DN 100	pipe DN
– larger than DN 100	100 mm

Half the above thickness is adequate for pipe lengths of up to 8 m
– at wall and ceiling penetrations
– where pipes cross

If a building obtains its hot water from a central installation, the hot Pipe layout water pipes mainly run parallel to the cold water pipes throughout the building and have more or less the same pipe cross section. The water temperature in the pipework is between 40 and 60 °C. To avoid energy losses, the hot water pipes should be kept as short as possible and always thermally insulated where they pass through unheated spaces. The extra space required for insulation must be taken into account when designing the pipework route.

The insulation thickness is approximately equal to the pipe diameter; with pipes less than 8 m long, half that thickness is adequate. This is also the case where pipes pass through walls or ceilings and where they cross, e.g. in the floor construction. > Tab. 5

Hot water systems can be central or decentralized in the building or Individual, group or central hot water supply provide hot water directly at the draw-off point. If a hot water source has only one draw-off point connected to it, this arrangement is called an individual supply, while with several connected draw-off points it is a group supply. > Figs. 18 and 19 With a central supply all draw-off points are supplied with hot water from a single, central boiler. > Fig. 20 It is also possible to combine individual, group and central systems, for example to switch off a central boiler in summer and yet have hot water available through individual supply points.

There are basically two types of boilers used to provide hot water: Boilers continuous flow or instantaneous water heaters, which heat the water directly as it is used; and storage water heaters, which keep the water constantly hot and ready for drawing off. A further difference between the types relates to the source of heat. Heat sources include solid fuel, oil, gas, electricity, geothermal, and solar energy. Heating takes place

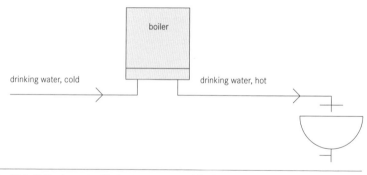

Fig. 18: Individual supply of hot water to one wash basin

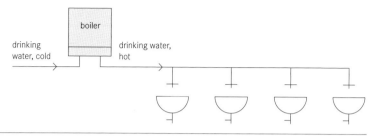

Fig. 19: Group supply of hot water to several wash basins

either indirectly through a <u>heat exchanger</u> and a heat medium, or directly by the application of heat to the water to be heated.

If possible, boilers installed in a central plant are used to heat the building and supply it with hot water. The plant consists of a hot water storage vessel, which stores service water and provides a source of heat for the heating circuit, and a connected boiler, which releases its heat to the service water. Hot water and heating energy are transported by

○ **Note:** A heat exchanger is used to transfer heat from one medium into another. The heat medium could be water, which releases its heat into the air, for example, as with a radiator. In hot water supply systems the heat exchanger is inside the hot water storage vessel.

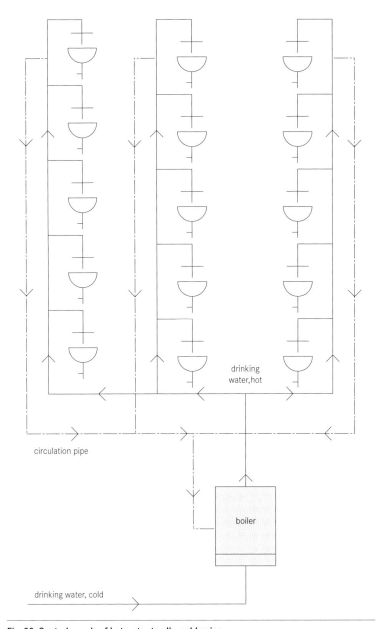

drinking
water, hot

circulation pipe

boiler

drinking water, cold

Fig. 20: Central supply of hot water to all washbasins

pumps through the pipe network to the draw-off points and heating radiators. Central plants have the advantage that a solar thermal energy installation can be connected or retrofitted at a later date and contribute to supplying hot water to the hot water storage vessel.

Continuous flow systems

Continuous flow systems, also called instantaneous or continuous flow water heaters, heat the water directly to a temperature of about 60 °C. > Fig. 21 Their advantage is that only the amount of hot water needed is heated. In contrast to storage systems, there are no standby heat losses with continuous flow systems, and the water cannot generally be classed as fresh.

Continuous flow water heaters are inexpensive to install and save space. They are highly efficient because they heat the water directly. The startup phase cannot be avoided: hot water can be supplied to the draw-off point only after a delay, which results in fresh water flowing unused with the waste water into the sewers. The pipes from the instantaneous water heater to the draw-off points should be as short as possible, so that this cold water phase is curtailed. It cannot be completely eliminated, however.

Instantaneous water heaters can be operated with electricity or gas. Electrical systems generally use an AC supply, while the gas systems require a flue or chimney connection. Electrically powered instantaneous water heaters are associated with high energy costs. As electricity is very expensive to produce, its use as an energy carrier should be restricted to providing small quantities of water or to situations when no other energy carrier can reasonably be considered. Gas, on the other hand, although it is a fossil fuel, produces the least amount of carbon dioxide

○ (CO_2) of all the fossil energy carriers.

○ **Note:** Coal, oil and gas are fossil fuels. When burned they produce carbon dioxide (CO_2) and contribute to global warming. There will also come a time when they are finally used up and are no longer available as energy sources.

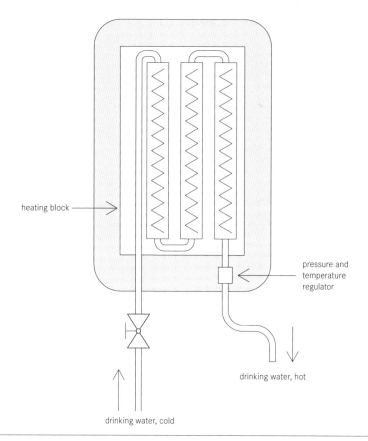

heating block

pressure and
temperature
regulator

drinking water, hot

drinking water, cold

Fig. 21: Principle of continuous flow water heaters

If designed as gas combination boilers, instantaneous water heaters can supply hot water and heating energy at the same time in a suitable system. Water quantities can be controlled hydraulically, thermally or electronically. Continuous flow systems can serve several draw-off points simultaneously and are used for individual, group and central hot water supplies. Maximum water flow is limited, however; when there is a high simultaneous draw-off, such as might be the case for hotels or sports halls, the output of a continuous system is too low. In this case a central storage system should be used.

Another hybrid form is an instantaneous water heater with a small, integral hot water reservoir holding between 15 to 100 l water. If more water is needed, e.g. for a bath, the rest of the bathwater is heated as if

Instantaneous water
heater with integrated
water storage

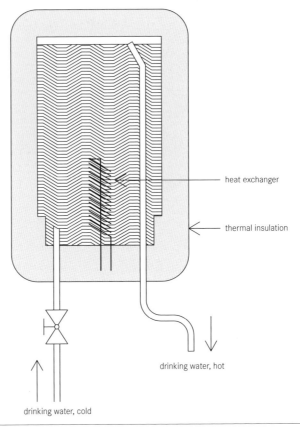

heat exchanger

thermal insulation

drinking water, hot

drinking water, cold

Fig. 22: Principle of storage water heaters

by an instantaneous water heater. Continuous flow systems with integrated storage are mainly used to supply smaller housing units with hot water and heating energy.

Storage systems

These storage water heaters continuously heat the hot water stored to keep it at a constant temperature of about 60 °C. > Fig. 22 The water is heated directly by a connected heat source or indirectly by a heat carrier, which could be an antifreeze solution in a thermal solar installation. > Chapter Hot water systems, Solar heating of hot water

Hot water storage must be located centrally in the building near the heating plant. It is thermally insulated and is able to supply several draw-off points as a closed, pressurized system. Open, unpressurized and uninsulated storage systems like boilers are designed for individual draw-off points.

○

Thermal solar installations can also be connected or retrofitted to hot water storage systems. As the storage and boiler are directly connected in these systems, the boiler reheats the water if the temperature rise achieved from the thermal solar installation is insufficient, or if the temperature of the hot water in storage falls below a particular set level. The disadvantage of hot water storage systems is that the water may go stale if it is stored for long periods.

Compared to instantaneous water heaters, which are located close to the points of use, central storage systems are associated with higher installation costs, as their pipework systems are usually considerably longer and therefore more expensive to install. However, overall costs can be reduced if hot water production is linked with heating the building, as it means only one boiler has to be installed.

Oversized pipework systems, drinking water heating systems with large storage capacities or poorly insulated drinking water pipes provide the right conditions for *Legionella* to multiply. *Legionella* are rod-shaped bacteria that are present in cold water in low concentrations but multiply quickly in warm water. Humans become infected not by drinking the water but by inhaling the aerosol created by agitating the water, for example, when showering. The symptoms of the illness are like those of a lung infection, starting with a fever, muscle pain, cough, and severe shortness of breath. It is very easily mistaken for influenza-type illnesses. If the illness is not diagnosed in time and treated with a suitable antibiotic, it can be fatal.

Legionella

○ **Note:** Unpressurized, uninsulated storage systems could be boilers or point-of-use water heaters, which are mostly installed as undersurface appliances below basins or sinks. They are suitable for producing small quantities of hot water quickly, e.g. in office kitchenettes.

If the water temperature in a hot water storage vessel falls to between 30 to 45 °C for an extended period, there is the risk of *Legionella* contamination. A simple but effective method of preventing the build-up of *Legionella* in drinking water is to thermally disinfect the stored water. This can be done by raising the temperature of the hot water to over 60 °C, which kills the bacteria, daily or weekly. Another method is electrolytic disinfection, which works by creating disinfecting agents in the water.

Solar heating of hot water

Solar collectors provide the most environmentally compatible form of heat energy because it is not accompanied by any emissions. Thermal solar installations are primarily used for the provision of hot water. Depending on the climate and given a favorable building, if the area is doubled the installation can also be used to support the heating system.

Thermal solar installations consist of flat plate or vacuum tube collectors, which differ in their efficiency and manufacturing cost, the fluid circuit for transporting the generated heat using a water-glycol mixture, and the hot water storage vessel in which the water is heated. A heat exchanger in the hot water storage vessel transfers the heat transported from the collector into the water in the vessel. > Fig. 23

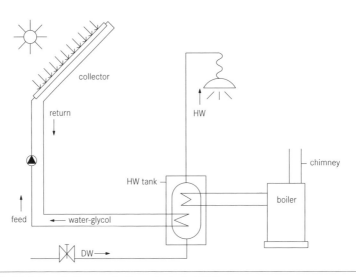

Fig. 23: Schematic diagram of a thermal solar installation

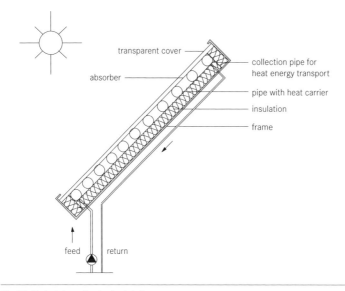

Fig. 24: Flat plate collector in detail

The design of the solar installation depends on the selected collector type and whether the intended use is hot water provision alone or also to support space heating.

Flat plate collectors consist in principle of an absorber layer with a highly selective coating, which allows the collector to absorb almost all of the solar radiation that falls upon it. The absorber is covered with a transparent cover of non-reflective safety glass with a high solar energy transmittance value and thermal insulation on the back and sides. The whole system is supported on a frame. Pipes filled with a heat transfer medium under the glass cover absorb the heat and transport it to the hot water storage system. > Fig. 24–26

Flat plate collectors

∎

∎ **Tip:** In a central European climate, a flat plate collector surface area of between 1.2 and 1.5 m² per person would be enough to provide hot water to residential buildings. Double that area would be needed to provide support to the space heating system in winter as well: 2.4 to 3.0 m² per person.

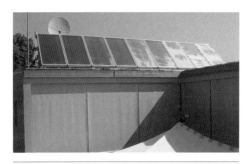

Fig. 25: Flat plate collector installed on a roof

Fig. 26: Flat plate collector integrated into a facade

Fig. 27: Vacuum tube collector

Vacuum tube collectors   With vacuum tube collectors, the absorber layer is inside airtight glass tubes to increase efficiency. > Fig. 27 The collectors consist of several glass tubes arranged close to one another and connected by a special

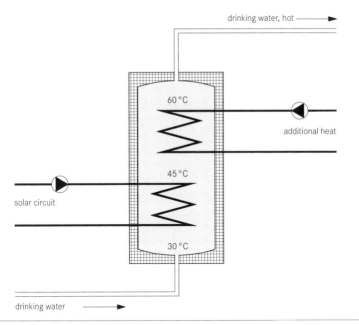

drinking water, hot ⟶

60 °C

additional heat

45 °C

solar circuit

30 °C

drinking water ⟶

Fig. 28: Stratification tank with different temperature zones

mount to the collection tube, which is filled with a water-glycol mixture. Vacuum tube collectors can be set at a particular angle by rotating them at the time of installation, so that a good yield can be obtained, even if the unit is at a relatively unfavorable vertical angle or less than optimum alignment. Metal plate reflectors attached to the sides can increase the amount of solar radiation the unit receives. The higher efficiency of vacuum tube collector systems means that an area of 0.8 to 1.0 m^2 per person is required for hot water provision in residential buildings.

Solar collectors are usually integrated into a southeast or southwest-facing pitched roof, or set at a vertical angle of 30 to 45° on a flat roof if they are intended to provide hot water all year round. If they are to provide support for space heating in Central Europe, the angle should be up to 60° as the winter sun is considerably lower in the sky. The units, in particular those with vacuum tube collectors, can also be attached in front of balconies, facades or similar alternative positions. If, for constructional reasons, the units cannot be installed at a suitable vertical angle or if the roof is not quite facing in the right direction, then a greater collector area should be provided. Alignment

If the amount of available solar radiation in winter is small, collectors can cover only part of the annual hot water demand and an additional means of water heating is required. One possibility that could be recommended is a combination of hot water provision and support to space heating. This system stores water in zones of different temperature in a <u>stratification tank</u> and can be used as a heat source for space heating. > Fig. 28

In a stratification tank, the hottest water is at the top over a middle mixed zone, with the coolest water at the bottom where cold drinking water is introduced. The feed to the heating circuit is taken from the top of the stratification tank, where higher temperatures prevail. When there is insufficient solar radiation, a separate boiler provides the additional heat through a heat exchanger. In this way about 25% of the heating energy demand can be fulfilled from renewable sources. Solar installations supporting space heating are most effective using a combination of floor or wall heating because this method of heating requires lower

○ feed temperatures than heating radiators.

SANITARY ROOMS

Hot water is produced by one of the systems described above, and distributed in parallel with cold water in a system of pipes to be ready for use at various draw-off points in kitchens, sanitary and other rooms with a hot water requirement. Sanitary rooms are mainly used for personal care and hygiene. Of all the rooms in a house, they are the most intensive in their use of building services installations, as they have cold and hot water supply and the associated waste water disposal systems. Depending on their design, they may be termed <u>rooms with wet areas</u> or <u>wet rooms</u>. To cut down the work involved in installing the pipework, the layout of these rooms should be chosen to reduce the number of installation shafts and shorten the water supply and disposal pipes, as far as possible. Grouping the pipes together not only simplifies the plumbing work, but also reduces the transmission of sound to neighboring rooms.

○ **Note:** Further information on the heating of buildings can be found in the chapter on "Tempering systems" in: Oliver Klein and Jörg Schlenger, *Basics Room Conditioning*, Birkhäuser Verlag, Basel 2008.

Noise from sanitary rooms often originates from WC cisterns, water flowing in waste pipes, faucets drawing off water, or activities in the room. These sounds are transmitted to other rooms through walls, ceilings and floors. Quiet rooms or bedrooms should not be positioned adjacent to bathrooms or toilets if disturbing noises are to be avoided. Walls with services in them next to bedrooms, for example, cannot be insulated to the extent that they emit no sound at all. Siting sanitary rooms next to separating walls between residential properties is only recommended if there is also a kitchen, bathroom or other room where noise is not an issue on the other side of the wall in the adjoining property, unless there is an acoustic isolation joint between the two parts of the building.

Wall chases are not advantageous in terms of sound transmission. Surrounding the pipes in the chases with insulation will certainly attenuate the noise, but the chase then has to be cut deeper, which is usually associated with structural stability problems.

Baths and lavatory pans standing on the floor should be bedded on an elastic isolating layer or a floating screed, so that the noises from them are not transmitted through the floor into neighboring rooms. Wall-hung sanitary appliances such as lavatory pans, wash basins or shelves should be attached to walls with a high mass per unit area using sound-insulating sleeves or plastic profiles or attached to false walls.

Faucets and valves in bathrooms are manufactured in two noise categories: low-noise faucets are category I; those that emit higher levels of noise are category II. For noise insulation, category I faucets are preferable, although they may sometimes give rise to higher costs.

The design of sanitary rooms is always a difficult task for architects, as it involves not only the layout and style but also the sound insulation and the integration of extensive pipework. This calls for great attention to detail, as a poorly thought-out arrangement of sanitary appliances and the resulting awkward pipework routes often cause technical, functional, and financial problems.

Arrangement of sanitary installations
When planning a sanitary room, an architect must take into account how far the sanitary appliances are from the drinking water risers and waste water stacks, and how directly and simply the connections can be made. While drinking water pipes generally have a small cross section and can even be installed in the floor structure without much problem, waste water pipes are more difficult to incorporate because of their relatively large diameters and required fall of 2% within buildings. Depending on the type of sanitary appliance, waste water pipes often start off

Fig. 29: Substructure of a double-sided false wall

slightly higher than floor level, which means connection to the stack is easy provided the distance is short.

Exposed drinking and waste water pipes create high levels of noise. On the other hand, false wall installations of various constructional types, or shafts that pass from story to story and conceal pipework, increase sound insulation and dispense with the need for expensive wall chases.

False wall installations   Instead of attaching sanitary appliances to a solid wall and forming the void around the pipe route with conventional masonry, most pipes are now installed behind false walls to preserve the structural stability of the main walls and provide better sound insulation. They consist of a metal supporting frame and a system for attaching the sanitary appliances. The remaining space inside them is filled with insulation and the frame is clad with plasterboard. > Fig. 29 False walls are normally between 1.00 m and 1.50 m high and are fixed about 20 to 25 cm in front of the real wall, depending on the diameter of the pipes behind them. They conceal only the pipework for that particular story and not pipes from other stories unless they are directly connected to an installation shaft. The top surface of a false wall can be used as a bathroom shelf.

Another version of a false wall installation is the modular assembly block system. This involves prefabricated, compact elements formed from polyester foam concrete, which encapsulate all the supply and disposal pipe connections, inbuilt flushing cisterns and all the fastenings for the sanitary appliances to be connected to them. They are about 15 cm deep and are either impact-sound insulated at their connections to the wall, or stand on supports on the structural floor. The cavities must be walled up or filled with mortar.

Fitting out sanitary rooms

The size and fitting out of sanitary rooms depends primarily on the number of occupants and their particular needs. The room dimensions of a bathroom, on the other hand, depend mostly on the sanitary appliances to be installed and the required distances between them. > Fig. 30

A separate bathroom and toilet arrangement should be considered for residential units with more than two occupants to allow more convenient everyday use. For a family with more than two children, there should be another shower in addition to the actual bath, as well as a separate WC. In all considerations of the size and position within the building of sanitary rooms, the designer should take into account that rooms with wet areas should generally be close to one another, so that pipes can be installed in groups and long pipes are not necessary to transport the water.

Sanitary appliances need to be spaced a minimum of 25 cm from one another or placed at different heights to allow them to be used without interference. Hence a washbasin, for example, may be positioned with an edge extending laterally over a bath at a lower level. Similarly, there should always be a clear area in front of each sanitary element to ensure freedom of movement. > Fig. 31

Wash hand basins and wash basins differ in their sizes. While small wash hand basins are found in lavatories and are intended for hand washing only, wash basins have larger dimensions. They should allow an arm to be immersed up to at least the elbow. Most are manufactured from sanitary ceramics or acrylic; in a minority of cases from enameled or stainless steel. The top edge of these appliances is normally between

Wash basins

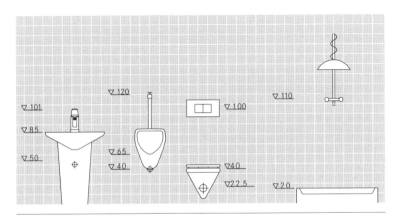

Fig. 30: Typical heights of sanitary room appliances

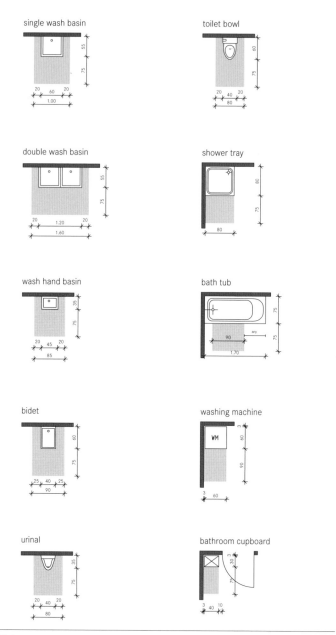

single wash basin

double wash basin

wash hand basin

bidet

urinal

toilet bowl

shower tray

bath tub

washing machine

bathroom cupboard

Fig. 31: Minimum movement areas in front of sanitary appliances

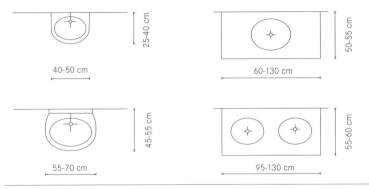

Fig. 32: Typical wash basin types

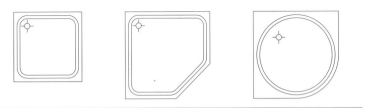

Fig. 33: Typical shower tray shapes

85 and 90 cm above floor level. Double wash basin units are more economic in their use of space than two separate wash basins; however, they must have a minimum width of 120 cm so that two people can use them unhindered at the same time. > Fig. 32

The corner valves for the hot and cold water pipes are installed under the wash basin and are used to turn off the drinking water to the fittings if repairs are needed. It is also possible to conceal waste and drinking water pipes and traps > Chapter Waste water, Waste water pipework in buildings in cupboards or behind panels under wash basins. Wash basins are also often built into specially designed bathroom furniture. This allows better use of the space in a bathroom and provides a more aesthetic way of concealing pipework.

Shower trays are normally manufactured from enameled cast iron, enameled steel plate or acrylic. Various shapes of shower tray are available. They could be anything from rectangular or square to circular or semicircular. > Fig. 33 The standard square shower tray is 80 × 80 cm in

Shower installations

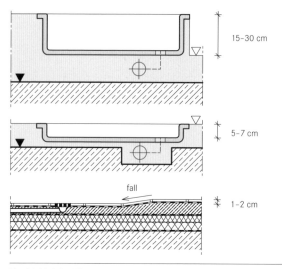

Fig. 34: Height differences in shower tray installations

plan with a depth of about 15 to 30 cm; larger dimensions and lower entry upstands offer more space and are easier to use. To reduce the step up into the shower, the recess in the floor structure must be made deeper to allow for the waste water connection, which normally fits conveniently under the shower tray. > Fig. 34 top and middle

Some bathroom designs dispense with the shower tray and have the shower floor at the same height as the bathroom floor. > Fig. 34 bottom This offers not only design and cleaning advantages, but is also part of a barrier-free bathroom. With these wet-room showers, the drainage outlet is at floor level. It is therefore necessary to have efficient waterproofing and edge seals, and a higher floor level to provide the required fall in the
○ waste pipe.

○ **Note:** The waterproofing and seals may consist of waterproofing membranes and sealing tape, or other waterproofing materials, which are spread on the substrate using the thin bed process. They should extend at least 15 cm above the top of the floor covering and brought up even higher in the indirect spray zone of the shower--even if the shower is in the bath. They must also extend at least 20 cm above the shower head on the walls.

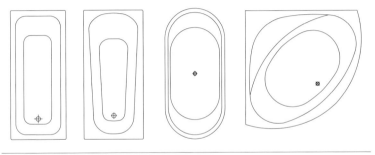

Fig. 35: Typical bath tub shapes

Bath tubs may be freestanding in the room, placed along one wall Bath tubs and clad in subsequently tiled boards, or set in a preformed foamed plastic bath panel unit. > Fig. 35 They are manufactured from enameled cast iron, steel plate or acrylic, and are normally 170 to 200 cm long, 75 to 80 cm wide and 50 to 65 cm high. If the entry height needs to be lower, the bath must be recessed into the floor to allow the waste pipe connection to be made. The bath can be made flush with the surrounding floor, for example by building a raised floor plinth around it, as otherwise the floor must be considerably lowered in the area of the bath tub.

The voids between the bath tub and cladding are generally filled with insulation. The gap between the wall and the edge of the bath tub is made watertight with a flexible seal. A clear area of about 90 × 75 cm should be provided in front of the long side of the bath tub to allow unobstructed entry.

Lavatory pans can be wall-mounted or stand on the floor. > Fig. 36 The Lavatory pans wall-mounted variety simplifies floor cleaning and is usually fixed to special framing members in the false wall construction so that its height can be adjusted. The shape of the lavatory pan depends on the type of flushing process. While older buildings mainly had shallow-flush pans installed, they are now increasingly being replaced by the less noisy deep-flush pans. > Fig. 37

Flushing cisterns range from false wall installations or exposed WC flushing cisterns pressure chamber cisterns up to wall-mounted, inbuilt or close-coupled cisterns. > Fig. 38 They can be installed at various heights above the pan. While high-level cisterns, which operate with considerable noise, are common in older buildings, new buildings have low-level cisterns or cisterns built into the walls, which are substantially quieter. Pressure cisterns use the pressure in the drinking water pipe and therefore do not require a

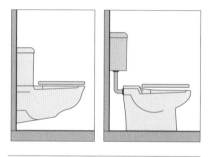

Fig. 36: Wall-hung and floor-standing WCs

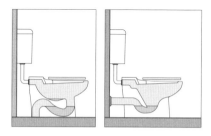

Fig.37: WCs with shallow- and deep-flush pans

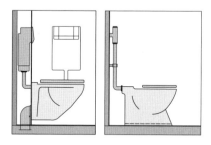

Fig. 38: Wall-hung WC with a cistern built into
the wall and floor-standing WC with pressure
chamber cistern

conventional box-like cistern. The self-closing valve provides flushing
water only as long as it is needed, i.e. as long as the flush lever is pressed.
Conventional cisterns, on the other hand, are automatically refilled after
every flush.

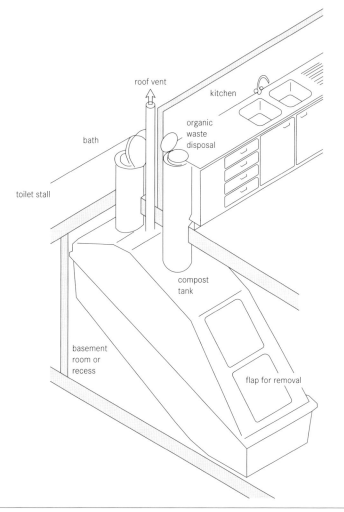

roof vent

kitchen

organic
waste
disposal

bath

toilet stall

compost
tank

basement
room or
recess

flap for removal

Fig. 39: Schematic diagram of a composting toilet

More than one third of the daily water demand per person, approximately 35 to 45 l, is used for toilet flushing. Reducing consumption of water for flushing offers great potential for saving drinking water. Older cisterns use between 9 and 14 l water per flush, while modern toilet systems require about 6 l. The quantity of flushing water can be set by adjusting the filling height in the cistern. It should also be possible to interrupt the flushing process by pressing the flushing button a second time (water-saving button). To reduce the quantity of water used per flush to as low as 3 l requires the cistern to be connected to a special type of lavatory pan, as otherwise noise may become a nuisance.

Water-saving toilet systems

Vacuum toilets need only 1.2 l water per flush. They have a history of use on board modern high-speed trains and ships. In residential buildings a pump sucks out the contents of the toilet and delivers it into a ventilated waste water tank. From there it is transported by another pump to the public drainage system. The lower drinking water consumption achieved using the vacuum process could result in high savings of waste water disposal charges. The smaller pipe cross sections make installation of vacuum toilets problem-free. However, the flushing process itself is considerably noisier than other types of WC systems.

Composting toilets do not use any water for flushing and therefore produce no waste water. They are used for ecological reasons or because the building is not connected to the public sewer. These toilets consist of a tank with one connected shaft for organic kitchen waste and one for toilet waste. > Fig. 39 Constant underpressure in the composting tank means that no odors can escape into the rooms. The decomposition of the material in the tanks over a period of months is initiated by air flowing through it. The nutrients resulting from this composting process can be used for soil improvement and plant food in the garden.

Fittings

The term fittings covers all shut-off devices fitted to a drinking water supply system such as stopcocks, gate valves or stop valves, as well as sanitary fittings on wash basins and showers, for example. Shut-off valves block or allow flow along lengths of pipework; they differ in the way they close off the pipe. Stop valves divide up a drinking water system into logical sections to allow parts of the system to be isolated and individual components replaced. Stop valves are therefore fitted before and after the water meter, filter and pressure reducer > Fig. 40 or at the lowest point of each riser and pipe supplying each story. In this way components can be replaced without having to shut down the whole pipe network. Stop valves are also installed at WC cisterns and under wash basins.

Tap fittings in sanitary rooms are available as wall- or surface-mounted. > Fig. 41 Wall-mounted faucets, which are mainly installed at bath tubs or showers, are fitted directly on to the wall concealing the water supply pipes, where a short connection piece is used to connect to the drinking water pipework. Surface-mounted models are attached directly to the top of the wash basin or sink and connected to the drinking water supply by means of corner stop valves. The type of tap fitting depends on the intended use; kitchen faucets, for example, have a longer spout then bathroom faucets.

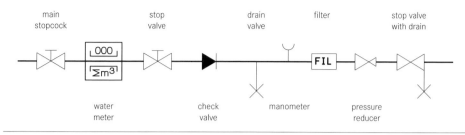

main stopcock		stop valve	drain valve	filter	stop valve with drain

Fig. 40: Shut-off valve arrangement after the service pipe enters the building

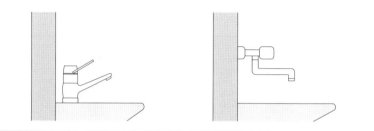

Fig. 41: Surface- and wall-mounted faucets on a bathroom wash basin

Conventional mixers consist of two rotating handles positioned close to one another; with the right and left handles controlling the cold and hot water flow respectively. The user controls the water temperature manually by adjusting the flow of each. More practical are the single lever mixers, which control the water temperature by rotation and the flow by an up or down movement of the lever.

Mixers

Contactless wash basin faucets are often installed in public toilets for reasons of hygiene. The movement of a hand in front of an infrared sensor opens the valve. Some electronically controlled versions just require a hand to go near the faucet to activate the water flow. A water flow regulator ensures that a constant amount of water issues from the tap. Contactless wash basin faucets require a source of electricity to work. This may be provided by batteries or an external power supply.

Contactless wash basin faucets

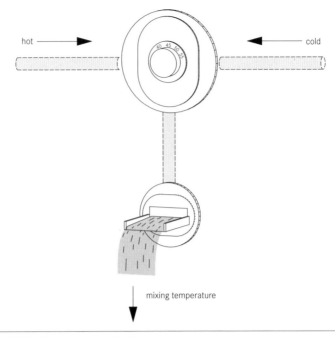

hot →   cold ←

mixing temperature

Fig. 42: Principle of a thermostatic tap

Thermostatic faucets   Thermostatic faucets allow the temperature of the water to be pre-set by a rotating handle, so that the water temperature remains constant even if the rate of flow alters. The faucet mixes hot and cold water at the correct ratio to achieve the set temperature. > Fig. 42

> ○ **Note:** All faucets and sanitary appliances should be
> aligned with the tile grid in the room to produce a
> pleasing appearance. Faucets should be positioned at
> a tile joint, a joint intersection, or in the center of a tile.

Barrier-free sanitary rooms

Barrier-free sanitary rooms have to satisfy special conditions. They should be fitted out in such a way that the occupant can use facilities in the room without help from another person. To achieve this there should be an adequate and barrier-free movement area of 120 × 120 cm in front of the wash basin, WC, shower and bath tub; for wheelchair use it would need to be at least 150 × 150 cm. Stepless shower trays level with the floor, wash basins that wheelchair users can drive under, and grab handles near all sanitary appliances make their use much easier. The door should have a clear opening width of at least 80 to 90 cm and should open outwards so as not to interfere with access to the sanitary appliances in the room. > Fig. 43

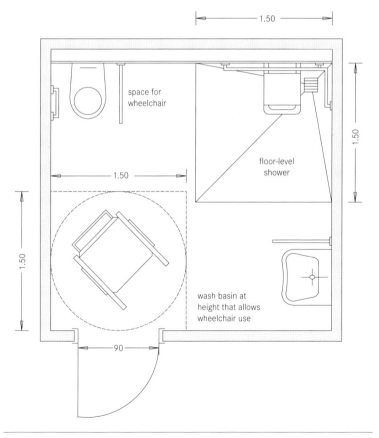

Fig. 43: Wheelchair-friendly bathroom

Waste water

After it has been distributed through the building's network of pipes, drinking water is automatically changed into waste water when it flows out of the faucets at draw-off points into wash basins, showers or bath tubs, even though it might be absolutely unused and clean. The description "drinking water" ceases to apply as soon as the water enters the waste water pipework.

The term "waste water" generally covers not only water that has become contaminated by domestic, commercial or industrial use but also relatively clean precipitation water (rain). Waste water is usually contaminated by solid particles, bacteria or chemicals, and must therefore be thoroughly treated before it can be fed back into natural bodies of water. This process is normally carried out at the public waste water treatment works.

Heavily contaminated domestic waste water from toilets and dishwashers that contains fecal and putrefactive substances is known as black water. Less heavily contaminated waste water from wash basins, showers and bath tubs is called gray water and contains only about one third the contaminants as black water. This difference is immaterial for the normal process of waste water treatment at the sewage works is concerned, as the plants are generally designed to purify black water. This difference is, however, very important for natural waste water treatment processes, as some facilities can only treat gray water.

Increasing awareness of our environment has shifted the focus, for several years now, to protecting the purity of groundwater, rivers and lakes. The biological self-cleaning process does not work above a certain level of contamination, so that waste water treatment methods of purifying heavily polluted industrial and domestic water are of the utmost
● importance in counteracting ecological damage. > Chapter Waste water, Methods of waste water treatment

---

● **Example:** A four-person household in Germany annually introduces about 100 kg of detergent into the sewage system. The development of more environmentally friendly detergents has lowered the pollutant load, but has only slightly reduced the problem.

But before treatment can take place, the used cold and hot water must be transported from sanitary rooms in buildings and fed into the public drainage system. This takes place through the pipe network described in the section below.

WASTE WATER PIPEWORK IN BUILDINGS

Waste water pipes are considerably larger than drinking water pipes and have the task of taking rain and dirty water away from buildings and conducting it into the sewers. A branched network of pipes of different sizes is required ensure that the sanitary appliances continue to work without problems. Buildings are generally designed to be drained by gravity, so all pipes are either vertical or are installed at a fall of at least 2% to transport the waste water down and out of the building. It is important that the waste water does not back up in the system. ○

The flood level is the maximum possible level up to which waste water   Flood level
may rise at a particular location in a drainage system. > Fig. 44 Normally the top of the road surface or the top of the curb at the connection point can be taken to be the flood level, unless indicated otherwise by the local flood prevention authority. This is the limit to which the water will rise in the event of a flood, and therefore it cannot back up any higher inside the building. A flood is most likely to occur during periods of heavy rain. Combined drainage systems are particularly at risk because they carry waste water and rainwater together. > Chapter Waste water, Methods of waste water treatment Flooding also occurs in separate drainage systems, for example if pipes become blocked.

In connected sanitary appliances that are below the official flood level in basements, there is always a risk that waste water from the drainage system will enter the building and cause serious damage. For this reason, each connection point must be protected with an anti-flooding valve or a waste water lifting plant. > Chapter Waste water pipework in buildings, ○
Protective measures, page 141

○ **Note:** If waste water backs up it is possible for the waste water in the public sewer to enter the building's pipework system connected to it, based on the principle of communicating vessels: if vessels or pipes that contain liquid and are open at the top are connected to one another, the level of the liquid will be at the same height in both—irrespective of their shape.

○ **Note:** European Standard EN 12056 applies to gravity drainage systems inside buildings. EN 752 applies to systems outside buildings. Both standards set out a general framework, which requires national annexes and allows regional departures.

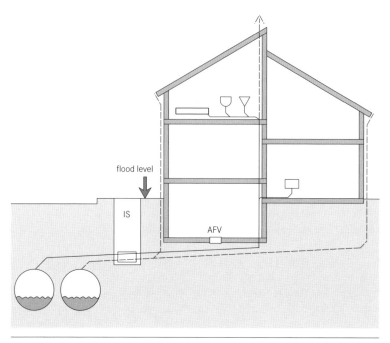

flood level

IS

AFV

Fig. 44: Flood level

System components and pipe runs

Individual and common waste pipes

A pipework system is made up of many different components, which are connected together to conduct waste water into the public drainage system. > Fig. 45 An <u>individual waste</u> pipe connects each sanitary appliance to a <u>common waste</u>, into which all the wastes in a sanitary room are brought together. > Fig. 46 The common waste has a fall of 2% and takes the shortest route to the vertical <u>stack</u>, which in turn carries the waste water downwards in a uniform diameter pipe with as straight an alignment as possible. The fall in horizontal waste water pipes is necessary to ensure that the flowing water leaves behind no residues in the pipe. All pipes are normally connected into the discharge pipe by 45° bends in the direction of flow to prevent water building up at the connection point. Neighboring common waste pipes must have staggered connections into the vertical stack to prevent water in one from entering the other. The individual pipework system components may be screwed together, solvent welded, or have push-fit connections.

Stack, drainage and vent pipes

The vertical stack pipe normally discharges below the level of the building's floor slab into a <u>drainage pipe</u>, which leads to the public drain-

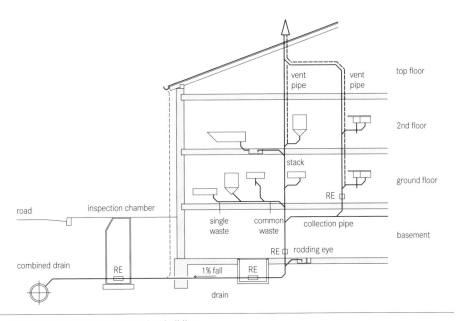

Fig. 45: Waste water pipework system in a building

age system or sewer. The stack must be vented to prevent backflow into sanitary appliances. This backflow is caused by underpressure in the stack resulting from the pressure differences that occur when the stack is suddenly used by several appliances at once. If the total length of stack is more than 4 m, it obviously runs through more than one story, and must therefore vent into the open air above the sanitary appliances in the top story and roof level without any reduction in cross section. Alternatively it could be fitted with a venting valve below roof level specially designed for waste water pipes. If the venting pipe is led through the roof to the open air, it must be at least 2 m away from a dormer window or roof window, or must project 1 m above the highest point of these features, so that no unpleasant odors can enter the building from the waste pipe.

At the lowest point of the stack, a drain sufficiently deep underground so as to be frost-free transports the waste water from the building into the connection drain, which is connected directly into the public sewer. If an ordinary buried drain is out of the question because the building has a basement and the public drainage system is too high to allow a normal connection, a collection drain can be laid to a fall below the basement floor slab.

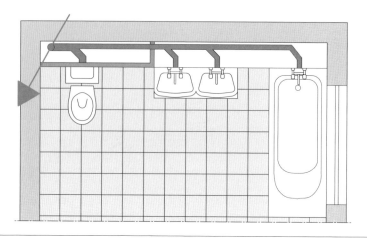

Fig. 46: Plan view of waste water pipes in a bathroom

Access for cleaning Only junctions with angles of up to 45° are permitted in buried and collection drains so that waste water can flow smoothly away. In addition, rodding eyes or similar openings must be provided at least every 20 m to allow any length of pipe to be unblocked and cleaned out without excessive effort. In vertical stacks, there must be a suitable cleaning opening at the lowest point, because this is where a blockage is likely to occur first.

Informative signage The position under the road of drains in the public waste water drainage system is indicated by sign plates usually fixed to building walls or marker posts. The numbers give the direction and distance of connection drains.

Drawing symbols Various symbols are used in plan and sectional views of planned waste water systems to improve the readability of the drawings and to show the numbers and arrangement of the connected sanitary appliances. > Fig. 47 In a similar way to that described in the chapter on water supply, the drawings should show the true position of objects in plan marked with the appropriate symbol in conjunction with the pipework system. The pipework system, including the pipe layout and sanitary appliances, is shown in a schematic sectional view as if the wash basins, showers, bath tubs or WCs were adjacent to one another and all connected to a single common waste. > Fig. 45 The pipes are shown with the 45° bends mentioned above, appropriately arranged for the actual direction of flow.

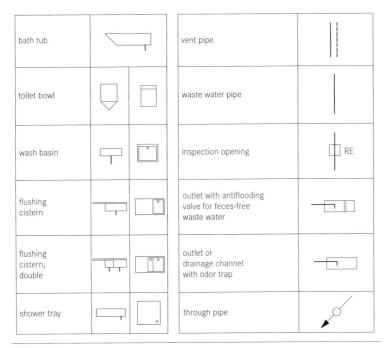

bath tub		vent pipe	
toilet bowl		waste water pipe	
wash basin		inspection opening	RE
flushing cistern		outlet with antiflooding valve for feces-free waste water	
flushing cistern, double		outlet or drainage channel with odor trap	
shower tray		through pipe	

Fig. 47: Representation and explanation of commonly used symbols

Calculation of pipe sizes

The cross section of the pipes depends on the type and number of connected sanitary appliances and the water demand, which in turn depends on the desired level of comfort and convenience in the building. Each appliance that generates waste water has a connection value (DU) and a minimum required pipe cross section. > Tab. 6 The estimated waste water outflow (Q_{ww}) in liters per second (l/s) of an appliance is the most important parameter in calculating the required nominal pipe size in waste water systems. The drainage index (K) is a measure of the frequency with which a waste water appliance is used. Hence the design of the system will vary with the type and use of the building. For example, sanitary installations in schools or public buildings will be much more frequently used than those in residential buildings.

The sum of the connection values of each appliance is used to calculate the pipe cross section of the common waste, stack or drain pipe. Therefore the required size of the drain is calculated from the sum of the connection values of all the waste water generating appliances connect-

Tab.6: Typical connection values of sanitary appliances and pipe diameters of single wastes

Waste water appliance	Connection value (DU)	Pipe diameter
Wash basin	0.5	DN 40
Shower with plugged outlet	0.8	DN 50
Shower with unplugged outlet	0.6	DN 50
Bath tub	0.8	DN 50
WC with 6-liter cistern	2.0	DN 100
WC with 4- to 5-liter cistern	1.8	DN 80 to DN 100

ing into it. A horizontal waste water pipe to which a WC is connected, for example, usually requires a nominal pipe size of at least DN 100; which means a pipe with an internal diameter of 100 mm. The vertical stack must therefore also have a diameter of at least DN 100. For a series of connections into a pipe, the total connection value can be calculated using the following formula:

$$Q_{ww} = K \times \sqrt{\Sigma\,(DU)} \text{ in } l/s.$$

Q_{ww} = Quantity of waste water (waste water outflow):
DU = Design units (connection value);
K = dimensionless drainage index, which represents the frequency of use (in residential buildings 0.5; in schools, restaurants, hotels 0.7; in public buildings with frequent usage 1.0).

Materials

Waste water pipes can be made from vitrified clay, cast iron, steel, fiber cement or plastic, while rainwater downpipes may be manufactured from lead. Vitrified clay pipes are generally used for buried drains, as they are resistant to load. Cast iron and fiber cement pipes are suitable for all types of building and land drainage systems. Their high mass per unit area makes them particularly useful for attenuating the noise of flowing waste water. Steel or stainless steel pipes are used where the waste water they carry is corrosive, which might be the case in laboratories, for example. The most economic material is plastic. Low weight and corrosion resistance means plastic pipes are primarily used in residential buildings, with higher-quality plastic pipes also finding use in industrial and commercial buildings. The plastic used for all pipe components must be heat-resistant.

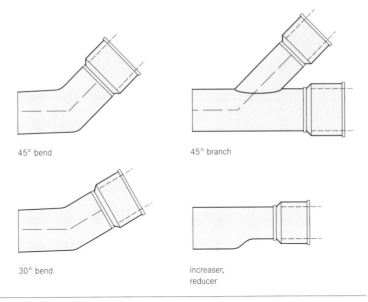

45° bend

45° branch

30° bend

increaser,
reducer

Fig. 48: Drainage pipe fittings

All materials are produced in short standard lengths and connected to one another by push-fit sleeves, threaded or sealed connections or, in the case of rainwater downpipes, crimped or soldered. They can be obtained as bends, branches, increasers and in other shapes. > Fig. 48

Protective measures

Traps ensure that no unpleasant odors can escape from waste water   Odor traps
pipes into rooms. They are fitted below the outlet of each sanitary appliance. Traps are available in various forms, but they all work on a similar principle to the pipe odor trap, which is the most popular due to its excellent flow characteristics. It consists of a curved piece of pipe of at least 30–45 mm diameter, which retains some water in its bend. > Fig. 49, left The bottle trap is more prone to blocking and therefore is less popular. > Fig. 49, right The standing water in double traps prevents odors from escaping out of the pipe into the room.

It is prudent to build floor waste water outlets in bathrooms in res-   Floor outlets
idential properties where washing machines or floor level showers are installed. They are specified for use in public buildings or swimming pools. They may be manufactured from cast iron, stainless steel, brass or plastic; they can be installed in the floor structure and require the least possible

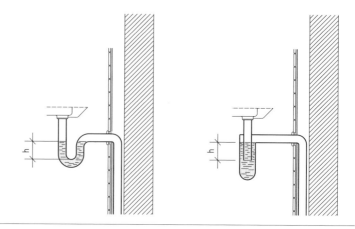

Fig. 49: Left: pipe odor trap, right: bottle odor trap

installation depth. When these floor outlets are installed, the floor must have a slight fall of 1.5% towards the outlet and be sealed so as to be waterproof. > Fig. 50 As the floor outlet is often in the middle of the room, it is not always an easy task to lead the connected waste pipe to the nearest stack. These outlets are usually only connected to DN 50 or perhaps DN 70 waste pipes, but they must be laid with the normal 2% fall.

Anti-flooding valves   As discussed earlier with reference to flood level, all waste water appliances that are below the flood level must have tightly sealing anti-flooding valves to prevent the backflow of foul water into the building. This may happen, in particular with combined drainage systems, when heavy rain takes the flow in the public drainage system to its limit. A high water level in the public drains can cause waste water from deep connection pipes to emerge from sanitary appliances. > Fig. 51

Anti-flooding valves usually consist of a motor-driven shut-off valve, a pneumatic gate valve, or an automatic or manually actuated stop valve (emergency shut-off). However, all the waste water pipes in the stories above flood level must not discharge through the anti-flooding valve, but must be connected downstream of it, as the building could otherwise be flooded by its own waste water.

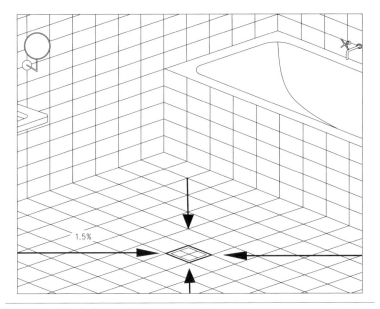

Fig. 50: Principle of a floor outlet

Waste water appliances situated below the flood level that cannot be connected with an adequate fall to the public drainage system because they are too deep underground have to be drained by a waste water lifting plant. This collects the waste water, which may or may not contain fecal matter, in a tank and delivers it by means of a pump and pressure pipes, through an anti-backflow riser with its highest point above the flood level, into the public drainage system. > Fig. 52 The height of the anti-backflow riser ensures that there is no way for the waste water to flow back into the building. The waste water is then taken in a drain connected to the plant's discharge pipe at the normal fall into the public drainage system.

Waste water lifting plants

METHODS OF WASTE WATER TREATMENT
Separate and combined drainage systems

Waste water is discharged into either a combined or a separate drainage system. In a combined system, domestic and industrial waste is led together with rainwater into the drainage system; in a separate system, rainwater flows directly into open water or watercourses, often referred to as outfalls, and only the contaminated water enters the public drainage system. > Fig. 53 Within the area of the building and in the design of the drainage pipework, rainwater is now assumed to be dealt with

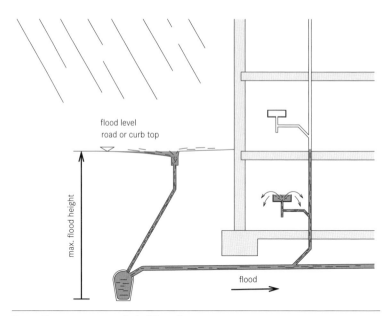

flood level
road or curb top

max. flood height

flood

Fig. 51: The consequences of a build-up of waste water

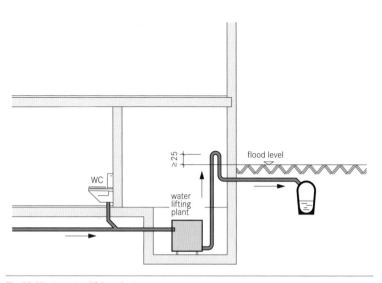

≥ 25

flood level

WC

water
lifting
plant

Fig. 52: Waste water lifting plant

separately from waste water, even if the public drainage system outside below the road surface is a combined system, as many countries are making plans to move to separate systems at some time in the future.

The reason for this is that precipitation water only turns into dirty water when it is mixed with ordinary foul water in combined drainage systems. As a result the volume of waste water increases greatly, which makes changing to a separate system worthwhile to reduce the foul water load on the drainage system and the costs of waste water treatment. The reduction in waste water volumes and the maintenance of natural groundwater levels are two good reasons why rainwater should be drained away if possible within the building curtilage, or be allowed to soak away locally.

Municipal waste water treatment plants first remove the coarse par- ticles from the waste water, and then clean it biologically to kill bacteria and treat it chemically to remove phosphates, heavy metals and nitrates. > Fig. 54 After cleaning, municipal waste water is discharged through outfalls into natural watercourses. But in spite of complex, costly water treatment systems, excessive amounts of plant nutrients and pollutants from treated waste water are entering natural watercourses, where they stimulate increased vegetation growth.

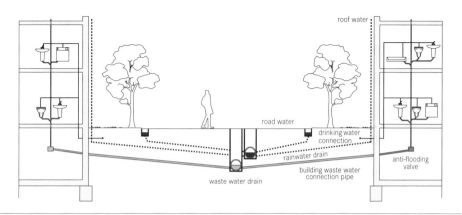

Fig. 53: Principle of separate drainage systems

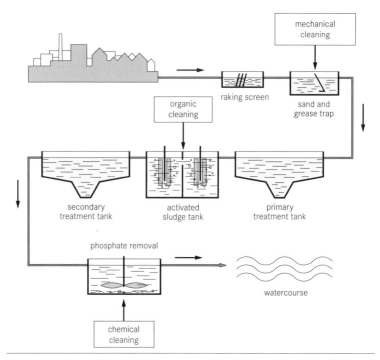

Fig. 54: Stages of waste water treatment

Natural waste water treatment systems

The idea of cleaning waste water using natural and less cost-intensive methods is not new. Water treatment facilities that work naturally are usually localized, small-scale disposal systems. Similar arrangements have been in use in rural areas for years, where the distance to a public drainage system may be too great to allow a cost-effective connection to be provided.

Increasing problems with the quality and costs of waste water disposal have meant that decentralized, natural water treatment methods have once again been considered as options by environmentally conscious planners over recent years. Numerous ecological housing developments have nearby reed bed water treatment systems, which clean all the waste water generated, within the boundaries of the site. These systems relieve the public drainage system, while sharpening our ecological sense of the natural water cycle and returning the responsibility for it to the individual.

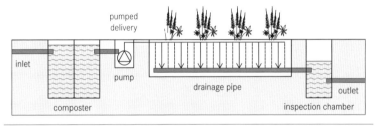

Fig. 55: Reed bed waste water treatment system using vertical flow

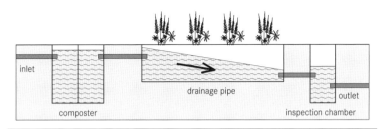

Fig. 56: Reed bed waste water treatment system using horizontal flow

Natural waste water processes have no need for the high energy and installation costs of conventional treatment works, but nevertheless produce excellent cleaning results. The actual waste water treatment process requires hardly any energy input from outside the site, but the systems themselves take up a lot of land. The design of the system largely depends upon the degree of contamination of the water to be treated.

Reed bed waste water treatment systems are the most common form of natural water treatment. They are generally based around waste water ponds with reeds growing in them and their cleaning effect is primarily produced by plant and animal microorganisms. Therefore it is not the plants themselves that purify the water; it is the microorganisms living in their roots that consume the nutrients in the waste water to produce the cleaning effect. The bed of the waste water pond is usually a sand filter through which the water flows either vertically or horizontally. A composting chamber or three-chamber septic tank may be installed upstream of the beds to remove solid matter. A continuous flow of air through the chamber ensures that composting takes place.

Reed bed waste water treatment systems

Fig. 57: Retention pond

First, the slightly soiled gray water from showers and wash basins or black water from toilets is carried along a separate pipework system by gravity, out of the building and through a buried composter, where the coarse particles are removed. From there the waste water is pumped out across the reed bed using the vertical flow principle, which takes up less area but the filter is further underground. > Fig. 55

Horizontal flow, on the other hand, involves a larger area of land but less depth. Here, the foul water flows out slowly across the system and is cleaned through the reed bed. > Fig. 56 The choice of system depends on the available space outside the building. Some waste water treatment methods use both flow types in series to achieve the best cleaning effect.

The reed bed is simply a sand and gravel filter bed. As most of the waste water seeps directly into the soil filter, the area does not look like open water but more like planted ground. The water from multistage systems can be passed through an inspection chamber, in which the water quality can be regularly tested before being taken to an outfall or a retention pond, where it could be used for recreation if the quality is adequate. > Fig. 57 The cleaned water could also be used as service water for flushing toilets. > Chapter Waste water, Uses of waste water

Natural waste water treatment processes require a great deal of space to be able to function properly, especially when used for cleaning black water. However, the aesthetically pleasing appearance and natural value of a reed bed are certainly more appealing than a conventional waste water treatment works. Reed bed waste water treatment systems should not be viewed just as an ecological alternative to conventional treatment processes. A natural treatment system is perfectly capable of handling all the waste water from buildings that are too far from the public drainage system.

DISPOSING OF RAINWATER

Rainwater is also part of the water cycle in buildings because it flows off roofs and impervious surfaces as dirty water and must be disposed of along with domestic waste water.

The solidly paved surfaces in urban areas prevent rainwater from simply seeping into the ground and becoming groundwater in the natural cycle, as would be ideal. Instead, it is conducted through pipes into the drainage system. > Fig. 58 During heavy rainfall the capacity of the drains is often inadequate, so that more and more foul water mixed with rainwater is flowing untreated into rivers and lakes.

Instead of rainwater being conducted rapidly into the drains, the modern approach is towards slower and more sophisticated systems of rainwater disposal that avoid mixing it with foul water. In choosing a suitable system, the designer must take into account the frequency and quantity of rainfall in the area, the character of the ground surface, and the height of the water table.

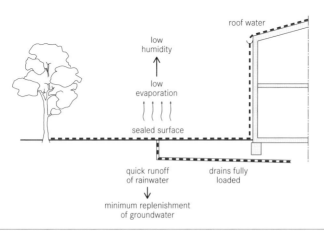

Fig. 58: Conventional rainwater drainage system

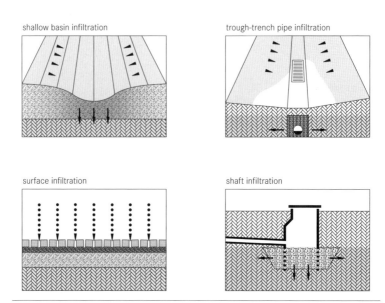

shallow basin infiltration

trough-trench pipe infiltration

surface infiltration

shaft infiltration

Fig. 59: Ways of promoting rainwater infiltration

Rainwater infiltration

To maintain the natural water cycle, ground surfaces that have not been built over, such as open ground, footpaths and squares, particularly in residential areas, should be designed to be as pervious to water as possible, for example as lawns or gravel. This can also be achieved by making built-upon surfaces less impervious so that rainwater can enter the ground in a natural way and contribute to a rise in the water table.

The character of the ground is critical to allowing rainwater infiltration. The more sandy a soil, the more pervious the ground is, and infiltration occurs naturally without any problems. If the soil is so loamy or clayey that rainwater is prevented from infiltrating, special measures may be required such as grass-lined basins, which store the water for a short time, trough-trench or pit infiltration systems, etc. > Fig. 59 These delay the runoff of rainwater and hold back the water in heavy rain, preventing the drains from becoming overloaded and reducing peak water levels. The urban climate benefits greatly from rainwater infiltration.

Costs can be saved in drainage by incorporating infiltration systems on the site. But costs may rise again due to the care and maintenance required for more complex retention systems such as green roofs in combination with rainwater ponds or extensive infiltration systems—for example, grass-lined basins.

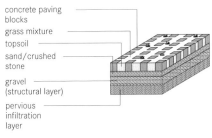

concrete paving
blocks

grass mixture

topsoil

sand/crushed
stone

gravel
(structural layer)

pervious
infiltration
layer

Fig. 60: Principle of surface infiltration

Fig. 61: Cellular grass paving for surface infiltration

With surface infiltration, rainwater seeps into the ground without having to be temporarily stored. Cellular grass paving is one method of surface infiltration; > Figs. 60 and 61 another is water-pervious blockwork; and both are particularly useful for parking spaces, gardens, or little used vehicular accesses. A lawn or gravel footpath can also aid infiltration where the underlying soil properties are favorable. Rainwater undergoes initial cleaning through surface infiltration, even in the top layers of soil. This cleaning effect continues as the rainwater flows slowly through further soil layers until it enters the groundwater.

Surface infiltration

Shallow basin or swale infiltration is a form of surface infiltration that delays rainwater runoff. An infiltration basin is a grass-covered hollow in which rainwater is stored for a few hours. > Fig. 62 During this time the water infiltrates slowly into the soil and eventually enters the groundwater.

Shallow basin infiltration

Shallow basin infiltration requires less land than surface infiltration. With a depth of 30 cm stored water, the area can be estimated as about 10 to 20% of the area of the connected roof surfaces. The rainwater is cleaned as it passes through the various soil layers. Infiltration basins are inexpensive to construct and require little maintenance. Furthermore, they can be integrated as design elements into leisure facilities and green spaces.

A trough-trench system combines two methods of infiltration: the grass-covered infiltration basin, and a gravel bed (trench) in which a drainage pipe is laid. The top, approx. 30 cm thick, layer of the basin acts as both store and filter for the rainwater. On leaving the basin, the rainwater is introduced at a single point or over an area into the trench, which is filled with coarse gravel and lined with a non-woven filter fabric. The rest

Trough-trench systems

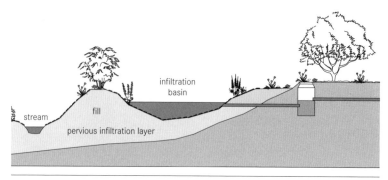

Fig. 62: Shallow basin or swale infiltration

of the rainwater is transported away slowly through the drainage pipe and is finally discharged at an outfall or into the public drainage system. On the way, the flow is dissipated through the porous pipe so that only a very small proportion of the rainwater arrives at the discharge point. Trough-trench infiltration is also suitable for handling high volumes of water in poorly draining ground conditions.

Rainwater retention

Retention is the holding back of rainwater. In large towns and cities, many millions of liters of waste water can be saved by holding back rainwater. Retention systems are intended to delay and reduce the direct flow of water into the drainage system. The water is delayed in most cases by green roofs or retention ponds. To an extent, and depending on the construction depth of the substrate, green roofs store precipitation water before releasing it, reduced by two thirds, into the drainage system. They improve the urban climate and in particular the local microclimate. The water evaporating from them can cool hot summer days and bind dust.

Green roofs   Green roofs may be extensive or intensive. While extensive green roofs have a substrate depth of 3 to 15 cm, an intensive green roof requires a substrate some 15 to 45 cm in depth. Both types of green roofs have a separating layer on top of the conventional roof membrane to prevent plant roots from destroying the roof construction. On top of this comes a drainage layer to remove the retained water, and finally the actual vegetation layer. > Fig. 63 Roofs may be designed as warm, cold, or upside-down roofs, which differ from one another by the position and ventilation of the insulation layer.

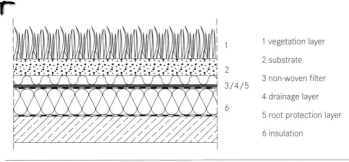

1 vegetation layer

2 substrate

3 non-woven filter

4 drainage layer

5 root protection layer

6 insulation

Fig. 63: Green roof showing typical construction

Extensive green roofs with a substrate depth of between 3 and 7 cm are planted with mosses and succulents with minimal water and nutrient demand. A somewhat deeper soil construction is necessary for low or medium water demand plants such as grasses or more leafy vegetation. Intensive green roofs consist of faster-growing grasses, perennials or woody species. The greater the substrate depth, the more effectively the roof retains and evaporates water. On the other hand, planting costs and the load placed upon the roof also increase proportionately.

Any flat roof can be a green roof provided that the roof structure is suitable, adequately sealed, and able to support the extra load of the substrate. Roofs inclined at up to 15° require no special safety measures; for more steeply sloping roofs, precautions must be taken to prevent the soil from shearing or sliding off the roof.

Plants and soil layers on green roofs mechanically clean the water. It could therefore be collected in a cistern and used as service water for toilet flushing. Since much of the water is retained and only about one third of the incident rainwater ends up in the cistern, it is normally not economical to install a second pipe network. Above and beyond the general relief of the drainage systems, rainwater retention by green roofs moderates extremes of temperature and improves the thermal insulation of the building during summer and winter.

Retention ponds generally have beds sealed with pond membranes. Hence they differ from infiltration basins or swales in that they always have water in them. Designed as natural habitats, retention ponds have planted banks and provide living space for a rich variety of wildlife. The

Retention ponds

Fig. 64: Rainwater drainage as a design feature

rainwater is mainly conducted by small watercourses from the roofs into the pond. The overflow from the pond during heavy rain is often taken to neighboring infiltration basins. Retention ponds can be a valuable feature in the design of public open spaces in residential developments.

Designing with rainwater

Elements of rainwater infiltration or retention works can also be used as design features to improve the utility value of open spaces and leisure parks. Instead of using underground drains, water is taken along open channels and streams, and can thus undoubtedly enliven the user's overall experience. > Fig. 64

○ **Note:** Suggestions and advice on the use of water in open space planning can be found in: Axel Lohrer, *Basics Designing with Water,* Birkhäuser Verlag, Basel 2008.

USES OF WASTE WATER

In view of the fact that drinking water treatment is becoming more and more expensive and complex due to the increasing pollution, and yet high quality drinking water is only required in very few areas, it is incomprehensible that millions of cubic meters of rainwater and waste water enter drainage systems without being used. Recent years have seen an increasing number of concepts for substituting rainwater or gray water for drinking water.

Using rainwater

The use of rainwater saves drinking water and relieves the load on drainage systems and water treatment plants. It poses no risk to hygiene when used for WC flushing, garden watering, and washing machines, as long as it contains no heavy metals or other toxic substances. The quality of rainwater depends on the place where it falls and the character of the surfaces over which it flows. For example, the roof surfaces could be contaminated with street dirt or bird droppings and therefore rich in microbes. The water from highway or car park drains is unsuitable for further use because it may be polluted with gasolene or oil residues. In this case it is better to forgo using rainwater. It should always be possible to design the components of any rainwater use system into a building with relatively little complication. > Figs. 65 and 66

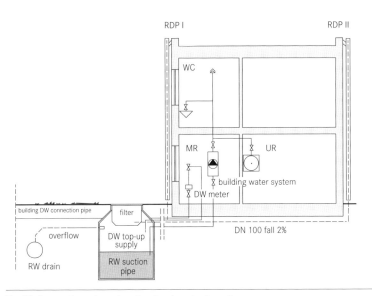

Fig. 65: System for using rainwater showing pipe layout

	roof surface and slope with high runoff coefficient
	unpressurized water tank/cistern
	downpipe with filter
	pipework system separated for DW
	automatically controlled pump
	drinking water top-up with open outlet (prevents back suction of drinking water)
	overflow, e.g. into public drainage system

Fig. 66: Typical components of a system for using rainwater

Roof collection area   The size and characteristics of the roof surface used for collecting rainwater are critical to its collection and use. If the roof surface is smooth, a large quantity of rainwater will be able to drain off, but if it is constructed from a porous material, part of the water is absorbed and evaporated. All commonly available roof materials, such as clay tiles, concrete roof paving or slate, are suitable for collecting rainwater. Rainwater collected from metal roofs can cause graying of washing if a washing machine is connected to the rainwater usage system. There are no harmful effects if rainwater collected from metal roofs is only used for toilet flushing.

The volume of rainwater delivered to the cistern depends on the intensity and frequency of rainfall events and the runoff coefficient of the

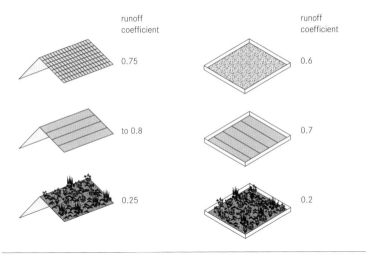

runoff coefficient 0.75

runoff coefficient 0.6

to 0.8

0.7

0.25

0.2

Fig. 67: Runoff coefficients of different roofs

roof. A runoff coefficient of 0.75 means that 75% of the rain falling on the roof flows through the downpipes and into the cistern. The runoff coefficient is between 0.0 and 1.0 and depends on the roof material. Smoother roofs have higher runoff coefficients. > Fig. 67

The collection tank is normally a cistern that accepts and stores water flowing off a roof through the downpipes and filters. Cisterns can vary in size and position. Buried cisterns are recommended if the building has no basement. Otherwise the tanks, manufactured from opaque plastic, are set up in a cool, dark basement room, so as to prevent the build up of bacteria and algae in the water. Cisterns are available in various sizes up to about 1000 l. For very high use, either several plastic tanks can be coupled together or a buried watertight concrete tank can be constructed to any size required.

Collection tank cisterns

The design of the storage capacity takes into account the rainwater influx and demand. Regional rainfall maps, which can be obtained from the meteorological office, are used for the calculation of the available rainwater. For example, in Germany the rainfall is between 600 and 800 mm per year depending on the region. The average length of a dry period is about 21 days. The calculation of the rainwater influx is based on the roof area and the runoff coefficient of the roof material.

Storage capacity

Calculation of the annual rainwater influx in l/a:

■ Collection area (m^2) × runoff coefficient (w) × annual rainfall (mm/a)

Calculation of the service water demand in l/a:

Daily personal demand × no. of persons × 365 days

Calculation of the required storage capacity in l:

$$\frac{\text{Service water demand} \times 21 \text{ days}}{365 \text{ days}}$$

With a balanced relationship between rainwater yield and service water demand, a storage capacity of about 5% of the annual yield has proved adequate.

During dry periods, drinking water can be topped up from the public supply, through an open, frost-free outlet directly into the cistern, or inside a domestic water station in the building. A domestic water station contains a pump for the delivery of rainwater, controls, pressure regulator, and further safety devices. During topping up, the drinking water pipework must not be allowed to come into direct contact with rainwater, to protect the drinking water in the public supply. It must be possible to conduct away excess water that the cistern cannot accept, through an emergency overflow into the public drainage system.

Gray water recycling
In highly impervious inner city areas, where there is generally insufficient space for a reed bed waste water treatment system, a biological gray water treatment system is adequate for cleaning slightly soiled water. They are best installed in a building's basement and are usually an assembly of various system components, specifically chosen and arranged to suit the cleaning process. Which system is installed depends on the amount of space available, the number of users and the budget. With these systems, black water must be separated and led into the public drainage system.

■ **Tip:** For rainwater use, the roof area is calculated from a projected view, in this case the view of the roof from above.

Fig. 68: Biological immersion contactor system

A typical biological immersion contactor system consists of a sed-imentation tank, a mechanical cleaning system in a holding tank, and a bucket wheel, which delivers the gray water continuously in a rotating biological immersion contactor. > Fig. 68 This is responsible for most of the cleaning action, and consists of polyethylene filter tubes, which represent the plant area in a microorganism carpet. The immersion contactor rotates at a speed of 0.5 revolutions per minute and is always half-immersed in the waste water tank, while the other half provides the microorganisms with oxygen by its contact with the air. The continuously growing biomass on the immersion contactor created by this process detaches itself from the rotating body in due course and sinks to the bottom of the tank. After the various purification stages have been completed, the cleansed waste water is no longer putrefactive and can be used as service water.

Biological immersion contactor systems

Another option for gray water treatment is a membrane filter system, which first mechanically precleans the gray water through a ventilated mesh, using microorganisms and an oxygen feed to remove the organic constituents, and then cleans the water by passing it through several microfiltration membranes positioned closely one after the other. The membrane filter system is a closed system and can be installed simply and easily into a compact space in a basement room.

Membrane filter systems

Gray water recycling is one of the most environmentally friendly waste water treatment processes. In addition to allowing more use to be made of rainwater, it also ensures that less drinking water has to be expensively cleaned and transported over long distances. Furthermore, the amount of waste water is reduced and the load on treatment works relieved. If the treated water is allowed to infiltrate, it replenishes ground-water and contributes to the natural water cycle.

The waste water treatment and the environmental alternatives given here connect to the end of the water cycle since the cleansed waste water is returned to natural water bodies. Drinking water recovery and resup-ply to buildings takes its place at the beginning of the cycle.

In conclusion

This examination of the subject of service water shows that there is a wide range of variation in how we handle drinking and waste water, and furthermore that complex and careful planning is called for from architects to integrate a drinking and waste water pipe system, including the connected sanitary appliances, efficiently into their buildings.

However, there is still much more to be done if we are to achieve sustainable development in our use of water resources, as is presently demanded by energy-saving buildings. Comprehensive solutions are required to ensure the long-term stability of the natural water cycle and to avoid burdening it, even if temporary or long-term droughts only occur in rain-starved countries. Instead of developing more and more complex and expensive cleaning and treatment techniques for drinking water, we should be ensuring wherever possible that no pollutants do enter the groundwater. To achieve this will require complex measures that are outside the remit of the building designer.

In this respect, architects can exercise influence on how water is used when they advise clients and point out to them the range of possibilities within their buildings—not only concerning a beautifully designed bathroom, but also how water could used more sparingly and reduce the volume of waste water produced. Simple measures to reduce drinking water usage, such as water-saving faucets or more extensive arrangements for the use of rainwater, different ways of using waste water, and rainwater recycling offer environmentally friendly alternatives to conventional fresh water and waste water technology. Moreover, they promote the sustainable protection of our valuable drinking water resources. In the future, if on the grounds of costs and environmental protection alone, further developments in this area will place great emphasis on water and energy savings. Systems that use solar energy to heat drinking water support this principle. If the will is there, concepts for rainwater and gray water use can be implemented quickly and easily. Overall, these measures make a major contribution to the protection of watercourses and the stabilization of the water cycle, even if, individually, they may appear to have no great effect.

Peter Wotschke

Electro-Planning

Introduction

With the advance of technical possibilities, the demands that contractors place on modern buildings are growing. Installation and operational functioning have to be carried out with a high degree of safety and great flexibility over the entire life cycle. Household functions are increasingly operated, monitored, and controlled electrically. At the same time, buildings are expected to have a low environmental impact and, above all, energy consumption should be kept to a minimum. Therefore, energy optimization is the most important measure for reducing the environmental impact of buildings.

For the architect, this means being informed about functional methods and technical developments in order to be able to implement the technical requirements of the contractors.

A particular challenge is the coordination of domestic engineering trades. The most important of these are: heating, air conditioning, fire protection, burglar protection, building control technology, and electricity distribution. The requirements cannot simply be divided among the individual trades but must be planned in a coordinated manner. A decisive factor is the networking of the components in electrical planning.

This volume provides an introduction to the planning of electro-technical installations and covers heavy current distribution and low current distribution, through to building control technology, in order to help architects attain a basic understanding of how they are all connected.

Basics of power supply

The standard power supply for residential buildings is usually pro- Voltage networks
vided by a 230/400 V low-voltage network. The medium-voltage network
(10,000 V or 20,000 V) supplies larger facilities, such as hospitals, administrative buildings, and department stores, while high-voltage networks (110,000 V) supply industrial plants.

In the case of electricity, depending on the current intensity and the Types of power supply
direction of flow, one can differentiate between various current types,
for example:

— Direct current: current and direction of the current flow do not
change over time. Solar cells and batteries supply direct current,
which is required for the operation of electronic devices.
— Alternating current: can change direction periodically. In Germany,
almost the entire electrical power supply is based on alternating
current. Plug sockets have alternating current and the majority of
household appliances are operated in this manner.
— Three-phase current: combines several phase-shifted alternating
currents. Households are supplied with three-phase current. Devices with higher power are usually connected via a three-phase
current socket or directly, without an electrical outlet, for example
an electric heater.
— Mixed current: direct current combined with alternating current

Furthermore, one can distinguish between different types of electricity, such as gray electricity from various electrical sources and green
electricity from renewable sources. The production of green electricity
is based on renewable biomass raw materials and sources, such as geothermal energy, sun, and wind.

The power supply can be subdivided into two areas according to its High- and low-voltage electrical currents
use: the supply of a strong current of electricity mainly for the connec-
tion of electrical devices via sockets, and the provision of low-level current for the operation of information and communication devices with
which the operation of the building can be carefully monitored and controlled.

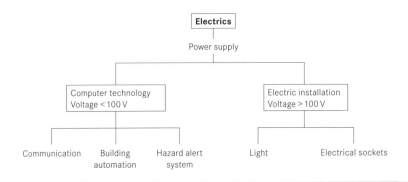

Fig. 1: Electrical technology in buildings

HIGH-VOLTAGE CURRENT EN ROUTE TO THE CONSUMER

The term "high-voltage current" is used for three-phase, alternating current. This principle is based on three interconnected, alternating currents, which enable the transport of electricity to the network. In order to be able to transport electricity, a certain amount of voltage is required.

If long distances need to be covered, then high or even maximum voltage is used. Due to its efficiency, it enables the transport of energy into regional or area-dependent networks.

High-voltage or three-phase current is thus required for the transport and subsequent distribution of energy. High-voltage current passes through various transformation processes before it ends up being used in households at a voltage of 230 V or 400 V. Voltages up to a maximum of 1,000 V are referred to as low voltage. Most electrical appliances in households, businesses, and industrial applications function with low-voltage current.

Technically speaking, a generator with three coils, arranged in a circle, is assembled for the generation of high-voltage current – hence the term "three-phase alternating current." This results in three alternating voltages, which can be employed at different times, thereby increasing performance.

This allows transport over long distances and the subsequent use – for example from the power station as a power generator – by the final consumer. > Fig. 2

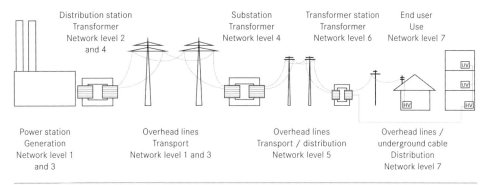

Fig. 2: Overview of a high-voltage network

Tab. 1: Grid-level structure in the network system of European electricity grid operators

Network level	Description	Classification	Voltage	Examples
NE 1	Transregional transmission network	High-voltage network	220/380 kV	Large power plants, wind parks, European network
NE 2	Distribution/substation	High to maximum voltage		
NE 3	District distribution network	High voltage	110 kV	Medium-sized power plants, e.g., bio and hydropower plants
NE 4	Distribution/substation	High to medium voltage HS/MS		
NE 5	Regional distribution network	Medium voltage	10/20/30 kV	Small power plants, e.g., wind, power, and photovoltaic systems
NE 6	Transformer station	Medium to low voltage MS/NS		
NE 7	Local low-voltage network	Low voltage	230 V/400 V	Small power plants, e.g., photovoltaic systems and fuel cells

In addition to high-voltage power plants, there are other voltage systems for energy transport. A heavy current system includes networks with a voltage of more than 50 V and currents of more than 2 A.

A high-voltage system can be divided into different voltage levels.
> Tab. 1

Depending on the power demand and the distance over which the power has to be transmitted, the appropriate voltage level is selected in order to minimize the loss of electrical energy from the power plant to the consumer. As a rule of thumb, it can be assumed that the maximum distance in kilometers is approximately the voltage in kilovolts. The alteration of voltage levels is achieved with the help of transformers in substations and, with smaller voltages, in transformer stations.

HIGH- AND MEDIUM-VOLTAGE SYSTEMS

For high- and medium-voltage networks, the primary components are the switchgear and the transformers. If large buildings or industrial plants are supplied with high-voltage current, this has to be integrated into the planning.

Switchgear

Switchgear can be described as the sum of all the components that are contained in control cabinets within a switchgear cabinet. In addition to various other components, control cabinets consist mainly of individual switchgear. Switching devices are devices for connecting (switching on) or interrupting (switching off) circuits, in order to disconnect them from the mains, or to ground them for short-term work. Switchgear for high- and medium-voltage networks is generally placed in its own room or container, where various safety regulations have to be observed.

Transformers

Transformers are one of the most important components for energy transmission and distribution. With the help of transformers, voltages can be increased or decreased. A transformer consists of an iron core that connects two coils (primary and secondary coil). If an alternating voltage is applied to the primary coil, this causes an alternating current, which in turn causes a changing magnetic field in both coils.

Depending on the number of turns in the respective coils, the magnetic field induces a secondary voltage in the secondary coil, which is increased or reduced relative to the primary voltage. Their layout depends on the application, the construction, the rated power, and the transmission ratio.

The changing magnetic field also causes induction currents in the iron core. These heat the core, resulting in a loss of energy and the necessity to cool. This cooling can be carried out in liquid or dry form. Accordingly, transformers are differentiated into oil-filled, alternating transformers (oil transformers) and alternating-phase, dry transformers (GEAFOL transformers).

Oil transformers

In oil transformers, electrical insulation and cooling takes place via mineral or synthetic oils. > Fig. 3 The use of such substances requires special planning measures for flooding and fire protection. For example, watertight collection tanks and collecting pits should be provided. Furthermore, rooms should be separated with fireproof walls and should have fire-resistant doors. Tanks and collection pits should be arranged to prevent the spread of fire.

Dry transformers

In dry transformers, electrical insulation is provided via substances such as epoxy resins or by solid insulating materials. Cooling is carried

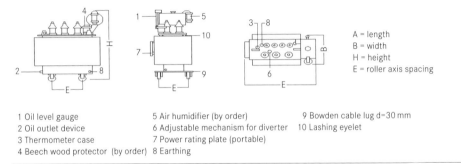

A = length
B = width
H = height
E = roller axis spacing

1 Oil level gauge
2 Oil outlet device
3 Thermometer case
4 Beech wood protector (by order)
5 Air humidifier (by order)
6 Adjustable mechanism for diverter
7 Power rating plate (portable)
8 Earthing
9 Bowden cable lug d=30 mm
10 Lashing eyelet

Fig. 3: Components of a transformer

out via convection in the ambient air, which ought to be taken into account when planning. Cast-resin transformers have an advantage over oil transformers, as the absence of an oil transformer eliminates the associated fire and groundwater risk. Moreover, they are nearly maintenance free and can be transported relatively easily. However, their use is limited to a power range of around 40 megavolt amperes (MVA) and an operating voltage of no more than 36 kilovolts (kV). > Fig. 4   ○

If transformers are housed in buildings, the design of the building must ensure that the transformers can be replaced. This involves correspondingly large external doors, access routes, and, if necessary, the ability for the transformers to be removed from the building on rails.

○ **Note**: Oil transformers are used as power transformers, for instance, in power supply systems, in transmission and distribution networks, in refineries, and on onshore and offshore platforms.

○ **Note**: Resin transformers are mainly used as distribution transformers in medium-voltage networks in the oil and gas industry, in foundries, aluminum production, and steelworks, as well as in public and commercial buildings such as airports, hospitals, etc.

Fig. 4: Example of a 40 MVA transformer

Fig. 5: Example of low-voltage switchgear

LOW-VOLTAGE SWITCHGEAR

Additional switchgear is required to supply low-voltage systems. Low-voltage switchgear and distribution boards provide the connections between equipment for generating (generators), transporting (cables, lines), and transforming electrical energy, on the one hand, and equipment such as heating, lighting, air conditioning, and information technology on the other hand.

As with medium-voltage switchgear, low-voltage switchgear is rarely built locally, but is rather delivered as ready-to-use switchgear. Most modular cabinet sizes are accommodated in separate switching rooms. > Fig. 5 It is sensible to schedule control-room floors as elevated floor systems, on which the control cabinets can be installed and below which the wiring supply can connect. > Fig. 6

Reactive-current compensation

Reactive-current compensation systems are of particular importance within the switchgear. Reactive current is a by-product of energy supply. It is the current required for supporting inductive loads (e.g., motors, transformers, ballasts, coils of any layout) necessary to produce a magnetic field. By means of reactive current, additional losses are generated in cables and transformers. Reactive current thus requires larger cable cross-sections, resulting in higher levels of energy loss during transmission. Therefore, in most industrial, commercial, and service industries – in addition to active energy – reactive current is also measured.

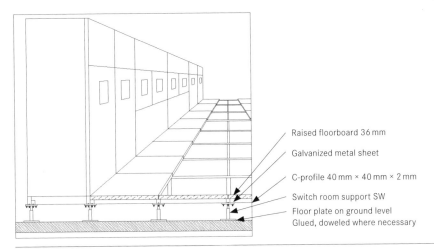

Raised floorboard 36 mm

Galvanized metal sheet

C-profile 40 mm × 40 mm × 2 mm

Switch room support SW

Floor plate on ground level
Glued, doweled where necessary

Fig. 6: Switchgear floor (Source: SYSBOTEC GmbH & Co. KG)

Reactive-current compensation systems can compensate for the generated reactive current by automatically adapting the necessary condenser capacity to reflect the current demand.

GROUNDING CONDITIONS

Central high-voltage and low-voltage systems require grounding to divert current flows into the earth. Depending on the grounding conditions of the current source, the kind of installation, the implementation of the neutral conductor, and the safety conductor, the kind of power supply is differentiated into TN, TT, and IT systems. _{> Tab. 2}

In this internationally consistent classification, the first letter indicates the grounding conditions of the current source (T: direct grounding of the current source (operating earth); I: isolation of all active parts in relation to earth).

The second letter classifies the grounding conditions of the operating installations and equipment (T: directly earthed body, independent of an existing grounding; N: bodies connected directly to the earth source of the current).

The basic network forms are derived from this, as summarized in Tab. 2.

Tab. 2: Network configuration

Network configuration	Power source	Body
TN System TN-S TN-C TN-C-S	Directly earthed	Grounded to the power source N and PE separately routed N and PE in one conductor N and PE partly combined, partly separated Neutral conductor (N)/Safety conductor (PE)
TT System	Directly earthed	Directly earthed
IT System	Isolated against earth	Directly earthed

Despite being hazardous in some instances, TN-C systems were frequently installed in households right up to the twentieth century. Nowadays, they are rarely used. TN-S systems, which are considerably more secure than the TN-C system, are mainly used in larger commercial plants. The TN-C-S system usually comprises a combination of a TN-C system, for example for the distribution network of the power supply, and a TN-S system in the customer installation.

The TT system is used as a standard in many European countries. IT systems, however, are mainly used in operating rooms of hospitals, in the chemical industry, or in the power supply of groundwater storage pumps.

The nature of the earth connection of medium- or low-voltage networks ought to be selected carefully, since it determines expenditure for safety measures. Furthermore, it also influences electromagnetic compatibility (EMC). Experience has shown that TN-S systems have the highest cost-benefit ratio for low-voltage electrical networks. > Chapter Elements of Low-Voltage Installations in Buildings, Earthing Systems

Types of power supply

In principle, power supply can be divided into four areas. The first two are responsible for the power supply of buildings.

— Public power supply: bulk of the electricity supply
— Private power generation: the largest group in numbers, but consumes the smallest share of total electricity generation
— Industry's own power plants
— Private systems, e.g., German Railways

Private power generators are relevant for the planning of buildings. Typical options are described in the following section.

PRIVATELY GENERATED ELECTRICITY

Privately generated electricity is fed into the public grid from wind-power plants, photovoltaic arrays, micro-hydropower plants, cogeneration plants (combined heat and power), and other small-scale power plants. This group, which is the largest in terms of numbers, nevertheless has the lowest share of total electricity generation. Direct photovoltaic (PV) and cogeneration (CHP) have primarily been used for direct electricity generation in buildings.

As a rule, private systems are connected to the public network in order for excess energy to be fed into the grid. However, electricity produced by private installations can also be used directly in the house without being connected to the public network. Such self-sufficient, network-independent systems (island systems) are common in remote buildings, such as mountain huts, where the effort or the costs associated with a network connection are prohibitive. The generation of power for direct consumption in buildings quickly reaches limits for regenerative sources (sun and wind), as energy sources are not continuously available in the required quantity, for example on windless or overcast days.

Connection to the public network

The demand for electrical energy is usually at its peak during times when the solar-based electricity generation yield is at its lowest. This applies, for example, to artificial light, when natural daylight is insufficient. Therefore, recovered energy must first be stored.

Storage of renewable electricity

The decentralized storage of renewable-generated energy still poses a particular technical challenge. Battery systems are usually space-, cost-, and maintenance-intensive, with short storage and discharge times. Therefore, batteries, rather than the public power supply network, are typically used as the storage medium. Thus, excess current is fed into the grid via a feed meter from the grid-fed inverter. This process is referred to as a network-coupled system.

Feed-in compensation The energy input is remunerated. The remuneration amount is stipulated by law, thus encouraging the consumer. As with all other consumers of electricity, homeowners draw the required electricity from the grid via a reference meter. The consumed quantity can be charged according to the amount of fed current. Thus, as a rule, the owners of privately owned installations do not use the self-generated energy themselves.

For each individual case, it has to be ascertained whether, or under which conditions, the use of private plants is economically justifiable and ecologically sensible. The most common installations used are photovoltaic plants and combined heat and power plants, which are described below.

PHOTOVOLTAIC SYSTEMS

Photovoltaic (PV) is the direct conversion of sunlight into electricity using solar cells, based on the so-called photoelectric effect. Light and negative charge carriers are released by light radiation in a semiconducting material (solar cell), thus generating a current flow in a closed circuit.

Since the resulting direct current cannot be used directly in households, it first has to be converted into alternating current by means of an inverter. The generated alternating current can then be consumed directly in the house or fed into the public grid. PV systems are fitted with shutdown and protective devices – against lightning strikes, for example.

The solar cells are interconnected with solar modules or solar panels, which are usually mounted on south-oriented roofs (in the northern hemisphere), integrated into the facade of buildings, or mounted on an open site. All solar modules are connected to one another to form the solar generator.

Solar modules or panels are available in various forms. In addition to the classic roof-mounted cells > Fig. 7, solar cells can also be incorporated into facade materials, roofing tiles, skylights, glass panes, and so on, thus providing scope for various architectural designs. In planning, however, optimal orientation should be considered in order to maximize efficiency. In addition, surfaces have to be cleaned regularly, in order to avoid any loss of efficiency due to the accumulation of dirt. When considering the life cycle of a building, it should also be noted that solar cells lose their efficiency over time, so that the possibility of replacement should be ensured.

Fig. 7: Installation of an array of roof-mounted photovoltaic panels (left) or as a building-integrated system (right)

COMBINED HEAT AND POWER PLANTS

The simultaneous production of electricity and heat in a single unit, which is mostly operated by gas, is referred to as a combined heat and power unit, or combined heat and power (CHP). In the plant, a gas combustion engine drives a generator that provides electrical power. The heat generated during this process is also used for heating and hot water treatment. CHPs achieve a high degree of efficiency through the double use of energy.

Depending on the application area, CHPs can be divided into different performance groups. For example, Maxi-CHPs are used for schools or administrative buildings, Midi-CHPs for small companies, Micro-CHPs for multifamily homes, and Pico-CHPs for single-family homes.

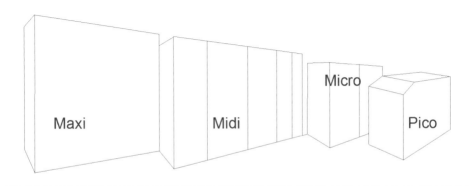

Fig. 8: Examples of combined heat and power plants (Source: ATN Hölzel GmbH)

This technology is mostly used in rural regions, or in urban housing schemes. The heat produced during the generation of electricity is used directly for heat supply in the vicinity of its production. As transmission losses are largely eliminated, CHP plants are thus able to achieve excellent efficiency levels of up to 92% – considerably higher than in the majority of large modern power plants, which have an efficiency of just over 60%. However, combined heat and power plants incur high maintenance costs.

Environmentally friendly combined heat and power plants have established themselves over the past few years, but due to their size, thus far they have predominantly been used for multifamily houses and commercial businesses. Economically viable plants suitable for single- and double-family houses, so-called Micro-CHP plants, have been on the market for only a few years. Like photovoltaic plants, combined heat and
■ power plants are being actively promoted.

■ **Tip**: If a replacement power supply system is being planned, it is imperative to check whether a combined heat and power plant would be economically viable with regard to the overall energy concept. An investment is generally worthwhile if the repayment period does not exceed seven years or, in justified cases, ten years.

PROTECTION OF THE POWER SUPPLY

Electric power can be supplied to buildings in various ways. Typically, three possible network structures can be distinguished:

1. The general power supply (AC) is the basic supply for all regular consumers.
2. The safety power supply (SV) supplements the AV supply and is intended to offer protection for the public, powering fire detectors or escape route lights in the event of a power failure or an emergency.
3. The uninterruptible power supply (UPS) supplies installations that have to be operated continuously even in the event of a power failure. These include, for example, electrical equipment in operating rooms, production machines in industry, or runway and tunnel lighting. The supply is then carried out via battery systems or emergency, diesel-powered units.

Generally, residential buildings only have one AC. A safety power supply is primarily used for large or public buildings.

A UPS system is required if the power supply has to remain uninterrupted for a maximum of thirty minutes even if, for example, the public power supply fails. One differentiates between a dynamic and a static UPS system. A risk analysis has to be undertaken as a basis for the planning of a UPS.

The two main components of a dynamic UPS are the electric motor and the generator, which are coordinated with each other as a machine set. Critical loads are supplied by the generator. Dynamic UPS

Through the use of flywheel storage accumulators and/or battery systems, voltage drops can be bridged for a limited amount of time, usually in the range of seconds or minutes. Bridging time can also be extended by coupling a diesel engine; however, the accumulators must supply the generator with energy until the diesel engine is running.

In static UPS, components of power electronics such as diodes and transistors are used to influence the supply voltage. Static UPS systems are classified according to the job, the quality of the UPS output voltage, and the performance in the event of power failure: Static UPS

- Classification 3: passive standby mode (off-line) as compensation for short-term mains failures, voltage fluctuations, and voltage spikes
- Classification 2: line-interactive operation as compensation for continuous low or excessive voltage
- Classification 1: double conversion operation (on-line), used, among other things, as compensation for short voltage surges, impact of sporadic lightning, and periodic voltage distortions

As a rule, larger UPS power units are used if spatial separation of electrical loads from the components of the electrical power supply is required.

For reasons of ventilation, electromagnetic compatibility (EMC), noise, maintenance, fire protection, and so on, the UPS and battery systems should be placed in discrete spaces.

Emergency power supply system (EPSS)
If the power supply must be maintained without interruption for more than thirty minutes, an emergency power supply system (EPSS) has to be installed, which can generate electricity over a longer period of time. An emergency power supply must be drawn up to take the utilization factor into account only for those consumers for whom it is imperative to have uninterrupted power. Emergency systems should be planned where extremely important plants must be supplied with electricity.

Parallel UPS systems can be used to increase performance and improve availability. It should be noted, however, that as the number of components increases, so the service effort is increased. The system's increased complexity can in turn create new possibilities for error.

Tab. 3: Comparison of energy sources

Power sources	Transformer	Generator	UPS
Selection	Number and power according to the required power for a normal power supply	Number and power corresponding to the total power of the supplied loads if the transformers cannot supply energy	Number, power, and energy depending on the time required to provide an independent power supply and the total power of all consumers powered by UPS
Requirement	− High security of supply − Overload capacity − Low power dissipation − Low noise level − No restrictions for installation − Compliance with environmental, climate, and fire protection regulations	− Cover the energy for the replacement power supply − In turbocharger engines, take over the load in phases − Availability of sufficient short-circuit capacity to ensure shutdown conditions	− Stable output voltage − Availability of sufficient short-circuit capacity to ensure shutdown conditions − Low-maintenance buffer batteries for power supply − Compliance with noise level limits − Low harmonic load for the prearranged mains
Advantages	− High transmission capacity − Stable short-circuit currents − Electrical isolation	− Decentralized availability − Self-sufficient energy generation	− Low losses − Voltage stability − Electrical isolation
Disadvantages	− High current surges − Dependency on the public network	− Network instability in network fluctuations − Small, short-circuit currents	− Very low short-circuit currents

Elements of low-voltage installations in buildings

In order to use and distribute electricity in buildings, many components are necessary to achieve a complete electrical installation. In addition to the components of low-voltage installations presented in this chapter, low-voltage systems (such as for telephone and data technology) and, increasingly, building installations for building automation are also required, as is explained in the following chapters.

RESIDENTIAL CONNECTION

Residential connections to houses link the public network with an individual building. For this purpose, a mains connection is established in the public area, which is routed via a house connection line through the house entrance to the connection box in the house. Generally, standardized components are used, which route the cables in a watertight manner into basement outer walls or floor slabs and, if necessary, are connected with further connection lines. > Fig. 9

House connection box and distribution

Residential connections terminate in a house connection box, which is the interface between the power supply and private electricity distribution within the house. Furthermore, a central electricity meter or current counter is installed in the main distributor for each unit, in order to charge the consumers according to their consumption. Fuses and switches for the further utilization units or circuit distributors are located in the mains distributor. > Fig. 10 and Chapter Electrical Circuits

Residential installation room

Depending on the size and type of the project, different rooms for household connections and installations are provided according to local regulations. In smaller residential buildings, a combined space is generally possible for all installations. > Fig. 11 In principle, the layout of the wall surfaces should be planned so that all installations are accessible.

The dimensions of the floor areas in technical rooms are determined by the dimensions of the required components and the corresponding safety regulations. > Fig. 12 Additional aspects, such as room ventilation, ceiling loads, and circulation routes, must also be taken into account when planning technical spaces and buildings. Oversized spaces will reduce the building's profitability, while undersized spaces can lead to a facility being refused council approval, or else create the necessity for expensive custom-made solutions in order for the system to be able to function.

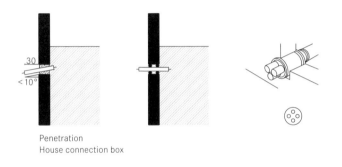

Penetration
House connection box

Fig. 9: Details of residential connections

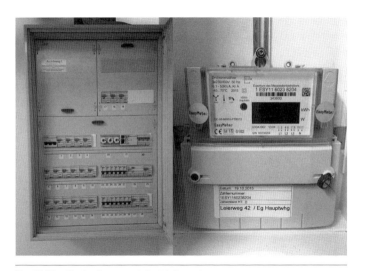

Fig. 10: Distribution boxes and electricity meters

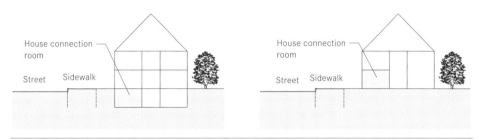

House connection room

Street   Sidewalk

House connection room

Street   Sidewalk

Fig. 11: Positioning of the residential connection room in the building

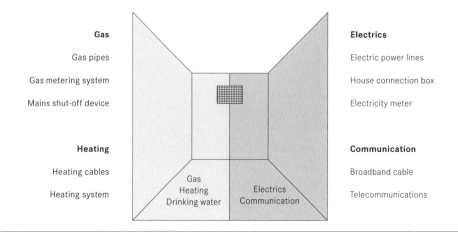

Gas		Electrics
Gas pipes		Electric power lines
Gas metering system		House connection box
Mains shut-off device		Electricity meter
Heating		**Communication**
Heating cables	Gas	Broadband cable
Heating system	Heating / Electrics	Telecommunications
	Drinking water / Communication	

Fig. 12: Installation principle of residential connections

EARTHING SYSTEMS

So-called "protective earthing" (PE) is an indispensable part of the power supply of buildings. PE provides protection against electric shock and lightning. Earthing provides for the conduction of electrical voltages or different potential energy (e.g., lightning strikes). Earthing systems must be connected to the potential equalization.

Ground (earth) rods, rings, and foundation earth electrodes can be used for grounding.

Ground/earth rods   A ground rod is generally perpendicular to the ground and inserted deep into the ground. The earth depth is the simplest solution for retro-fitting a grounding or lightning protection system. A depth of 9 m is rec-ommended. If several ground rods are used, then the required earthing depths can be divided into several parallel lengths. All ground rods have to be connected with a ringer.

Ring ground   A ring ground is a surface electrical ground that is laid at a distance of 1 m and a depth of 0.5 m around the outer foundation of a building. In order to be effective, the ringer must be in contact with the earth along at least 80% of its total length.

Depending on the type of soil structure, however, all these earth grounders are subject to a greater or lesser degree of corrosion. Dam-age caused by earthworks can also not be ruled out.

In order to avoid these disadvantages, a foundation grounding sys-tem should be provided for new buildings. The foundation grounding is inserted into the building foundation and improves the efficacy for protection against electrical shock. The main potential equalization thus becomes far more effective.

The foundation earth electrode must be taken into account when Foundation earth electrode contractors tender for structural work. Generally, the implementation is carried out by foundation manufacturers in conjunction with competent electricians. Since the foundation earth electrode is a component of the building's electrical system, responsible specialists of both trades should sign off on it before any concrete is employed on-site.

A foundation earth electrode consists of non-insulated conductors, usually made of strip or round steel, embedded in the foundations of the exterior walls or in the floor slab of the building. It is connected to the earth across a large area via the relatively well-conducting concrete.

The foundation earth electrode must be executed as a closed ring ground. It must be connected to the main potential equalizing rail – usually in the house connection area – via a prominently marked, corrosion-resistant connecting jumper lug (hot-dip galvanized steel with plastic sheath or stainless steel) with a minimum length of 1.5 m. Additional connecting lugs must be provided to ensure lightning protection.

The galvanized or non-galvanized steel must be surrounded by at least 5 cm of concrete on all sides. This achieves a high level of corrosion resistance, which generally corresponds to the longevity of the building. Round bar steel should be at least 10 mm in diameter and strip steel (at least 30 × 3.5 mm or 25 × 4 mm) should be positioned upright.

In the case of large buildings, subdivision of the spanned surface area is recommended by creating cross-connections in widths of approximately 20 × 20 m. For terraced houses, a small closed ring should be formed beneath each house, depending on the size of the site.

In the case of waterproof concrete tanking, a "black tank" (sealed with bitumen), or a tank with perimeter insulation (thermal insulation), a ring ground outside the foundation is required to create a reliable connection with the earth. Please note that the ringer should be made of *stainless steel* as it is not surrounded by concrete and is therefore not protected against corrosion.

A prerequisite for effective overvoltage protection is electrical bond- Electrical bonding ing. > Fig. 13 Electrical bonding is the practice of intentionally electrically connecting all exposed metallic items (housing) in a building that are not intended to carry electricity as protection from electric shock.

Fig. 13: Electrical bonding rail with connecting lug (right)

Electrical bonding is usually installed in the basement, usually in the building's internal terminal box, and connects:

— the grounding/protective conductor of the electrical system,
— the grounding system,
— all dissipation of the excess voltage protection devices of the energy and computer networks,
— the conductive screens of wiring and cables,
— metal construction, gas, water, and heating systems, and
— the external lightning protection system.

ELECTRICAL CIRCUITS

The circuit is the total of all electrical loads supplied by the same distributor and protected by the same fuse. In residential buildings, each room is usually supplied with a circuit for luminaires and sockets. For household appliances such as electric cookers, ovens, dishwashers, washing machines, and so on, a separate circuit must be provided, even if the appliances are connected via sockets. Connections for three-phase, alternating current also receive their own circuits.

As with the number of sockets and connections, the number of circuits should correspond to the equipment values. If additional sockets and connections over and above the minimum are specified, then the number of circuits should be increased correspondingly.

Circuit distributors   Circuit distributors distribute the electrical energy already detected by the meter to the individual circuits. Installation distributors are used for this purpose. Installation distribution boards – also called residential distributors – are generally installed in apartments. In single-family houses, it is customary to combine circuit distributors and counters in one cabinet. > Fig. 14

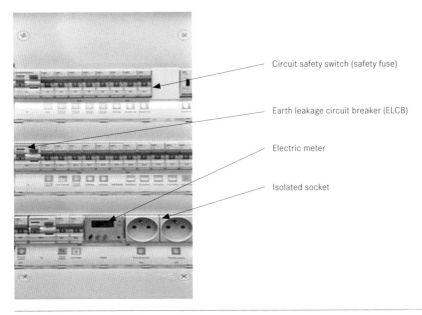

Circuit safety switch (safety fuse)

Earth leakage circuit breaker (ELCB)

Electric meter

Isolated socket

Fig. 14: Structure and arrangement of fittings in a distribution box

The following devices are accommodated in circuit distributors:

— Excess current protection devices, that is, line circuit breakers or fuses with a maximum rated current of 63 amperes
— Residual current circuit breaker
— Connection terminals
— Remote switch
— Switch contactors, time-delay switches, etc.

Most of these installations are designed in such a way that they can be clipped onto rails, so-called DIN rails, as a time-saving measure. Depending on the type of rooms in which the distributors are installed, safety categories from IP 30 (dry rooms) to IP 54 (for damp rooms or outdoors) are stipulated.

Distribution boards are available for wall mounting, recessed wall mounting, and cavity wall assembly (symbol: H). Since the dimensions of the products vary and do not correspond to the standard masonry dimensions, niches should be made large enough to accommodate a relatively large distribution box. Alternatively, it is necessary to coordinate at an early stage with the electrical installer regarding the product specification and its size. All cavities are plastered.

When planning distribution boards, it is important to make sure they are positioned in an easily accessible place. Because of the switching noise of relays and switchgear, distributor boxes should not be fitted in walls adjacent to bedrooms. The layout of the distribution boards should also correlate with the position and size of the house connection box or electrical room to permit optimal configuration of the wiring routes.

All control cabinets and distribution boards should be dimensioned with a 20% reserve tolerance for future components.

CONDUITS AND CABLES

Electrical energy is generally transported via wires and cables. It is transported from the power station via various intermediate stations to the electrical equipment and systems and then into the building.

Strands   A bundle of several strands in a sheath is referred to as a conduit. A wire is a conductor covered with plastic insulation. If a conductor is enclosed in an additional fixed coat, then it is referred to as a cable.

In residential buildings, copper cables are used exclusively. Alternating-current users are supplied with triple-wire, three-phase alternating current, or special circuits with 5-wire cables. The wires differ in their structure and their insulation, which is usually made from plastic or rubber. The wires are color-coded for ease of identification. The following combinations are generally used:

— 3 wires: green-yellow, black or brown, light blue
— 5 wires: green-yellow, black, light blue, brown, black

The green-yellow-colored conductor should be used strictly as a protective conductor (PE) or for the neutral conductor that has a protective function (PEN). > Chapter Earthing Systems

Cables and wires are marked with letter combinations, which provide information on the type and intended use. The plastic cable "NYY" is most frequently used in residential schemes. > Fig. 15

If a cable is to be used as a grounding cable, then it is covered with an additional plastic sheath. Such a grounding cable can then be placed directly in the ground.

Circuit networks and   The connection of wire cables with devices is primarily achieved by
connections   means of screw terminals and screwless terminals, though press connectors or plug connectors are also used. > Fig. 16

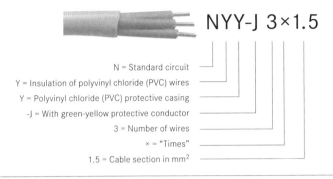

$$NYY\text{-}J \ 3 \times 1.5$$

N = Standard circuit
Y = Insulation of polyvinyl chloride (PVC) wires
Y = Polyvinyl chloride (PVC) protective casing
-J = With green-yellow protective conductor
3 = Number of wires
× = "Times"
1.5 = Cable section in mm^2

Fig. 15: Annotated structure NYY-j 3 x 1.5

Fig. 16: Connection options for electrical wiring

In principle, wire connections or junctions can only be carried out on an insulating mat or with an insulating covering. The connection points must remain accessible. Suitable terminal compartments – connecting sockets or boxes – are required for this. The route of the wiring varies, depending on the type of boxes used.

Cables are connected in special junction or device connection sockets.

WIRING LAYOUT

There are various options for the installation of electrical wiring:

Surface mount/flush installation

— visible as a surface-mounted installation,
— visible on installation channel systems, or
— concealed as a flush installation chased into the masonry or concrete,
— in wall cavities, or
— in installation ducts, underfloor ducts, or hollow floors.

Installation is forbidden in ventilation ducts or in chimney vents or flanks.

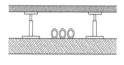 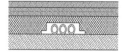 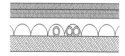

Raised floor   Underfloor conduit   Cavity floor

Fig. 17: Concealed cable routing in floors

Wiring is predominantly flush-mounted in residential buildings. Here, cable routing is recommended in empty conduits, which allows for subsequent installations or extensions to be carried out without causing any damage.

In nonresidential buildings, the wiring is predominantly accommodated in suspended ceilings, raised floors, or parapet channels. > Fig. 17 This facilitates maintenance and allows for the flexible organization of switches, sockets, and lights, permitting, for example, a change in use.

INSTALLATION ZONES

In order to minimize conflicts with other connection pipes, such as gas, water, or heating conduits, and to prevent damage to cables, e.g., by drilling of dowel holes or nailing, cable routing of flush-mounted wires in walls is only installed vertically or horizontally. If possible, installations are also restricted to defined installation zones. Wiring in floors and ceilings, however, can be installed in the shortest possible way.

A low, horizontal installation zone is allocated in a 30-cm-wide zone, 30 cm above the floor, and a similar, upper horizontal installation zone runs below the ceiling. Light switches, sockets, and switches above working surfaces are arranged in a central horizontal installation zone. In the vicinity of door and window openings, and in the corner junctions of rooms, vertical installation zones have to be provided. Within these zones, in addition to the electrical wiring, it is preferable that connections, switches, and sockets be arranged centrally. > Fig. 18

When laying cables, special care must be taken to protect them from physical damage (which could lead to further injury and/or damage to property). This can be achieved either by their careful positioning or by the use of cover paneling.

Sockets, switches, or installation sockets located outside the installation zones must be supplied with a vertical branch cable extending from the nearest horizontal installation zone.

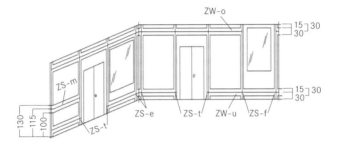

ZS-t: vertical installation zones around doorways:
10–30 cm from the building shell

ZS-f: vertical installation zones around windows:
10–30 cm from the building shell

ZS-e: vertical installation zones on the walls:
10–30 cm from the building shell

ZW-u: horizontal installation zones:
15–45 cm above the floor

ZW-o: horizontal installation zones:
15–45 cm below the ceiling finish

ZW-m: central horizontal installation zones:
100–130 cm above the floor

Fig. 18: Installation zones for electrical cables, switches, and sockets

INSTALLATION SYSTEMS

If cables are to be installed in a concealed manner, then no exten- \
sive fixing or protective equipment is required, as long as suitable cable \
types are installed. The cables can then be placed, for example, in walls \
and ceilings. Either slots are chiseled from walls and ceilings before plas- \
tering, so that cables can be installed flush to the surface, or flat cables \
are used, which can be fixed inside the plaster. > Fig. 19 Care ought to be \
taken not to compromise the loadbearing strength of the loadbearing el- \
ements when creating slots.

> Flush-mounted installation

In drywall and gypsum-board walls, the wiring is usually installed in \
the cavity, so that initially only one side of the wall is built during the con- \
struction process and is then closed after the successful installation of \
all the wiring.

If there are no fire protection requirements on ceilings, then it is pos- \
sible to route cables (e.g., for a light outlet) through holes in the floor \
above the ceiling. However, in this case, empty pipes should be used, to \
obviate the removal of the entire floor construction in the above story in \
case of subsequent installations.

Fig. 19: Installation methods for walls and ceilings

Fig. 20: Examples of grid channels (left), cable clips (right)

Fig. 21: Surface-mounted installation with an express clamp, cable clamp, cable collection holder, gripping iso-clamp, and empty conduit

The following cable structures and installation types are available for surface-mounted installations: > Figs. 20 and 21

— Cable channels
— Grid channels
— Conduit channels
— Cable conductors
— Collection brackets
— Cable clips
— Steel-armored conduits

For cost savings, cables are often routed in bundles in a single channel. > Fig. 22 This allows for access in the event of malfunctions and the ability to easily reinstall the cable. However, in order to ensure service reliability, the number of cables in a cable channel should be limited to the quantity authorized by the manufacturer. In particular, redundant systems should be routed in separate channels.

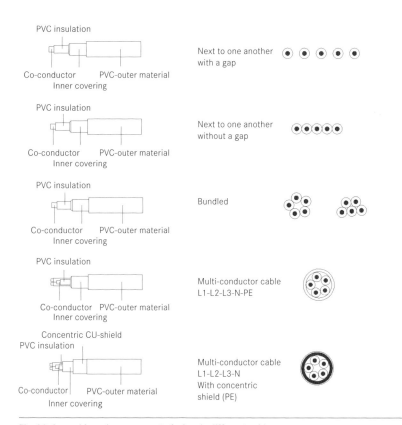

Fig. 22: Assembly and arrangement of wires in different cables

In certain instances, such as in office buildings, commercial complexes, or shopping centers, flexibility in the layout of units is an important parameter. This allows for changes in the energy distribution and the position of the power consumer. When they are laid visibly, cables allow this to a certain extent. However, this option is less visually pleasing and is comparatively complex. A less costly alternative is the use of rail distribution systems to distribute power.

The following table compares two energy distribution systems.

Tab. 4: Comparing rail and cable central power distribution

Characteristic	Rail distribution system (RDS)	Cable installation
Reaction to fire	Very low fire load density	Up to 10 times higher fire load of PVC cables than with SVS
Flexibility	Variable tap-off units; installation also possible under applied voltage	Changes and extension possible; installation work only possible in a "voltage-free" state
Material	Halogen-free rail boxes	Standard cables are not halogen or PVC free
Effort to install	Uncomplicated assembly with simple tools	Complex assembly with numerous auxiliary tools
Network installation	Linear design with outlets via tap-off units	A star-shaped supply of loads, thus cables accumulate at the feed-in point
Space requirements	Compact design, standardized angle, and offset elements	A lot of space is required for bending radius, type of layout, accumulation, and current load capacity
Price	Comparatively high installation costs	

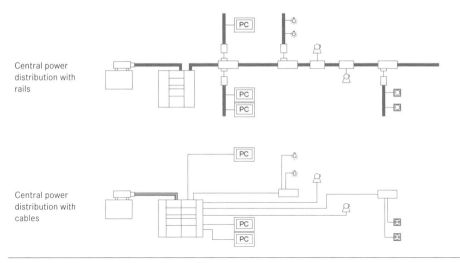

Central power
distribution with
rails

Central power
distribution with
cables

Fig. 23: Central power distribution with rail and cable

SOCKETS

Installation sockets are classified according to their intended use, as follows:

— Connection sockets – also known as distribution boxes or joint boxes – are used to accommodate connection terminals for conductors with a cross-section of up to 4 mm².
— Equipment sockets, so-called switch sockets, are used for mounting installation devices (switches, sockets, dimmers, actuators, etc.) in the wall and can also be used as connecting sockets without built-in devices.
— Device connection sockets – also known as appliance sockets or transit sockets – are intended for installation devices and additional connection terminals for through wiring.
— Sockets can be used with terminals for connecting a limited number of portable devices (such as electric heaters or wall lights) to the fixed installation.

Fig. 24: Conduit box

Fig. 25: Device connection boxes

Fig. 26: Shockproof plug

Conduit boxes

This standard form of installation provides for a separate junction box with a diameter of 70 mm and a depth corresponding to the device sockets for each connection point. This allows for subsequent changes or additions to the layout without great effort, thus requiring a relatively high investment in material, since more cables and branch outlets are required in order to use the conduit boxes.

Connection boxes

Connection boxes have sufficient space to accommodate the additional branching of cables in the device box for switches, sockets, dimmers, etc. This allows for a low-cost installation, since in this variation junction outlets are no longer required.

Shockproof sockets and plugs

Shockproof sockets and shockproof plugs are combined with three-wire connection cables to securely connect movable electrical devices with a protective conductor. Two opposite protective contacts in the socket and in the plug ensure a secure connection with the protective conductor. Thanks to their special geometrical design, it is guaranteed that during insertion the protective conductors of the plug and socket will always connect *before* the voltage-carrying sockets and plug pins.

In order to ensure that the protective measures in buildings are effective, shockproof sockets should be used. Socket inserts for flush mounting are available with hooks (e.g., for masonry or concrete) as well as with screw fastening (e.g., for drywalls). The attachment must be carried out in such a way that the socket cannot be pulled out of the mounting when the plug is removed. Also, the insulation of the conductors should not be damaged during installation.

Plugs, sockets, and extension cables (with plugs and coupling) must always be connected in such a way that the plug pins cannot be live under any circumstances when unplugged. Sockets, switches, remote control sockets, and so on are often combined with one another for functional reasons and due to their uniform design. In addition, they must be designed in such a way that the high-voltage part is protected against direct contact by separate, detachable covers.

SWITCHES

A wide variety of switches and sockets is available on the market. In residential installations these are often the only visible elements of the electrical installation. The variety, therefore, lies in particular with the design, as they can be adapted to any conceivable style of apartment or to the design and color of the walls.

Installation switches

Installation switches visible in the building, mounted in or on the wall, usually serve to switch light circuits on or off. A wide range of technical features is available with manually operated switches for fixed installations. Depending on the method of assessment, the following distinct types are available. According to the function, there are single, double, or triple-ended switches corresponding to basic circuits.

Circuits

■ **Tip**: In addition to the protective contact plugs, so-called "European plugs" fit into shockproof sockets. European plugs fit into sockets in all European countries.

■ **Tip**: Most manufacturers offer different sets of installation devices, each with a uniform design, often with a range of variations and combinations for different levels of interior design and requirements. It is therefore necessary to check if all necessary functions are covered by the desired switch series.

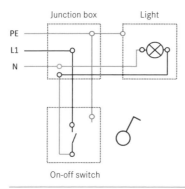

Fig. 27: Schematic diagram of the off-switch

— Off-switch, which is switched off from a switch point. This is the most common application in the private sector, where a luminaire is switched on or off with a switch. > Fig. 27

— Group switches, with which two luminaires are switched from one switching point, so that only one or the other luminaire is operated. Such a circuit is used, for example, for operating garage doors or blinds.

— Series switches, e.g., in versions with two compensators, where several lamps are switched on independently from a single switching point. Series switches are used, for example, in bathrooms to switch on mirror and ceiling lights. > Fig. 28

— Changeover switches – also called hall or hotel control – operate from two switching positions. This circuit is used in small lobbies or rooms with two entrances. > Fig. 29

— Intermediate switches can be operated from three or more switching positions. This connection consists of two changeover switches and any number of intermediate switches. These are mainly used in rooms with more than two entrances. > Fig. 30

The switches can usually be equipped with a glow control lamp (pilot light shines when the light is switched on) or with an orientation light (switch lighting, which shines when the light is switched off).

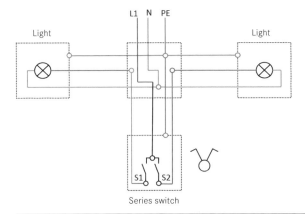

Fig. 28: Schematic diagram of the series circuit

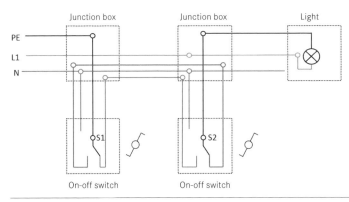

Fig. 29: Schematic diagram of changeover switches

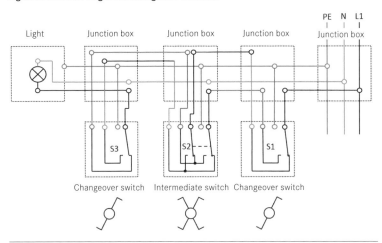

Fig. 30: Diagram of cross-connections

Fig. 31: Examples of rotational, rocking, tilting, push, and pull switches (from left to right)

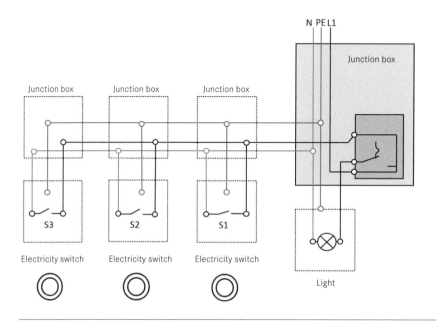

Fig. 32: Diagram of the impulse/push-button/relay circuit

According to the technical design, a distinction is made, for example, between rotational, rocker, tilting, push, and pull switches in the surface or flush-mounted design, also for cavity walls, door frames, and control panels. There are versions with screw covers and screwless covers, for rigid and flexible conductors. > Fig. 31

Special versions for different purposes include: push buttons for installation remote control, electronic switches, remote-controlled switches, switches in combination with dimmers, time switches, and so on.

Push-button   The so-called installation remote control is a light circuit with electromagnetic remote control, which functions with the aid of a latching relay. > Fig. 32 Instead of conventional switches (off, serial, change, and

Fig. 33: Variety of installation devices with uniform design

cross-connections with corresponding wiring), simple push buttons are used here. A current surge circuit consists of the main circuit with the lights and the control circuit controlled by any number of push buttons.

When a push-button device is pressed, the installation remote switch, which is also referred to as an impulse switch or a current impulse relay, receives a pulse, or a current surge. This current surge triggers the switching operation in the circuit. The installation remote switch has two (or several) switching positions, which are changed by the pulses produced by the push buttons. At the next current surge, the following position is assumed. Installation remote switches are generally placed on the DIN rail in the circuit distributor.

The advantage of this is that any number of push buttons can be connected to the installation remote switch. This is particularly useful, for example, in long corridors or extended stairs, where you can control lights from various positions.

Dimmers are used to control the infinitely variable brightness of light- Dimmers ing. Dimmers differ in the manner in which they are operated (e.g., by rotating, by touch) and the type of light, since not every light can be combined with every kind of dimmer.

In addition, there is a variety of special switches. These include, for Other switch types example, key switches, motion detectors, twilight switches, and radio switches, which are generally also supplied by the manufacturer via the same switch programs. Furthermore, there are low-current elements for telephone, network, audio/video, intercom, loudspeakers, blinds, heating control, time switches, etc. > Fig. 33

Tab. 5: Examples of minimum protection systems

Protection against foreign bodies	1st digit	Moisture protection	2nd digit	Protection type	Example
d > 12.5 mm	2	None	0	IP 20	Socket in living area
d > 1.0 mm	4	Water splash	4	IP 44	Covered light in bath or shower
Dust	5	Water jet	5	IP 55	Distributor in a swimming pool

PROTECTION SYSTEMS

Sockets are required to house switches, sockets, dimmers, and so on, in walls. Equipment boxes for switches, sockets, or other devices are offered in flush-mounted versions and are not included in the purchased parts package for flush-mounted sockets or switches. On the other hand, surface-mounted appliance sockets are usually included as part of the installation equipment, e.g., for the installation of damp-proof installations that have protection grade IP 44.

LIGHTING SYSTEMS

In addition to fixtures for general and accent lighting, lighting systems also include fixtures for safety lighting (safety lighting system, safety light, single-battery light).

In addition to safety lighting, which usually has its own, secured circuit, all cables for luminaires must be integrated into the layout planning. Here, it is specifically the routing of the light outlets that should be planned when, for example, ceiling lights need to be arranged in exposed concrete ceilings. Some luminaire types function with low-voltage systems or ballasts, so that the setting of the luminaires and lights is useful at an early stage in the planning process. Recessed luminaires are often installed in hollow boxes, which need to be fitted at the same time as the concreting of the ceiling. > Fig. 35 Rapid developments in the area of LEDs mean that lighting concepts can be completely reconceived due to the longevity and extremely low current requirement of LEDs.

○ **Note:** Lighting systems and coordination with natural daylighting are described in detail in *Basics Lighting Design*, from page 231 in this compendium. Therefore, only the relevant content for electrical planning is discussed here.

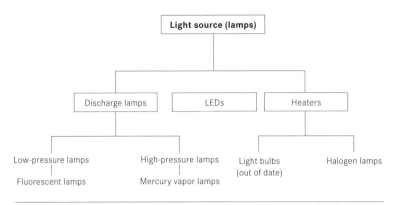

Fig. 34: Classification of light sources

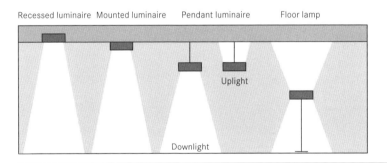

Fig. 35: Types of luminaires

Emergency lighting is required in the event that the power supply to the general artificial lighting fails. Therefore, power sources for emergency lighting must be planned independently from the power supply for general artificial lighting. When designing the emergency lighting, a distinction is made between safety lighting and replacement lighting. In order to meet safety regulations, safety lighting must fill the following roles in the event of a failure of the general power supply, to ensure that people can safely leave a building, to avoid panic, and to ensure safety in potentially perilous workplaces: > Tab. 6

Emergency lighting

Facilities where people congregate	Switch-over time max. (S)	Rated operating time Power source for safety purposes (h)	Lit or backlit Safety symbols in continuously operated buildings	Central Power Supply System (CPS)	Power supply system with service description	Single battery system	Power generation unit without interruption (0 s)	Power generation unit short interruption (<0.5 s)	Power generation unit medium interruption (< 15 s)
Public places, theaters, restaurants, airports, railroad stations	1	3	X	X	X	X	X	X	
Hotels, hostels	15	8	X	X	X	X	X	X	X
Schools, high-rise buildings, underground garages, parking lots	15	3	X	X	X	X	X	X	X
Rescue routes in workplaces	15		X	X	X	X	X	X	X
High-risk workplaces	0.5		X	X	X	X	X	X	

- Lighting or backlighting of safety signs for escape routes
- Illumination of rescue routes
- Lighting of firefighting and signaling systems
- Facilitation of rescue operations

Depending on the specifications, a separate, fire-retardant cable network may be required. This can be arranged in F90 components without a fire load or as a protected E30/E90 cable. If necessary, battery solutions can also be used.

Safety lighting ought to be provided, among other reasons, to illuminate rescue routes in workplaces, accommodation facilities, homes, restaurants, and public places such as theaters, stages, cinemas, exhibition halls, underground garages and parking lots, airports and train stations, as well as schools.

Standby lighting Replacement lighting is used so that economically and/or technically important work can be carried out in the event of the failure of normal lighting. Therefore, the requirements applicable to safety lighting must be met and, furthermore, the power of the replacement lighting must correspond to the power of the normal lighting. At lower lighting levels, standby lighting can only be used to shut down or halt work processes.

Lightning protection systems

Surge voltages are short-term voltage impulses – so-called "transients" (from Latin *transire*, "past") – that occur for only fractions of a second. These achieve voltage values of several 10,000 volts. They have very short rise times of a few microseconds (µs) before they drop relatively slowly over a period of up to several 100 µs. Excess voltage

The causes of voltage surges are:

— direct or indirect lightning pulses at distances of up to several kilometers (LEMP, lightning electromagnetic pulse)
— switching operations in the energy network or in residences (SEMP, switching electromagnetic pulse)
— electrostatic discharge (ESD, electrostatic discharge)

In the case of a lightning strike, it is usually assumed that approximately 50% of the lightning current is discharged into the earth via the external lightning protection system (lightning arrester). Up to 50% of the remaining lightning current flows into the building via electrically conductive systems such as the main potential equalization. Therefore, despite the presence of an external lightning protection system, it is always necessary to install an internal lightning protection system as well.

External lightning protection is formed by means of structural measures such as capturing devices, static eliminators (lightning arresters), and earthing systems. > Figs. 36 and 37 It protects buildings only against mechanical damage and fire; it does not prevent the rise of the electrical potential of the building hit by the lightning to around tenfold, from approximately a few 10 kV to some 100 kV compared with the environment. These potential differences exceed the insulation resistance of low-voltage consumer systems many times over, frequently resulting in their total destruction. External lightning protection

Internal lightning protection, on the other hand, is implemented by means of protective elements such as a lightning arrester (so-called coarse protection), a surge diverter (medium protection), and device protection (fine protection). Internal lightning protection

A risk analysis is required for risk management based on lightning protection. This initially determines the need for lightning protection. Later, technically and economically optimal protection measures will be defined. The building in question is subdivided into one or more lightning protection zones (LPZ).

Fig. 36: Lightning conductor on a house

Fig. 37: Lightning protection devices mounted on the roof

The protection zones are defined as follows:

Zone 0 (LPZ 0): In this area, outside a building, there is no protection against electromagnetic interference impulses (LEMP). There is a differentiation between the two LPZ 0 areas: LPZ 0A refers to the area subject to impact. Here, there are aboveground devices and wiring outside buildings and areas of protection. LPZ 0B, on the other hand, refers to the area protected from direct lightning strike by an external lightning protection system. Affected are: underground cables, external devices, and cables within 20 m of the protection zone of the building, or devices and cables more than 20 m outside the protection zone, if they are situated within the protection area of a lightning protection system or an insulated air-termination system.

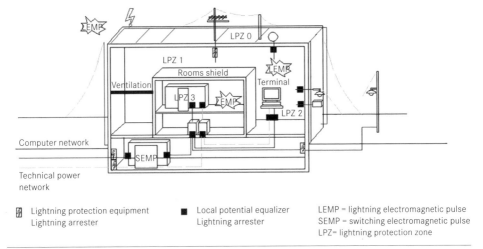

Fig. 38: Protection zone concept in lightning protection

Zone 1 (LPZ 1): The transition from LPZ 0B to LPZ 1 is effected by means of a lightning current arrester that can be installed, for example, in the main distributor or at the entrance to the building and which provides protection from direct or nearby lightning strikes. Zone 1 relates to equipment and cables within buildings (including basements).

Zone 2 (LPZ 2): The transition from LPZ 1 to LPZ 2 is effected by means of a lightning arrester that is installed, for example, in the current distribution or sub-distribution and protects it against excess voltages caused by lightning strikes over the supply network. Zone 2 only mitigates for slight voltage excesses.

Zone 3 (LPZ 3): The transition from LPZ 2 to LPZ 3 is effected by means of a device protection, that is, a mobile surge arrester, which can be installed, for example, on sockets or electrical devices. It protects against excess voltages in the power supply of the end user. In Zone 3 there are no interfering impulses due to LEMP or excess voltage.

For each lightning zone, the geometric limits, the lightning data, and the type of damage to be considered are specified. The assumed risk is reduced by the use of protective measures until an acceptable residual risk is reached, proceeding from the unprotected state of the object. Protective measures must be considered for, on the one hand, structural installations, the people within the building, and electrical and electronic equipment and, on the other hand, for the supply circuits.

Low-voltage installations in buildings

Low-voltage systems are electrical installations which, as a rule, do not carry currents that are hazardous for humans or can cause serious damage to property. In practice, such low-current systems function with voltages of less than 50 volts and currents of less than 2 amps.

NETWORK AND COMMUNICATIONS TECHNOLOGY

Phone/Internet connection
The connection of a building to the external communications technology usually takes place via a telephone/ISDN or DSL connection, if necessary also over high-capacity glass-fiber or satellite connections. The telephone network provider installs a line in the house. Additional networking of the connection sockets in residences or other buildings takes place within the framework of electrical planning. Usually, a telephone connection unit (TAE socket) is installed in the apartment or unit at a central location, from where routers manage the internal network operation with Internet, telephone, fax, etc.

Router solutions in residential buildings
In apartments, routers are normally connected to the TAE socket, which has additional connections for analog terminals (telephone, fax, etc.) and network cables. Other devices can be integrated into the communications network by radio-based means via Wireless Local Area Network (WLAN) and Digital Enhanced Cordless Telecommunications (DECT). In upmarket housing, it is now customary to supply all rooms with Ethernet cabling and to provide corresponding sockets as well as a patch field in the area of the telephone/Internet connection for setting up a home network.

Server solutions
In larger buildings, such as office buildings, more complex network systems are built, which generally have their own server cabinets/racks or server rooms. All LAN-bound data cables are distributed from this point into the units, resulting in a high installation density in the area of the servers and patch fields. > Figs. 39 and 40 If necessary, separate rooms are planned for central usage units (such as enterprise-wide data storage), which can have autonomous energy and air supply, fire protection measures, and high security standards for accessibility.

Server cabinets/ racks
The central units of a network are the server cabinets (also called racks), which usually have an installation dimension of 19 inches (approx. 48 cm) and 21 inches (approx. 53 cm). The outer dimensions of server cabinets are usually 60 cm or 80 cm wide and stand-alone cabinets are usually between 200 cm and 220 cm high. The depth varies between 60 cm and 120 cm, depending on the installation components and on

Fig. 39: Network sockets RJ45

Fig. 40: Networking a Local Area Network (LAN)

Fig. 41: Network cable CAT with an RJ45 plug (left) and a fiber-optic cable (right)

whether they have two-sided operability. A 100 cm-wide area in front of and behind the server cabinets should be provided for their installation and maintenance. In smaller units, only patch fields can be used, which can easily be accommodated inside cabinets.

A typical Ethernet cabling consists of RJ45 patch cables or optical fibers (FO) > Fig. 41, which connect the network distributor/patch panel to the socket or terminal. It is usually practical to configure the cabling of networks in such a way that access to the cables is provided during operation for maintenance and exchange purposes. This can be done by means of cavity conduction paths (in cable ducts, cable planks, or double-layer/hollow floors) or empty conduits.

Ethernet

An alternative that is increasingly specified is networking via the sockets of the existing low-voltage installation (also called power LAN). Here, additional cabling of networks can be dispensed with.

Power LAN

Door/house communication | Door and room-to-room communication generally comprises speech and video systems for entrance doors. In addition to the simple buzzer, which allows door opening via an electrical voltage, there are various communication systems. Intercom devices are usually situated radially outward from the doorbell of the entrance door to listener intercom systems at the entrance doors of the apartments or units. However, they do not allow communication between one another. Hands-free devices, on the other hand, do not require a handset and can also be mounted as a home communication system. Additional video features are often added nowadays, which make it possible to view the caller without the necessity for audio contact. However, extra video cabling is necessary for this.

TV/video/audio | TV reception can be via Internet, cable, satellite, or antenna. Cable connections are placed parallel to the telecommunication via the street into the house, while antenna reception is usually decentralized. The use of satellite systems requires more precise planning of the route and the positioning of the parabolic antenna, since this must have an undisturbed, direct connection to the satellite for interference-free reception.

The classic distribution of video/audio signals in houses is via coaxial cables and corresponding sockets. > Fig. 42 Coaxial cables (abbreviated: coax cables) are bipolar cables with a concentric composition. They consist of an inner conductor (also called a soul) that is surrounded at a constant distance by a hollow, cylindrical outer conductor. The outer conductor shields the inner conductor from interference radiation. Today, digital lines are standard on most end devices, enabling network connections to be used. In addition, loudspeaker cabling is installed in a flush manner to ensure high-quality transmission paths from amplifiers to loudspeakers.

○ **Note**: The current, standard digital video broadcasting (DVB) is differentiated according to the following categories:
– DVB-C: connection via cable
– DVB-S: connection via satellite reception
– DVB-T: terrestrial connection via antenna

Fig. 42: Connection sockets for coaxial and loudspeaker cables

ELECTROACOUSTIC SYSTEMS

Apart from voice alarm systems (VAS), electroacoustic systems (EAS) also include electroacoustic emergency warning systems and public address systems (PA). If possible, the entire electroacoustic system should be available in a building to perform different functions. For instance:

— Emergency call and announcements with freely selectable and programmable gong introductions
— Targeted alarming with evacuation instructions
— Music transmission with high sound quality

For this purpose, the device is divided into loudspeaker circuits for individual calls to all the auxiliary rooms. When connected to a loudspeaker circuit, the switched programs in the remaining areas should not be interrupted.

The triggering of an alarm signal by the fire alarm system should take place automatically in the event of an emergency, using preprogrammed loudspeaker lines. A common hazard signal is used as an alarm signal. Targeted evacuation instructions are stored digitally as a sound file and are automatically triggered in the respective building sections by the fire detection function of the fire alarm center via monitored interfaces.

Sub-master stations in remote buildings with independent programs must be connected to the main center and integrated into the monitoring of the main center. External systems for music recording as well as background music programs via the alarm system are to be muted to ensure high speech intelligibility in the event of an emergency.

For the mobilization and evacuation of personnel, police and fire-fighters need an emergency system that remains functioning in an emergency. The alarm system is therefore to be equipped with a UPS system, which ensures functionality for at least thirty minutes. The reserve power supply must also be considered.

VIDEO SURVEILLANCE

Video surveillance is the observation of objects, people, or property by video camera and monitor. Video surveillance is usually designed in a closed system via fixed cables (closed-circuit television, or CCTV).

In the simplest form of video surveillance, only a video camera and monitor are connected. Depending on the required task, however, it might be necessary to integrate additional components into the video surveillance system.

Analog video   In the case of analog video systems, the video system signals (video, control, and parameterization) are transmitted via coax cables or two-wire lines, or modulated via glass fiber. The information of these signals consists of analog (non-graduated) voltage values in the transmitted frequency. In traditional analog video systems, numerous cameras with crossbars are connected to numerous monitors. This results in a point-to-point connection, the signal direction of which has already been defined in the planning phase.

The cabling is usually star-shaped, allowing subunits (satellite systems) to be formed. The quality of the analog video is generally high. If, however, the analog video signal is transmitted over longer distances, the signal level decreases and the image loses contrast. Likewise, high-frequency components are dulled, which results in increasing loss of clarity. If additional amplifiers (equalizers) are used, then the signal noise increases. Video quality therefore decreases with increasing transmission distance.

Video over IP (VioIP)   In contrast to analog video, video system signals are digital at video IP and are transmitted via an IT network (local/wide area network – LAN/WAN – or Internet). These IT networks typically consist of active components (switchboards, routers, etc.) and interconnections. These are usually UTP (Unshielded Twisted Pair) cables, balanced, unshielded cables with twisted and colored paired wires (Cat 5, 6, or 7), fiber (optical fiber), or wireless connections.

The quality of the IT network digital video signal is independent of the distance of the transmission path and is thus always maintained. The direction of the signal path is determined by the terminal used (camera, monitor, recorder, etc.) and can therefore be changed. Thus, it is also possible to integrate other devices into the IT network, provided that the permissible network load in the affected sector is not exceeded.

HAZARD WARNING AND ALARM SYSTEMS

Hazard warning systems are used to reliably recognize and report danger to people and property. > Fig. 43 They automatically or manually trigger the processing, transmission, and emission of danger reports. The transmission paths in ring technology or DC technology are permanently monitored.

Burglar alarm systems are hazard detection systems that automatically monitor property for theft, as well as for unauthorized entry into areas and rooms. If the building envelope is to be monitored, then magnetic contacts, sensors, motion detectors, and glass break detectors, etc., must be integrated into the system. In their planning, architects must take into consideration that all windows, doors, and other entrance openings must be suitably electrified.

Burglary and holdup alarm systems are hazard detection systems that are used to make a direct call for help in case of an attack – usually directly to the police. Furthermore, this alarm can also be used as a secondary alarm by an external safety control unit.

Fire detection systems are hazard detection systems that are used to make a direct call in the event of a fire or to report a fire at an early stage.

These systems consist of fire detectors, a fire alarm control center with access to an emergency power supply, a transmission device, alarm devices for internal alarm, and control devices, which close fire protection doors, open smoke and heat outlets, control fire extinguishing systems, switch off machines, and so on.

The role of automatic fire detectors is to detect evidence of fire, such as visible or invisible smoke, heat, or flames, and to report this to the fire detection center.

One distinguishes between the sizes of fires depending on optical, thermal, and chemical fire detectors or combinations thereof, flame detectors, and special detectors and smoke suction systems. In addition, there are also handheld detectors that are used on escape routes for the manual triggering of alarms. The detectors are connected individually or in groups for the transmission of signals. These are routed to the fire alarm center as a branch and/or ring line.

Burglar alarm systems

Burglary and holdup alarm systems

Fire detection systems

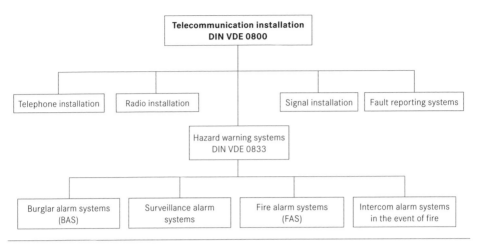

Fig. 43: Structural classification of hazard reporting systems

The fire detection center records, evaluates, and processes the pretested signals from the detectors. In the event of a fire, the optical and acoustic signaling of the triggering detectors via the transmission device is sent to the fire department or somewhere that can provide assistance. Precise fire detection is achieved through the use of targeted detectors. Further tasks of the fire detection center include functional monitoring of the entire system and warning of possible faults, as well as activation of electrically controlled extinguishing systems.

In addition to extensive fire alarm systems in larger buildings, smoke detectors should be installed in apartments. These should be attached to ceilings in all living rooms and bedrooms. Here, cable-free battery solutions are also an option. > Fig. 44 High-quality smoke detectors can also be connected so that, in the event of an incident, all smoke detectors can give a signal simultaneously.

Voice alarm systems   To alert individuals or the occupants of an entire building, the use of acoustic signal generators with DIN-tone is preferable. > Fig. 45 In production areas with sound levels exceeding 110 dB(A) and in public areas, optical signal transmitters are also required, since hearing-impaired people must also be taken into consideration. Optical alarm devices include revolving signal lights or flashing lights.

Acoustic alarm devices for fire warnings include: sirens, horns, electronic signal transmitters with adjustable tones, PA systems, and voice alarm systems.

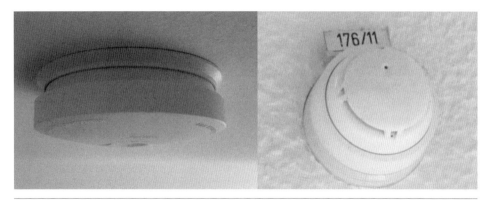

Fig. 44: Smoke detector (left) and fire detector (right)

Fig. 45: Alarm installation loudspeaker in a suspended ceiling

Building automation

BUS SYSTEMS

Facilities that are used for the automatic control and monitoring of technical installations and processes in buildings, as well as for checking their consumption data, are grouped under the term "building automation." The system is divided into three areas: > Fig. 47 and Chapter Levels of Building Automation

1. Management level
2. Automation level
3. Field level

Building system engineering/bus technology should be regarded as part of building automation, which carries out automatic functions within the premises of the building. This is possible across rooms, within a building, and between separate buildings. The concept of building automation emerged in order to differentiate it from conventional electrical installations. The previous installation of individual components has now been replaced by systems technology, or the "system bus."

In contrast to conventional electrical installations, the two-core, low-current bus system is used for information transmission and, irrespective of its low-voltage supply, carries the circuit of the terminals. Sensors send the recorded information to the actuators, which convert it into switching signals for the terminals (e.g., air conditioning). > Fig. 46 Since all actuators and sensors are connected to the same line, complex control processes can be managed via a single (bus) system. The most important bus systems are EIB/KNX, LON, and LCN.

EIB/KNX   EIB/KNX was originally developed under the auspices of the European Installation Bus (EIB) as a common standard for the application of building automation in commercial and residential buildings. After the system was modified, it came onto the market as KNX. KNX is the only global standard that enables the connection of products from different manufacturers. The system consists of so-called "participants": the sensors and the actuators. Sensors detect physical variables such as temperature, pressure, or air pressure, convert them into information, and pass it on to the network. Actuators receive this information, convert it into physical quantities, and trigger a function, for example with lamps, heaters, or blinds.

The smallest unit of a KNX system is a line. This can consist of a maximum of 64 participants and can have a maximum length of 100 m.

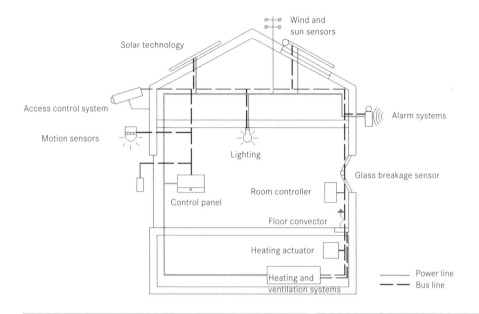

Fig. 46: Application areas of building automation

The origin of the Local Operating Network (LON) was decentralized automation with the help of a control unit, which can be used for all devices, so-called "nodes." In addition to sensors and actuators, there are also controllers in a LON. In this way, information that is only required locally is also processed locally. LONs are mainly used in measurement and control engineering (MSR). This technique is rarely found for domestic technology such as heating, ventilation, and air conditioning.

The Local Control Network (LCN) is also used in building automation. In this system, the sensors and actuators are equipped with microcomputers that are compact enough to fit into sub-distribution boxes or circuit distribution. The LCN is characterized by the ease with which it can be planned, installed, and programmed – not least as the sensors and actuators can be accommodated in a module.

The 230 V network is used as a bus, but it ought to be equipped with an additional wire. If this is taken into account during the electrical installation, then no further cabling is required. Also, the LCN modules do not require power supplies as they are connected directly to the power cables. An LCN segment consists of a maximum of 250 modules, which allows several hundred rooms to be controlled on a regular basis.

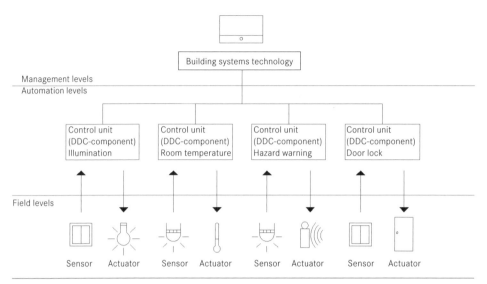

Fig. 47: Levels of building automation (BA)

LEVELS OF BUILDING AUTOMATION

The three levels of a BA system mentioned above are distinguished by the size and complexity of the building or the properties to be automated. Due to advances in digital control and control technology, the boundaries between the levels are becoming increasingly blurred. Functions of the automation level have become increasingly decentralized with more powerful digital systems, that is to say, integrated into the various zone levels.

Field level   At the lowest field level of the building, its various technical installations are operated with the help of the field devices: sensors and actuators. Sensors record information and transmit it to the actuators via a bus system (see above). The actuators receive the data and convert it into switching signals. Information is processed at the field level and prepared for the higher levels.

Automation level   With its control units (DDC – Direct Digital Control), the automation level monitors the limit values, switching states, counter reading, control, and regulation of the building's technical installations. Automation stations process the resulting data and communicate it to the field or management levels. These are small, powerful devices that can be implemented in digital technology and configured with standardized software tools.

The management level involves the higher-level operation and monitoring of activities and the signaling of faults should they occur. Information on building automation is collected here and evaluated, for example, on the terminal screen and printed out on the log printer. The management level includes the implementation of system-wide and high-level control and optimization algorithms. In addition to a computer, the necessary equipment includes a redundant data storage incorporating possibilities for data backup and, if necessary, an uninterrupted power supply. Management level

HIGH-LEVEL MANAGEMENT FUNCTIONS

A management system can be implemented as a central control room or as distributed systems with several operator stations based on client-server architecture. The management system software consists of a multitasking operating system, a powerful database system, user software, and process visualization software. The software communicates between the management and automation levels via a defined transfer point – the building automation node – and exchanges data with its databases.

The use of high-level management functions requires the interconnection of all related BA systems into an interoperable system, which must be available for the connection of various systems. For this purpose, the system requires an open communications interface such as, for example, the neutral data transmission system FND or the BACnet, so that, if required, it is possible to connect further automation devices to the operating and management devices.

BACnet/IP provides a method for BACnet automation networks to expand over building and property boundaries. An Ethernet network, which is generally used for data transport, is set up via routers, hubs, switches, repeaters, and transceivers. BACnet/IP networks

A BACnet/IP network is a virtual network consisting of one or more IP subnetworks (IP domains) that share the same BACnet network number. It contains a number of nodes that communicate using the BACnet/IP protocol. The BACnet/IP nodes may belong to different physical networks, which in turn are part of a larger IP network and are exclusively connected by IP routers. Several BACnet/IP nodes can belong to the same BACnet network.

With the help of bus systems, control systems for lighting, roller shutters and blinds, heating, etc., can be installed and programmed easily, using fewer cables. All devices and systems in the building communicate via the bus line. Central functions use this line and control a selected number of devices, or all of them, via a single control command – the bus telegram. The corresponding bus commands have to be programmed. Central functions

Examples of central functions:

— All lights in the building on or off
— Close all windows
— Lower the thermostatic valves of the heaters
— Close or open blinds

All functions can be combined as desired. In conventional installations, for example, a central switching off of the lighting in conjunction with the down-regulation of the heaters would only be possible with additional wiring. If a bus system is to be installed, then the contractor must inform the system integrator who is programming and commissioning the system of the specific connections required. Some examples:

— "Lights off": all the lights in the house are simultaneously switched off by pushing the button when sleeping. Individual lighting, such as aquarium lighting, can be excluded.
— "Lights on": all lights are switched on, either by pressing the button or automatically, e.g., when the alarm system is activated.
— "Heating on/off": when leaving or entering the house, all radiators are adjusted down or up to a predefined value (e.g., anti-freeze position).
— "Blinds up/down": in the morning and in the evening or automatically, such as during storms (signal from the wind monitor), all blinds are raised and all awnings retracted.
— "Close windows": when a person leaves the house, all windows do not have to be checked individually; they all close at once or automatically with corresponding signals from the rain/wind monitor.
— "Leaving the house": for safety reasons, all electrical appliances (except refrigerators and freezers) are switched off; lights are switched off (except aquarium lighting); all windows are closed; blinds are switched to the random mode to make it look as if the house is occupied; radiators are reduced to a minimum.

The ability to program central functions can contribute to energy savings. They can also be operated remotely – via Internet, mobile phone, and so on – for example to switch on the heating before arrival.

Comfort functions   In addition to increased safety and energy savings, one of the primary objectives of building automation is to achieve a higher level of comfort for the user. A high degree of automation is achieved when the BA system automatically adjusts to the user's predefined settings and, under normal circumstances, does not require manual user interventions. Some examples:

- Brightness- and presence-controlled switching, which switches lighting on or off with the aim of creating uniformly lit spaces when people are present in the room.
- Storage of "scenes" that can be activated at the push of a button depending on the use of the space, for example dimming down the light and/or closing the shutters when a presentation is given in a seminar room.
- Use- and presence-activated heating control, where the desired comfort temperature is automatically controlled and maintained.
- Automatic control of the blinds according to sunlight, so that glare does not occur and/or the rooms are not overheated during the summer period.

Implementation of electrical planning

Electrical planning includes the sum of all electrical wiring, connections, and other elements. Even though most elements of electrical planning might play a key role in the planning and the determination of qualities, the requirements of electrical planning must be integrated into the design right from the outset.

The location and dimensioning of the house connection area and the cable routes are particularly important parameters in the design process. In addition, early predefinition – for example, regarding the extent of electrification of components – enables architects to estimate heights of ceiling and floor constructions, in order to determine room proportions and overall building heights.

Thus, close coordination between electrical planning, architectural design, and the other technical planning with experts during the planning process is necessary in order to attain a holistic solution.

PLAN OF EXECUTION

Ultimately, the project planning should result in the implementation of all of the contractor's functional specifications. Moreover, the plan of execution should be so clear and comprehensive that the contractor can derive the assembly planning from it without having to carry out any further calculations or measurements. In addition to the electro-planning based on the architecture planning and electrical drawings, the calculation and determination of systems, and definition of quality levels are also necessary. > Figs. 48 and 49

Special attention must be paid to coordination with other trades. This doesn't only mean that the planning is carried out to a high technical level and on schedule; but the various trades companies must not obstruct one another. Care must be taken to prevent clashes, particularly with other domestic engineering trades. This applies in particular to the management of cabling routes, but also to fire partitioning and the positioning of slots, recesses, and ducts.

DIMENSIONING

With regard to the electrical power supply, estimation of the required power is the most important task in the basic determination. In order to achieve high efficiency, the components should operate at a capacity of approximately 70% to 80% of maximum power. Insufficient dimensioning leads to malfunctions and excess dimensioning to inflated costs.

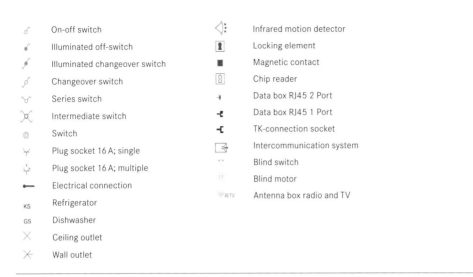

♂	On-off switch	◁:	Infrared motion detector
♂	Illuminated off-switch	🔒	Locking element
♂	Illuminated changeover switch	■	Magnetic contact
♂	Changeover switch	🔲	Chip reader
⌄	Series switch	⊣	Data box RJ45 2 Port
⌄	Intermediate switch	⊣	Data box RJ45 1 Port
⊚	Switch	⊣	TK-connection socket
⌣	Plug socket 16 A; single	⊡	Intercommunication system
⌣	Plug socket 16 A; multiple	··	Blind switch
▬	Electrical connection	M	Blind motor
KS	Refrigerator	⌣R/TV	Antenna box radio and TV
GS	Dishwasher		
✕	Ceiling outlet		
✕	Wall outlet		

Fig. 48: Annotation symbols in electrical planning

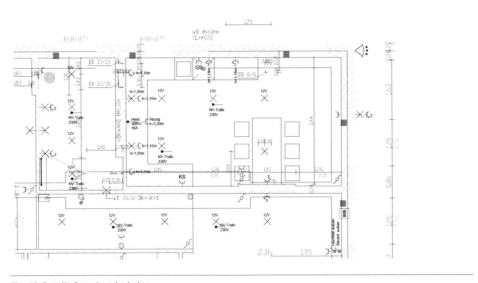

Fig. 49: Detail of an electrical plan

The dimensioning of networks and electrical systems is undertaken via the so-called "power requirement calculation," which takes into account the connections that the respective installation components have. In order to be able to configure the installation components, user requirements, building regulations, technical equipment, and technical installations for the design planning must first be compiled roughly and then compiled in detail for the execution planning.

The total connection value of the building is calculated as the sum of the connected values of individual devices. This represents the maximum required electrical power. Examples of the electrical values of electrical appliances in a typical residential building are shown in Tab. 7.

The power requirement is determined as the sum of the installed capacity (ascertained by the electrical supply data) and the concurrency factor. The fact that not all electrical equipment or electrical systems are simultaneously switched on or operated at full load is taken into account. The concurrency factor "g" is the ratio of the power consumed at a point of the network, or the electrical system, to the power installed behind this location.

Tab. 8 contains benchmark values of the concurrency factor for residential buildings and public buildings. These assessment values are not concrete, project-specific values, since individual energy requirements lead to entirely different factors, taking daily and annual changes into account in specific cases. For dimensioning, the least favorable load case – that is, the case with the highest simultaneous energy requirement – should be determined.

In addition to electrical household appliances, sockets, outlets, and connections should also be taken into account during planning. Every living room, dining room, and bedroom should be equipped equally, with at least one socket per wall. Each room should be equipped with at least one switch for the lighting. Sockets near water, e.g., in kitchens, bathrooms, and garages, must be fitted with a residual current device (RCD).

Depending on the equipment, electrical installations in residential buildings should be provided with a minimum of sockets, outlets, and connections. > Tab. 9

The value of the equipment is generally defined for a single residential unit. Each individual room must correspond to the respective minimum requirements of the equipment value according to its use. The allocation of space is possible once the value has been defined.

Tab. 7: Power consumption of household appliances

Household appliance		Connection value in [W]	
		from	to
iron	Alternating current	12,000	1,000
water heater	3-phase current	2,500	21,000
built-in oven	3-phase current	6,000	5,000
built-in cooker	3-phase current	8,000	8,500
electric oven	3-phase current	1,600	14,000
fryer	Alternating current	120	2,300
freezer	Alternating current	3,000	200
dishwasher	Alternating current	700	4,500
coffee machine	Alternating current	100	1,200
fridge	Alternating current	1,000	130
microwave oven	Alternating current	4,500	2,000
sauna	3-phase current	300	18,000
vacuum cleaner	Alternating current	1,000	1,000
hot water storage 15 l – 30 l	3-phase current	1,000	4,000
hot water storage 50 l – 150 l	3-phase current	3,000	6,000
clothes dryer	Alternating current	2,000	3,600
washing machine	Alternating current	2000	3,300

Tab. 8: Simultaneity factors for the main feed

Type of building	Concurrency factor	
	from	to
Residential building		
Single-family houses	0.4	0.4
Multifamily houses		
— General requirements (without electric heating)	0.6	0.6
— Electrical heating and air conditioning	0.8	1.0
Public building		
Hotels, guesthouses, etc.	0.6	0.8
Small offices	0.5	0.7
Large offices	0.7	0.8
Shops	0.5	0.7
Schools, etc.	0.6	0.7
Hospitals	0.5	0.75
Meeting rooms	0.6	0.8

Tab. 9: Equipment values for electrical installations in residential buildings
(according to RAL-RG 678)

Equipment value	Identification	Quality
1	*	Minimum equipment according to DIN 18015-2
2	**	Standard equipment
3	***	Convenience equipment
1 plus	* plus	Minimum equipment according to DIN 18015-2 and preparation for the use of building system technology according to DIN 18015-4
2 plus	** plus	Standard equipment and at least one functional area according to DIN 18015-4
3 plus	*** plus	Convenience equipment and at least two functional areas according to DIN 18015-4

The equipment value is ascertained according to the number of sockets, the lighting connections, and the telephone and radio/TV/data connections for the different room types in the living area. Indicated in Fig. 50 and 51 below are the equipment values proportional to the number of sockets > Fig. 50 and lighting connections > Fig. 51.

CALCULATIONS

Calculations made in the design planning are constantly updated on the basis of findings obtained during the course of detailed planning. However, the complete calculation of all equipment and equipment components takes into account all interfaces for noise protection, heat protection, and fire protection. These include, for example:

— cable cross-section calculation
— creation of the system performance levels, call-by-call, fire alarm, public address system, antenna installation
— transmission networks
— design of the central devices

DIMENSIONING

All measurements are based on the above-mentioned calculations. On this basis, central devices such as antennas, fire alarm centers (BMZ), electroacoustic systems (ELA), data distributors, etc., are dimensioned and the cables are designed with corresponding structural systems.

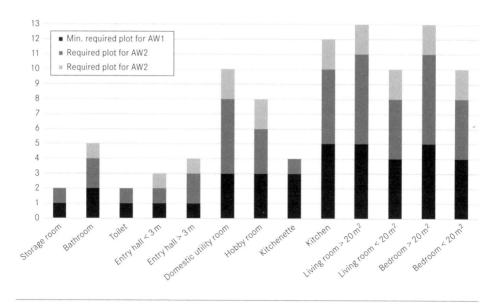

Fig. 50: Number of sockets for equipment values 1-2-3 (according to RAL-RG 678)

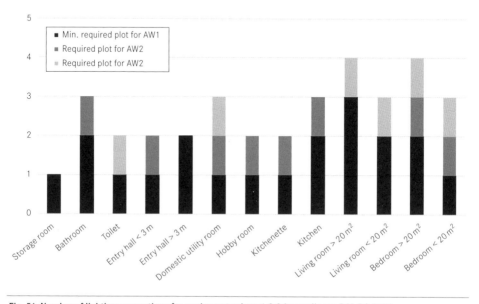

Fig. 51: Number of lighting connections for equipment values 1-2-3 (according to RAL-RG 678)

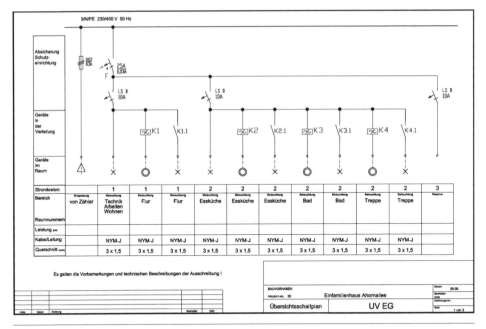

Fig. 52: Overview diagram for a single-family house

DIAGRAMS

Diagrams must be drawn up that indicate additional performance data, dimensions, functions, and components, including the building automation components required to create the data. These include:

- overview diagrams for all electrical equipment > Fig. 52
- system diagrams
- function flow diagrams or descriptions for each system with function components and the principle of distribution
- power consumption lists of the electrical components provided

PLANS AND SECTIONS

A graphic representation by means of sections or enlarged details of the plans is required so that the various trades can be coordinated. These include, in particular, the laying of cables and wires, as well as their intersections.

A symbolic representation of the components (loudspeakers, fire detectors, station antenna, panels, data connections, etc.) is made in the drawings. However, for example, central units are shown in a standardized manner in order to plan the occupancy of house connections. In doing so, ground plans are created to a scale of 1:50, sections and details to a scale of between 1:50 and 1:1.

INSTALLATION DESCRIPTION

Finally, a description of the equipment components and other fixtures is provided. The performance values and specifications and, if necessary, the chosen manufacturer must be clearly documented.

In conclusion

Nowadays, electrical planning is no longer a peripheral aspect of the planning of buildings, carried out by appointed trade companies, as was the case a decade ago. With the increasing complexity of our buildings due to increasing energy standards and expanding building maintenance requirements, buildings have become highly networked and digitally controlled. The logging of climatic data, the monitoring and control of previously manually operated components, such as windows and heating systems, the generally high degree of automation, and extensive safety and hazard monitoring ensure that cable lengths and the number of components per building have increased exponentially. Completely networked building concepts, such as Smart Home, which integrates all devices not connected to the building, including household appliances, into integral planning, show that this development will continue.

Thus, an integrated electrical planning approach is essential in order to take these issues into account from the outset. For practicing architects, it is imperative to understand the structures and principles of electrical planning and to integrate the systems. *Basics Electro-Planning* provides a clear overview of the fundamental aspects, enabling architects and engineers to coordinate and update their knowledge of electrical planning.

Roman Skowranek

Lighting Design

Introduction

Light is of vital importance for human beings. For in addition to our ability to see, our bio- and circadian rhythms are shaped by light.

Hence, within the context of planning buildings and exterior spaces, light planning is not only a central element in design, it is also of immense importance to the way we feel in these spaces.

It is therefore important to note that for every imaginable use, new requirements arise and normative standards take effect, which can restrict our plans and goals. Furthermore, prevailing circumstances may vary from case to case. Consequently, adopting a general categorical approach to light planning is very difficult; normally, individual planning will be required in every case.

Whereas historical light planning was primarily concerned with introducing daylight into interior spaces, illuminating predetermined areas with sunlight at certain times of the day, and ensuring that night illumination was available with natural sources of light, contemporary lighting design can offer a far greater choice of variations and technical options. At the same time, demands are constantly growing. Guidelines have to be followed and minimum and maximum values complied with. Human sensitivities adapt to new lighting situations, and, last but not least, the energy efficiency of artificial light and sunlight need to be taken into consideration. As a result, the complexity of planning tasks has increased in the field of interior planning and architecture, resulting in an ever higher degree of specialization in the domain of lighting design.

The foundations of lighting design

The question of how we employ naturally available as well as artificially added light raises certain design issues that need to be clarified in advance: which specifications does a particular light source fulfil or have to fulfil, and which measurable values are available. Above all, and as far as planning specifications are concerned, the physical properties must be addressed, since they form a crucial part of the planning background. Furthermore, it is necessary, as far as the actual planning is concerned, to establish which properties are to be utilized. Moreover, it is essential to identify which tasks the light has to perform. In addition, certain specifications may have to be met with regard to basic lighting, as well as room and accent lighting, which may differ quite considerably, or have to be achieved through a variety of means.

THE PLANNING PROCESS

The individual stages of light planning are barely distinguishable from the standard sequences of architectural planning. The fundamental data, as well as the design and its execution, define the process. During the first stage, the client or user specifies the desired functions and defines, above all, the areas to be illuminated and the specific colour scheme required. In the draft stage, the components are primarily considered from the standpoint of artificial lighting, such as the types of lighting and illuminants, since the daylight components are – in the case of pure lighting design – generally defined by the position, size and style of the windows. The components and furnishings are then put in position. To this end, computer-aided simulations can be generated – when required or desired – that reflect the room's spatial effect. These simulations cannot, however, serve as a substitute for sampling individual components in a specific installation context, for only here can the individual installation situation be chosen definitively. Interaction between light planners and electronics planners is essential, since the cable routes and the positioning of the switches must also be considered.   ○

○ **Note:** Owing to the growing opportunities in computer-aided design, many situations in the planning process can now be illustrated, as in the case of rendering, illumination scenarios, calculations, etc. These are not, however, a substitute for sampling or for reexamining work on the spot, because the individual's perception of a light situation cannot be simulated down to the very last detail – despite photorealistic renderings.

PHYSICS TERMINOLOGY AND PARAMETERS

Owing to light's complexity, many different parameters are used to describe and do justice to the various aspects of this subject. > Tab. 1

The light and colour spectrum

To the human eye, only a minuscule part of the electromagnetic spectrum is perceptible. This field is known as the light or colour spectrum. It is also frequently referred to as real "light". Higher-frequency ranges with short wavelengths (such as UV or X-rays) and low-frequency ranges with long wavelengths (microwaves and radio waves) are invisible to the human eye. Within the range of the visible light spectrum, it is possible to determine the diverse wavelengths of the colour tones. > Tab. 2

Luminous flux, luminous efficacy and the quantity of light

Luminous flux Φ [lm] shows how much light is radiated from a light source. In order to establish this fact, the human eye is needed as an evaluating organ. When calculating the luminous efficacy, the quantity of light, the light yield and the luminance, it is essential to regard luminous

Tab. 1: An overview of the photometrical parameters

Parameter	Symbol	Unit
Luminous flux	Φ	lumen [lm]
Luminous efficacy	η	lumens per watt [lm/W]
Luminous energy	Q	lumen seconds [lms]
Light yield	I	candela [cd]
Illuminance	E	lux [lx]
Daylight factor	D	percentage [%]
Light density	L	candela per m² [cd/m²]
Colour temperature	–	Kelvin [K]
Colour rendering index	R_a	–

Tab. 2: The wavelengths of the colours of the spectrum

Hue	Wavelength [nm]
Red	710–630
Orange	630–580
Yellow	580–560
Green	560–480
Blue	480–420
Violet	420–380

flux as a baseline value. In the case of artificial light sources, the luminous flux levels used for the <u>light calculations</u> are stated — depending on the product — by the manufacturers. In order to balance the energy and perform investment appraisals, it is necessary to calculate the <u>luminous efficacy η</u> [lm/W] — an essential source of light. This, in turn, calculates the energy required to reach the nominal value. <u>The quantity of light Q</u> [lm × h] states the entire luminous flux emitted by a light source over a defined period of time. A light source with highly concentrated luminous flux thus produces a greater quantity of light per unit than a light source containing very little luminous flux.

<u>Light yield I</u> [cd] determines the ratio of light emitted by a light source moving in a certain direction. The luminous intensity of natural light sources can be influenced by the use not only of sun-shade and glare protection, but also of glazing and light control. In the case of artificial light, these are the essential light models and light sources/illuminants used. > Fig. 1

Light yield

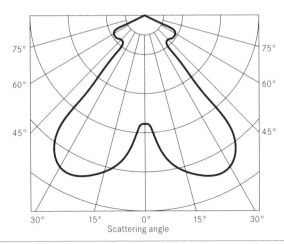

Fig. 1: The light density distribution curve of a rotationally symmetrical reflector

235

In the case of <u>illuminance E</u> [lx; lm/m²], the luminous flux represents a specific illuminated area. Above all, when illuminating workplaces, extensive normative specifications apply that determine which values are reached, or should not be exceeded. In the case of daylight design, the decisive values are generally the readily available illumination intensities of natural light sources; when planning artificial lighting, calculations should be made and simulation models calculated to ascertain which lights and illuminants will be needed to produce the necessary illumination intensity. > Tab. 3

The <u>daylight factor quotient D</u> describes the relationship between a room's illumination intensity (the centre of the room) and illumination intensities outside and beneath a cloudy sky. In both cases, the quotient is always derived from specific measurements and/or detailed calculations. In both cases, a pattern of grids containing a number of points can be laid out in the rooms observed in order to arrive at a distinct surface display. This makes sense in rooms that are exposed to natural lighting from different directions.

$$D = \frac{E_{interior}}{E_{exterior}} \times 100$$

D   Daylight factor [%]

$E_{interior}$ Lighting intensity interior [lx]

$E_{exterior}$ Lighting intensity exterior [lx]

Tab. 3: The illumination intensities of natural light sources on the ground

Light source	Luminance [lx]
Clear sky, sunny (summer)	90,000–130,000
Clear sky, sunny (winter)	19,000–25,000
Cloudy sky (summer)	15,000–20,000
Cloudy sky (winter)	5,000–8,000
Dusk	3–750
Moonlight	0.02–0.30

○ **Note:** Tables and values on specific parameters can often be found in the norms and guidelines. When reading the set values, please note that quite different demands are shown for both the minimum and medium illumination intensities, as well as for the horizontal and vertical areas.

Light density is the parameter within physics that describes the brightness experienced by human beings. It is one of the few units that is extremely dependent on the direction of a source of light. Hence, luminance is always dependent on a generator and not — as in the case of most other parameters — on the recipient of the light radiation, i.e., the human eye. Furthermore, the awareness of darkness and glare through the perception of diverse sensitivities of the eye varies according to the eye's sensitivity. Not only that: the eye adapts itself to certain situations over the course of time. In addition, the wavelengths of light, that is, the perceived colour, ensure that similar light densities trigger differentiated feelings. > Tab. 4

Luminous colour or colour temperature (unit of measure: Kelvin) describes a colour impression produced by a light source. A lower value alludes to a large share of red in the existing colour spectrum, in which subjective perception is experienced as warm. Above all, in the planning of the temperature, the colour plays a major role in determining the artificial light sources, since the planning goal generally is to simulate natural light. The technical capabilities, however, generally end with colour temperatures well below those of natural light. > Tab. 5 Light sources with a colour temperature of under 3,300 K are registered as warm-white, and have a neutral white spectrum fluctuating between 3,300 and 5,000 K; higher values result in warm "daylight white" or "cold white" light sources.

The colour rendering index R_a serves to display the quality of the colour rendering of diverse light sources. In the process, it describes the impact evoked by light directed at objects and other people. Good colour renditioning is achieved when a natural colour environment is optimally reproduced (value $R_a = 100$). In high-quality interiors with good residential quality and/or workplaces with light sources, an $R_a < 80$ should not be used. > Tab. 6 The colour rendering index R_a refers to the eight most frequently used test colours. The index makes this quite clear and means in this context: "in general".

Tab. 4: The perception and sensitivity of the human eye

Viewing task	Light density
Night vision	$3-30\,\mu cd/m^2$ – $3-30\,mcd/m^2$
Twilight	$3-30\,mcd/m^2$ – $3-30\,cd/m^2$
Daylight	$> 3-30\,cd/m^2$
Dazzle	$> 100,000-1,000,000\,cd/m^2$

Tab. 5: Exemplary colour temperatures of natural and artificial sources of light

The source of light	Colour temperature [K]
Candle	1,500
Light bulb (60 W)	2,700
Light bulb (200 W)	3,000
Halogen lamp (12 V)	3,000–3,200
Fluorescent lamp (neutral white)	4,000
Morning/evening sun	5,000
Cloudy sky	6,500–7,500
Fog/haze	7,500–8,500
Clear sky	9,000–12,000

Tab. 6: Colour reproduction index with diverse light sources

Source of light	Colour rendering index R_a
Light bulb	Up to 100
LED	80–97
OLED	80–90
Fluorescent lamp	50–98
Metal halide lamp	60–95
High-pressure sodium lamp	18–85
High-pressure quicksilver lamp	45
Low-pressure sodium vapour lamp	< 44

ILLUMINATION TASKS

Planning with lamps and illumination basically calls for a holistic approach to many different types of illumination. Initially, the general lighting (or basic illumination) is intended to ensure uniform illumination for a predefined area. Accent lighting is more differentiated in the next step, because it means creating — within what are now generally illuminated area zones — a foreground and background. In addition to this, special points of emphasis and accentuated surfaces can be created.

Lighting in general   General lighting is planned with the aim of ensuring equally good orientation in all parts of a room. It fulfils the basic task of making things visible and ensures that the room is perceived in this way. > Fig. 2 Since primarily diffuse sources of light are used here to create or minimize contrasts, for example by casting shadows or directing the light rays in a

Fig. 2: Overall lighting/illumination in a living room and a conference room

Fig. 3: Examples of the accentuated lighting of objects and room zones

certain manner, an exclusive form of general lighting will not suffice in most cases to emphasize the room's function or highlight the activities of the person inside the room. To this end, more ambitious steps must be taken. All-purpose lighting is planned so that it can still be used even if there is a change in functions or use.

The accentuation or arrangement of light sources on specific zones or objects is referred to as accentuated illumination. In this case, contrasts are created that – due to the general lighting – do not have a sufficient impact, as yet. > Fig. 3 Here, illumination systems are used that direct or bundle daylight or, in the case of artificial light sources, rely on narrow beams and adjustable lamps. In order to illuminate and stage the surfaces, a combination of the brightness from the lamps and the emerging shadows is used to emphasize the structure, the colouring and the

Accentuated illumination and the illumination of surfaces

239

Fig. 4: Examples of the illumination of surfaces

materiality. To this end, lights are often used that are not directed straight
● at the surface, but appear as scattered light or rays of light. > Fig. 4

The illumination of interior and outside spaces

    The tasks of lighting design differ from those of urban lighting design, and frequently extend to the illumination of a single object in a display case. The catalogue of requirements encompasses – in the case of all plans – the general situation with regard to interior and exterior space, the use of space and rooms, the desired and required illumination, as well as its useful life. Consequently, a concept needs to be developed that takes into account the amounts of daylight and artificial light, the types of artificial lighting and the existing buildings, as well as objects and surfaces. In the following, the available planning elements will be presented and an overview of the potential areas of use for diverse plan-
○ ning scenarios underlined.

● **Example:** In the case of street lighting, equipping a street area with an adequate number of street lamps at regular intervals will ensure a sufficient amount of lighting. The siting of a large number of lamps at or near crossroads, and using reflecting signs at danger spots, will make the latter stand out and encourage people to pay greater attention to these zones.

○ **Note:** The growing significance of light planning can also be seen in the fact that urban authorities are increasingly developing light concepts that define the functionality and design of light in open space. The goal of these concepts, which are now obligatory up to a certain point, is to create a harmonic overall impression of urban lighting.

DAYLIGHT

The use of natural sunlight and night light is one of the core tasks as far as the planning and illumination of interior and exterior spaces is concerned. As an exclusive light source, or as a light source supported by artificial light > Chapter Artificial Light, it is the task of light planners to ensure that there is a user-specific degree of light available for end users. In many cases, such as secretarial work with screens and monitors, a certain degree of glare-protection light is essential; this can be provided through glare protection or light guidance. In the case of daylight planning, it is almost equally important in most naturally illuminated rooms to keep an eye on thermal insulation, which makes sun protection measures necessary, depending on which way the room is facing. The overall concept of light planning ought to have as its goal the minimal employment of artificial light in order to create the required degree of brightness.

Daylight is subject to natural fluctuations. In this regard, both the temporal aspects (the time of day, a specific season), which determine, above all, the angle of incidence and the refraction of daylight, as well as superordinate and subordinate local issues play a role. The superordinate aspects cannot be influenced by the planners, or only to a minor degree: the latitude and longitude of the location, the topography, the distance and height of the surrounding buildings/vegetation. The subordinate points can be influenced during the design and planning stages (the alignment of buildings and spaces, as well as rooms and exposure areas).   O

The use of daylight in interiors

The use of daylight in interior spaces has a considerable impact on people's well-being. The human organism adapts to the daily disappearance and return of natural light; this process controls not only our sleeping-waking rhythm, but also the release of hormones and the operation

O **Note:** When planning the alignment of buildings and the resulting irradiation factors, a solar altitude diagram can be consulted that shows the day and year in which certain dependent values are stated. (> Fig. 5) These values are cited in DIN 5034-2 for this core region of Germany.

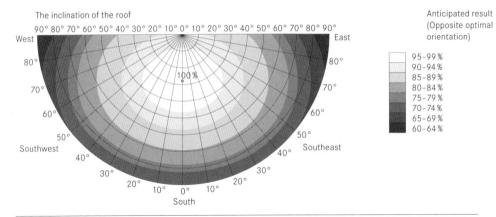

Fig. 5: An exemplary sun chart

of our metabolic functions. This rhythm, which is linked to the presence or absence of sunlight, not only controls our general perceptions but also has an influence on our physical and psychological health. The human eye also evaluates certain light situations.

Thanks to this connection, the inclusion of daylight in lighting design has a positive effect on those who want to use space. From an energy standpoint too, the use of natural light is advantageous, because every time a source of artificial light is used, additional electrical energy is required. The sun's light also reaches colour temperatures that are agreeable to human beings, but very difficult, if not impossible, to reproduce with the means of artificial light.

The aforementioned problems encountered by light planners (the limited natural daylight available during the course of the day, seasonal irregularities, etc.) necessitate complex solutions. Measures are taken to guide and control delivery of light in order to prevent a light fall-off in the depths of the room, to avoid glare and to regulate heat input. In the planning phase, it is important to focus on the ways the space will be utilized, as workplaces, in particular, present normative challenges that can hardly be dealt with by the use of sunlight alone.

Planning elements for daylight use
Daylight design involves diverse methods of making natural light available. As far as outside areas are concerned, this is generally a question of restricting irradiation in order to avoid glare, whereas for interior rooms it is a matter of providing protection from the sun. Consequently, precise analyses of interior rooms must be carried out with regard to the creation of daylight apertures.

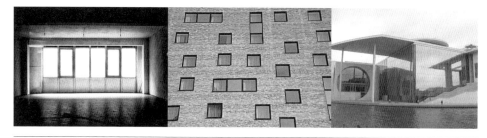

Fig. 6: Diverse windows and types

An obvious way to supply rooms with daylight is to create openings Windows in the room-encompassing shell. The windows' size, position, partitioning and materials influence how it is possible – despite the windows – to allow only an essential amount of light into interior rooms in order to avoid glare or an excessive generation of heat. As far as daylight design is concerned, the window is the element that offers the greatest variation. It is also the one that has to fulfil the most demands:

— Size
In contemporary architecture, windows can be made to almost any size. With some constructive effort, facades and roofs can be designed with the greatest degree of transparency. Large window areas, however, also place greater demands on statics, solar protection and thermal protection.

— Form
In window design, many variations are possible. Round and trapeze-shaped windows can be realized, as well as arching elements and wide ribbon windows with countless individual windows arranged alongside one another. > Fig. 6

— The position and arrangement
Both the window's position within the building's shell (in the outer wall, cellar, or roof, as a skylight, or in an interior courtyard) and its positioning within the assigned room (the middle of the room, for example, or a corner) must be taken into account. Furthermore, the window can be located in a specific part of the building and positioned in the reveal (exterior, interior, glass curtain wall). > Fig. 7

Fig. 7: The fenestration in the inner courtyard, the corner of the building, and the skylight

Fig. 8: Windows with diverse glass/frame elements and sash windows

— The relationship of the glass, the frame and the distribution of the windows

  The following basic principle applies here: the larger the window, the greater the share of glass in relation to the frame profile. With additional steps, rungs and bolts, a creative or structural distribution can be achieved. > Fig. 8

— Materials made of glass and frames

  Glass plays a very special role in antiglare and solar protection measures, as well as in heat protection. Clear glass ensures intense lighting, as well as high heat input. With the aid of colour dyes, the light input can be reduced, and with the aid of multiple glazing the insulation properties can be improved. In the case of frame constructions, wood, artificial materials and metals (such as aluminium and steel), or a combination of these, can be installed.

In addition to introducing direct daylight via apertures in the outer shell, indirect systems of <u>light control</u> and <u>guidance</u> ensure a well-moderated, scattered or channelled incident light. Daylight is primarily regulated outside or inside window levels by directly reflecting or scattering sunlight. In this case, standard systems employing lamellas and shutters can be used, which also perform the function of solar protection. Alternatively, light-guiding glass can be used, in which the cavity between the glass panels plays a key role as a light reflector. In order to bridge greater distances in longer rooms, additional light-guiding measures must be undertaken. These do not necessarily have to be structurally complicated or expensive solutions, such as light wells, light pipes or solar lamps > Fig. 9, which usually tend to be overly complicated or technically unfeasible. By carefully selecting not only the appropriate surface structures for the interior walls and ceilings, as well as coats of light paint with a highly reflective quality, even an unfavourably designed ground plan can be supplied with sufficient daylight.

○

In the case of natural indirect lighting, where interior rooms have no direct contact with the outside world, such as corridors in office buildings, <u>translucent elements can be built into the walls and doors</u>. Here, as in the case of window glazing, clear and toned glass, as well as translucent glass elements can be used. Only in rare cases, however, is this type of illumination satisfactory. With regard to mobility and access, as well as for safety reasons (escape routes, safety lighting), permanent artificial lighting is advisable.

Light management for daylight design always raises technical issues. Generally speaking, light management also involves connecting a room's artificial illumination sources. With the aid of a daylight-dependent lighting control system, such as a DALI control (Digital Addressable Lighting Interface), an independently operating system can be used to support or

---

○ **Note:** A major disadvantage of light-guiding systems is that they only function in direct sunlight; diffuse sky light (under a cloudy sky) cannot be passed on. This is particularly problematic when the sun is not shining, since that is when the need for light in interior rooms is greatest. Hence, a location must be chosen in which an indirect system can be meaningfully employed. In Central Europe, for instance, sunny hours account for 45 to 60 % of the total.

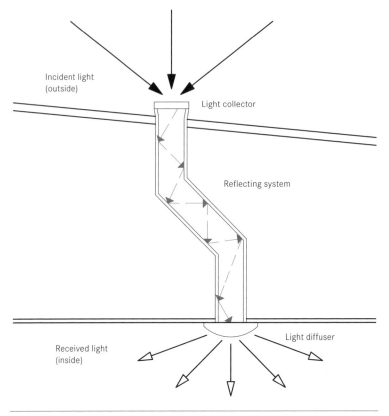

Incident light
(outside)

Light collector

Reflecting system

Received light
(inside)

Light diffuser

Fig. 9: The functional principle behind the light flue and the light pipe

replace a manual light management system (using switches and dim-mers), by following (or replacing) appropriately programmed rules. Data is collected on the room lighting/brightness via sensors, which – on reaching certain thresholds – switch the room lighting on or off. Light-ing <u>control systems</u> of this nature are generally used in offices and com-mercial businesses, since their light scenarios are pre-programmed and assignable to specific scenarios and illumination groups. These types of control systems, however, are frequently installed in private contexts. The DALI lighting system can be used in conjunction with certain inter-faces (Bus-systems; EIB (Europe)/LON (USA)), and also integrated into a superordinate, household building management system, in which solar protection, air-conditioning systems, air-conditioning technology, heating and cooling are controlled independently of one another. > Fig. 10

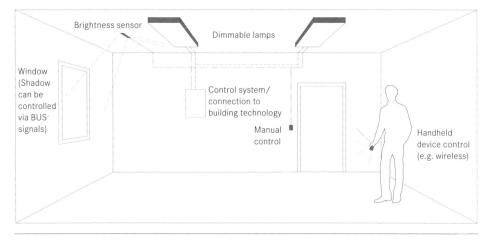

Fig. 10: An exemplary construction of a DALI-control system

Solar protection and antiglare protection

External factors, such as neighbourhood development, vegetation, the form of a building and the location of a room within a building, can result in a reduction and moderation of light in the area to be planned. If, however, these measures are not enough to sufficiently contain the light and heat input, additional systems for providing sun and glare protection will have to be provided. Diverse systems can be positioned in front of the facade or window, on the inside or at window level. There may also be a desire to block out the sun completely, to deflect its rays, or to filter a certain amount of its light. Ideally, the system should be individually regulating; in other words, it ought, if necessary, to be adapted to diverse requirements internally and to the weather situation externally, have an appropriate ventilation system (even when it is "shut down"), and be easy to use. Last but not least, economic and design considerations should be taken into account.

From the standpoint of heating, external systems are the most use- External structures
ful since they capture the sun's rays before these reach a window element, thus preventing the elements in the facade from overheating. Systems such as shutters and daylight control systems use rigid or mobile
horizontal lamellas, which either deflect or irradiate a user-optimized
share of the radiation. With reflecting or matte lamellas, it is possible to
manipulate the share of irradiation by redirecting it or fading it out. One
great advantage is that – depending on the sun's position in the sky – one
can reduce the direct radiation while at the same time preserving a view
of the surroundings.

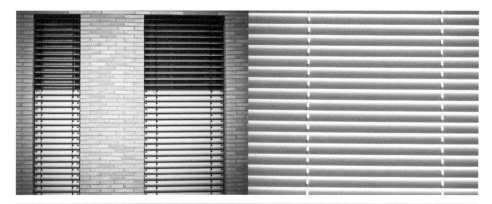

Fig. 11: External venetian blinds in laminated metal

Fig. 12: Canopies designed to shade the window elements

Awnings operate on the principle that the formation of shadows on the facade opening prevents or limits irradiation. Awnings, too, can generally be rolled in and out (roll-up and folding awnings) and provide additional protection from the weather. The materials used – mainly synthetic fibres such as acrylic or polyester, enriched with variously coloured dyes – determine the degree of radiation and translucence.

As with all external structures, wind susceptibility increases the need for cleaning. Furthermore, lamella structures have to be monitored to establish the effects of the wind. Frequently, therefore, wind sensors are fixed to the facade, because any transgression of predefined limits would automatically cause the shutters and awnings to retract.

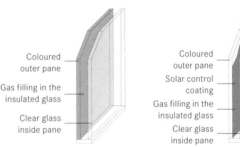

Coloured outer pane
Gas filling in the insulated glass
Clear glass inside pane

Coloured outer pane
Solar control coating
Gas filling in the insulated glass
Clear glass inside pane

Fig. 13: Interior glare protection provided by fully or partially pleated blinds

Fig. 14: Examples: Coated glazing/dyed glazing

The systems installed in the interior often consist of blinds – or roller blinds – assembled immediately before glazing. > Fig. 13 Standard curtains and drapes provide antiglare protection and, in some cases, a certain diffusion of light. As in the case of awnings, they allow for a choice of materials and colours. Easy accessibility, cleaning, and mounting give them a distinct advantage over outside elements. Often, interiors and exteriors are combined in order to gain the greatest degree of individual adaptation to the desired light situation. Interior constructions

The most common variation consisting of glazed window elements (and one that limits the sun's radiation inside rooms and buildings) is that of solar control glazing. The manufacture of anti-sun glass involves a dying process in which a part of the radiating sun's energy is absorbed, whereas the process of coating the glass (generally using multi-sheet windows on the inside of the external pane) results in a reflection of the sun's radiation. > Fig. 14 Solar control glazing makes it possible to keep the Glazing

○ **Note:** This applies to sun sensors too, which, in case of excessive energy inputs, shut down the sun-shading elements, thereby creating an undesirable situation for light planners. Hence, in certain cases, and despite the lack of sunlight, venetian blinds have to be lowered. Circumstances of this nature must be taken into consideration during the planning phase.

Fig. 15: Examples of milk glass and capillary glass

sun's radiation level at around 50 to 80 %; the manufacturer's own estimation is represented by the g-value of the respective glazing process.

If, in addition to ensuring overall protection from the sun, the aim is
to avoid being able to see through the glazing without, however, entirely
restricting the transport of light, frosted glass, or translucent panes of
glass, are generally used. In this case, etching techniques, screen printing,
sandblasting, diverse coatings, and foiling allow for a variety of designs.
If a very high spread of entering light is to be achieved, capillary glass
can be used as an interesting – albeit costly – design variation. In this
case, a translucent glass solution offering thermal insulation based on a
fabric with hollow cavities has been employed, ensuring a higher degree
of transmission of the overall construction.

○ **Note:** The g-value indicates the overall amount of
escaping energy of the total solar energy transmittance
of the antiglare protection, or, in other words, both the
direct transmission share of the sun's energy as well as
the share of energy in the radiation and heat transfer,
which is transferred – via the glazing – to the room.
A low g-value indicates a high degree of solar protection. Sun-protection glasses generally have a g-value
of 0.3 to 0.5, which means that 30 to 50 % of the sun's
energy has reached the internal space. Nowadays,
high-grade glasses can be manufactured with a g-value
as low as 0.15.

Fig. 16: Double-shell facade profile construction with interior, translucent insulation

Fig. 17: An example of deactivated/activated switchable glazing

Profile glass is a special type of translucent glass. The latter is manufactured in a U-form cast, making it particularly stable and relatively easy
to produce at considerable construction heights. In addition to its use as
a light-diffusing element in a facade aperture, it is also frequently chosen
for facade cladding. As a double-shell element used in connection with
translucent insulation material, it can also be employed as a non-bearing
external wall element. > Fig. 16

Switchable glasses reduce the sun's light and glare — and especially
its heat input — by changing or blurring the colour with the aid of an electrical or thermal impulse. In contrast to sun-protection glasses, which
are permanently coloured, switchable glasses are clear in a non-activated
state. Since diverse variants are still in the development phase, or in a
very expensive stage of manufacture, they are seldom employed in housing projects and office buildings. > Fig. 17

ARTIFICIAL LIGHT

In interior rooms, artificial light sources are often the only types, and they are highly sought after owing to the great diversity of light colours they offer and the wealth of opportunities for adjustment, control and modelling. However, people often find it difficult to remain for long in rooms equipped exclusively with artificial light. Artificial lighting can emphasize a room's use by designing and creating focal centres, or by deliberately changing and manipulating a familiar situation. In contrast to daylight, artificial lighting is available for long stretches of time.

Economic factors and environmental criteria also play an important role in the use of artificial lighting. With the aid of refraction and by simulating light, the distribution of light and light quantities must be calculated in exactly the same way as the consumption of electricity and sustainability (maintenance and disposal) in order to compare the costs and uses. Furthermore, there are comprehensive standards and guidelines on the varying uses of light, which the planners have to deal with.

Planning elements for the use of artificial light

Artificial sources of light   Artificial light sources produce light by supplying electrical current. Great diversity with regard to requirements has led to the appearance of a wide variety of illuminants, which can be used for many purposes.

Thermal radiator   Sources that generate light via hot filaments are referred to as thermal radiators. > Fig. 18 In terms of energy, however, electric light bulbs and halogen lamps are not very efficient in comparison with other sources of lighting, because their luminous efficiency and lifetimes are very short. Thermal radiators, nevertheless, are counted among those sources whose light we find warm and generally experience as pleasant. Their light also resembles white light, in the absence of natural light. If an area is partially lit by daylight, however, and a light bulb glows, the yellow colour's impact will be far greater than that of the sunlight. The classic standard light bulb, which is no longer bought and sold in shops, forms the basis of all artificial-light planning and the development of modern lamps.

Discharge lamps   Discharge lamps generate light by guiding electrical current through a gas contained in a sealed, illuminating body. > Fig. 19 A distinction is made with regard to the pressure between high-pressure discharge lamps (halogen-metal halide lamps, high-pressure sodium lamps and mercury vapour lamps) and low-pressure discharge lamps (induction lamps, fluorescent/low-pressure lamps and low-pressure sodium vapour lamps). Low-pressure sodium vapour lamps in particular are distinguished by the fact that they — as thermal radiators –have a far greater life expectancy. As they emit a comparable quantity of light, their energy requirement is much lower. On the other hand, discharge lamps are quite limited with

Fig. 18: Thermal radiators – standard light bulbs and halogen lamps

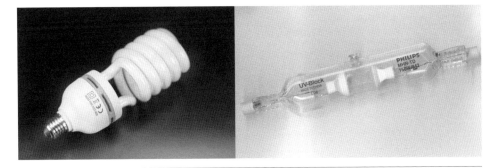

Fig. 19: Examples of discharge lamps

regard to their colour reproduction. Whereas low-pressure discharge lamps – especially those in the form of the neon tube – are very frequently used in the non-private sphere, high-pressure discharge lamps are generally used in streets and for industrial lighting.

In the case of electroluminescent lamps, radiation is generated by a build-up of voltage and electricity on a semi-conductor, yet without releasing any thermal energy as is the case with thermal radiators. In the process, the light source radiates constant brightness in all directions. The most commonly used form is the light-emitting diode (LED), which is able, by filtering or selecting the semiconductor, to reproduce the various colour tones. LED lamps, manufactured in the form of a standard light bulb, have meanwhile replaced the classic light bulb and are manufactured with the same sockets and screw threads. > Fig. 20 The higher price of materials is offset by the far longer life and equal distribution of

Electroluminescent lamps

light. Special forms such as <u>organic light-emitting diodes</u> <u>(OLED)</u> and <u>electroluminescent displays</u> have primarily found their use in computer and monitor technology. They are characterized by their great flexibility, while their luminous flux and luminance are far lower than that of standard LEDs. In the domain of architectonic light planning, their main use is for rooms designed to provide light uniformly and two-dimensionally.

Lamps   A fixture that serves to house light sources is referred to as a lamp. Lamps are not generally designed for just one type of illumination or one specific illuminant, but are able to use various sockets and connections, depending on the lamp concerned. The products are categorized in line with the type of product and assembly. Owing to increasingly differentiated demands, requirements and designs, manufacturers nowadays combine most types of lamps — depending on the form and design — in individual ranges.

Outside lighting   As far as outdoor use is concerned, very diverse designs in both the private (garden and path lighting) and public domain are being produced. For public functions such as street and path lighting, light columns (lanterns) are mostly used, which are spanned above the street or pathway on pendant luminaires. > Fig. 21 They are also used privately as wall luminaires for entrance lighting and as radiators to accentuate house facades.

Parks and public spaces offer considerable opportunity for experimentation. Illuminated and self-lighting stelas, bollard luminaires, as well as adaptable lamps are used just as much as floor and wall lamps dug into the ground, bollard luminaires (adjustable), and projectors, as well
○   as variants built into plinths and steps. > Fig. 22

○ **Note:** Due to their ever-greater use, external lamps designed for the public sphere are now being manufactured to make them vandal-safe. This is done by using more stable materials for the boundaries and mounts, as well as unbreakable covers for the lamps. Nevertheless, no one can guarantee these materials against deliberate acts of destruction.

Fig. 20: Examples of electroluminescent lamps

Fig. 21: Examples of mast lights and hanging lamps

Fig. 22: Bollard lighting, recessed luminaires and illuminated stairs in the public domain

Tab. 7: IP – ways of protecting lamps according to BS EN 60529

Protection from foreign bodies/touch protection		Protection from the effects of water	
Code	Protection class	Code	Protection class
0	Not protected	0	Not protected
1	Protection against solid foreign bodies > 50 mm, protection against extensive touching.	1	Protection against dripping water.
2	Protection against solid foreign bodies > 12 mm, protection from touching with one's finger.	2	Protection against dripping water (below 15° deviation from the perpendicular).
3	Protection against solid foreign bodies > 2.5 mm, protection against being touched with tools, wire, etc.	3	Protection against dripping water (below 60° deviation from the vertical).
4	Protection against solid foreign bodies > 1 mm, protection against being touched with tools, wire, etc.	4	Protection against splashing water.
5	Protection from dust, fully protected against touching under tension.	5	Protected against water out of a nozzle.
6	Protected from dust, fully protected against touching under tension.	6	Protected against heavy sea.
		7	Protected against the consequences of immersion.
		8	Protected against continuous immersion.

When choosing an appropriate external lamp, attention has to be paid to the protection type required. The type defines the degree to which a luminaire is protected against external impact (mechanically and from water). This information is derived from the designation "IP", and from two consecutive numbers. > Tab. 7

Ceiling lamps   The most frequently used type of lamp in both the private and commercial spheres is the louvre luminaire, which often permits free positioning and allocation to specific functions and areas of use. If the lamps are attached flush to a suspended ceiling, for example, they are referred to as recessed luminaires. A specific form of lamp, fixed to the ceiling, is the raster luminaire. Within the framework of a grid ceiling system, the raster luminaire replaces single ceiling elements and can even form the ceiling itself. In contrast to fitted lamps, those mounted directly onto the ceiling with visible luminary are referred to as surface-mounted luminaires. Surface-mounted ceiling systems come in all imaginable forms and colours. > Fig. 23 They not only serve as a pure source of light but have also become an integral part of architectonic design. Another special form of ceiling lamp is the pendant luminaire, or suspended lamp. This solitary lamp, which is also hung in rows from the ceiling, is used to

Fig. 23: Examples of ceiling lamps

Fig. 24: Examples of wall lamps

lend emphasis to a specific area. In rooms with high ceilings, such as multi-story foyers and halls, it is also used to prevent light from spreading too far. In private apartments, lamps of this type are generally hung above the dining table; in offices they are hung above tables or in conference and discussion rooms. Owing to their position inside the room, pendant lamps can illuminate both the areas beneath the luminaires, and the ceiling area if the selected product allows light to escape upwards.

Wall lamps are used in interiors to supplement basic illumination in otherwise insufficiently lit rooms, or to accentuate lighting in areas that require special emphasis. Radiation is generally directed upward and/or downward; direct rays of light are usually avoided. Externally, directly radiated light is used more frequently. > Fig. 24

Wall lighting

257

Fig. 25: Examples of standing lamps

Fig. 26: Examples of table and desk lamps

Standing lamps   For reasons of flexibility, standing lamps are designed for private use or in offices where they are not assigned to any particular place. Depending on the room's use or allocation, lamps can be positioned anywhere. In existing buildings with low ceilings, where suspended ceilings or ceiling surface-mounted luminaires cannot be used, standing lamps also serve as an ideal alternative. > Fig. 25

Table lamps   Similar to standing lamps, but smaller and more flexible in format, table lamps are used as freely positionable illumination. The desk lamp is a typical example. Nowadays, table lamps and standing lamps are sometimes equipped with built-in sensors and automatic dimmer functions. > Fig. 26

Standard illumination control systems are by no means restricted to the standard light switch, which can, at best, only be supplemented by additional dimmers. Depending on the lamps and illuminants, electronic control equipment, transformers, and/or manual releases may be required and have to be taken into consideration in household planning. Furthermore, integration into the building's overall technology is necessary if interaction with artificial lighting systems and other functions is envisaged, such as house intelligent building technology, or an optimized daytime and artificial-lighting mixing system is desired. ■

The positioning of the controlling elements (sensors, detectors, etc.), the controlled elements (lighting, solar protection, ventilation, etc.), and the types of controllers are meanwhile very diversified. Types of control include time-based control systems, which also operate through pre-programming, as well as motion sensors, controlled on-off switches, and light-dependent systems. With the aid of external sensors, they regulate the illumination times and illumination intensities in the interior (luminous intensity).

> ■ **Tip:** An important and, unfortunately, frequently neglected aspect of planning is the expedient positioning of switches and other control elements. In many instances – and not only in the case of constructions, conversions and the redevelopment of existing buildings – light switches have been found behind doors or in inaccessible places.

Planning scenarios

The goal of light planning is to use the planning elements – daylight and artificial light – in a meaningful way for the planning task at hand and to combine them. There are many different public and private fields of application, each of which uses specific elements that are appropriate and others which – for technical and design reasons from the standpoint of design – should not be used.

STREET LIGHTING AND EXTERNAL LIGHTING

The main task of street lighting is to ensure the safety of road users. The basis of planning lies in values that constitute the norms and guidelines which are to be applied – especially in the presence of pedestrians. The essential elements of standard illumination are loadbearing systems, housings, ballast, ballast units and ignitions, light-guiding systems (mirrors) and sources of lighting. The most common of these is the "lantern", with a ballast unit made of fibre-reinforced composite synthetic material. > Fig. 27 An operating device for upstream installation or ignition is necessary because it uses sodium vapour, mercury vapour and fluorescent lamps as an illuminant. In contemporary street lighting, high-pressure sodium-vapour lamps/LED lamps are now being used with ever greater frequency. The use of high-pressure sodium-vapour lamps is still the most economical choice, since they not only have a very long lifetime but also a far more compact design than low-pressure lamps.

In general, street lighting is switched on and off via a central control that triggers the switching procedure following a time signal, or by brightness sensors that trigger the switching procedure at dusk.

Car park lighting and parking lots   In principle, the above-mentioned modes of street illumination can also be used in car parks if they are located outside. > Fig. 28 Here, too, the light column remains the most common type. The height of the light source has to be adapted to the size of the car park. In the case of small parking lots, structures of up to 4.50 m in height make sense. With larger parking spaces, they may be as high as 12 m. The lighting should not be manipulated, but radiate horizontally to achieve an equal distribution of light over the entire area. The same benchmark should apply to all parking areas > Tab. 8 in order to ensure a general sense of security, and to make sure that the faces of approaching people can be recognized.

Fig. 27: Examples of street and exterior lighting

Fig. 28: Examples of parking lot lighting

Tab. 8: The required lighting level for parking spaces and multi-story car parks

Area	Luminance [lx]
Parking lot (outside) (semi-cylindrical illuminance)	1.5–5
Multi-story car parks / car park	10
Carports / parking spaces (medium illumination strength)	75
Entries and exits (daytime)	300
Entries and exits (nighttime)	75

○ **Note:** Benchmarks must be established for the overall lighting of parking lots, which can be measured at any given point within the space. For security's sake, the necessary illumination intensity refers to a semi-cylindrical area to the height of 1.50 m, in which a face turned toward the observer is identifiable.

Fig. 29: Examples of lighting for underground car parks and multi-story car parks

In the case of multi-story car parks, and especially underground garages, planning is far more complicated. In addition to overall illumination,
the illumination of the driveways, the entrances and exits, the parking
spaces and pedestrian routing has to be considered. In order to respond
to the eye's need to adapt to modified illumination when entering and
leaving the car park, transitional areas with varying illumination intensities for day and night operation are necessary. > Fig. 29

The illumination of
parks and squares

Apart from the overall need for powerful lighting to ensure public
safety, it is difficult to make general statements regarding the illumination of parks and public squares. Indeed, very few universally valid com-
ments have been made regarding the design of such spaces. There are,
for instance, a number of individual scenarios related to the environment,
the use of the park and the volume of traffic. For example, not only the
square itself, but also the surrounding buildings, can be illuminated and
serve as a source of light. Apart from illuminating pathways, certain aesthetic objects can be singled out not only by lighting, but also by certain
types of colouring. > Fig. 30

In order to gain the necessary illumination capacity, street mast luminaires are frequently employed, provided there is sufficient space to
obtain the necessary illumination intensities for general lighting. In this
case, column luminaires can be used to obtain the required illumination
intensity for general lighting, and assuming there is sufficient capacity. If
required, these can be supplemented not only by bollard luminaires, but
also by installing and mounting lights in floors, wall areas and stairs in order to brighten up the areas used by people. To achieve the anticipated
impact, it is very important to use lamps with a suitable protection class.

Fig. 30: Examples of illuminating public spaces

PUBLIC BUILDINGS

If areas are publicly accessible, the needs of many different people will have to be taken into account. Among other things, illumination designs must support people with diminished sight. Diverse usages and types can also create various expectations, which must be fulfilled by the light design.

Access to public buildings such as hotels, offices and academic institutions is gained through an easily identified reception area, behind which lies a foyer and other access zones, as well as the further-reaching areas of use and access. The architecture of these areas must be clearly identifiable from a distance, and the lighting good enough to ensure visibility even under conditions of poor or non-existent daylight. > Fig. 31 Furthermore, an entrance serves as a transition zone between the inside and the outside. In other words, lighting design has to help the eye in latently adapting to the changing light situation. Daylight-dependent controls now prove their full value, providing powerful illumination during the day and adjusting the lighting at night to that of the darkness outside.

The illumination of entrance areas and foyers

If the building or the reception zone is accessed via stairs, the lighting must be illuminated accordingly so that the steps stand out from one another. In addition, the individual steps can be individually illuminated by recessed luminaires or strip lighting in order to emphasize the route.

In the foyer, the aim is to create a form of illumination that assists orientation. Additional accentuation can be achieved by illuminating individual areas such as the walls, ceilings, columns and the stairs. Above all, it is in multi-story foyers that pendant luminaires and ceiling luminaires

Tab. 9: Exemplary, necessary illumination intensities for public areas

Area	Luminance [lx]
Entrance/foyer (depending on the traffic)	100–200
Stairs	150
Waiting areas	500
Cash points/counters/bars	300–500
Shop windows	> 2,000
Supermarkets/DIY stores	> 1,000
Dining rooms/restaurants	200
Buffets/self-service counters	300

come into their own as a design element, since there is a multitude of brands to choose from. LED lamps are ideal for the routing and orientation because they generate warm-white and pure white colours – depending on the landscaping. > Fig. 31

If there are reception zones, reception desks and waiting areas, they should be viewed independently, since a greater luminous intensity is required in these areas than in the surrounding area.

The lighting of museums and exhibition rooms

The illumination of exhibition rooms presents light planners with one of their most complex tasks. Thanks to the architecture, the basic concepts have been defined here, since the basic concept has already been outlined: i.e. whether a pure art-light plan can be defined by the draft plan, whether a pure art-light plan is to be realized, or whether daylight is to be made available in the exhibition areas. The ground plans vary from hall-like spaces (with installations and mobile room dividers, in some cases) to smaller single rooms with clearly defined routes. In specific cases, the room measurements and heights, as well as the types of exhibit, call for special planning. Since museums and other exhibition areas often do not merely display a permanent collection, but have to rely on changing exhibitions, a considerable degree of flexibility is required with regard to the illumination (e.g. via live lines, mobile spotlights, and flexible grids). > Fig. 32

For the overall lighting, diffuse illumination is recommended: in other words, measures that take advantage of the daylight and artificial lighting. In this way, uniform room lighting can be achieved with a minimum amount of shadow. Ceiling luminaires and luminous ceilings with a diffuse covering (for example, frosted glass) are particularly suitable for this purpose. Owing to their longer operating life, fluorescent lamps are

Fig. 31: Examples of illumination in the entrance area and the foyer

Fig. 32: Examples of the illumination of museums and exhibitions

recommended, because they provide sufficient amounts of illumination and excellent visual impact. If visitors wish to move freely through the exhibition area without having to choose a specific direction, a more general form of illumination will suffice to start with. If there is a concept for guiding visitors around the exhibition, an additional constellation of path luminaires can be chosen in the form of floor and wall lamps, or in the design of strip lights.

In the next planning stage, the prime focus will be on the illumination of the exhibits themselves. Planning of this kind also depends greatly on the nature and material quality of the choice of exhibits. Paintings and pictures have to be handled quite differently from sculptures and show-cases. Audio and video installations are increasingly being used as supportive media, or as art in themselves. All these exhibits share a common feature: they can be emphasized with highly focused lamps such as spotlights and downlights. It is worth noting that the visitor may well be focusing on a specific exhibit, without there being any reflections, shadows or glare. Radiation effects, which emanate from daylight, as well as artificial

Fig. 33: The illumination of exhibition objects

sources of light, can damage exhibition items and paintings in the long term, since they can trigger chemical processes. The latter must be minimized by using a suitable choice of illuminants and additional filters with the aim of diminishing infrared and ultraviolet radiation. If an exhibit is displayed in the wall area, the beam angle of the light concerned must be set at a slight angle of 25° to 30° to the lower edge of the exhibit.

The illumination
of restaurants The illumination of restaurants varies considerably depending on the type of gastronomy. For example, a cafeteria offering self-service requires different lighting levels and light colours than a posh restaurant with a dining room. In this case, the planning tasks include general lighting, accent lighting, and the illumination of bars and tables, while in the case of restaurants, exterior lighting also plays a role: not only because gastronomy must be acknowledged as such, but also because the type and quality of the illumination influences customers' expectations even before they enter the restaurant.

The overall lighting generally assumes the form of ceiling lighting (as individual illumination, or in the shape of power rails with a number of directed spotlights). Additional ambient light and spatial designs can be introduced in the form of wall luminaires. In order to realize a variety of usage scenarios, plans should include variable illumination involving a dimmer and, in some cases, lighting that can be switched on and off as required. In self-service areas, far higher illumination levels (200 lx) will be provided than in a restaurant with service staff. Here, too, there is a lack of uniformity regarding illumination levels: some areas will be emphasized. In the lounges, the lighting is often supported – or even largely replaced – by accent lighting. The illumination of the room zones, columns, walls and individual objects, such as pictures and other features, is to be planned and integrated into the overall concept. > Fig.34 In the process, the lighting levels, light colours and, consequently, the choice of lamps

Fig. 34: The illumination of dining rooms, bars and buffets

Fig. 35: The illumination of restaurant tables

and lighting, may vary considerably. With regard to the illumination of a wall painting, completely different measures will have to be taken from those designed for accentuating glasses or porcelain.

Particularly bright-but-dazzle-free lighting should be chosen for the bar and buffet areas. > Fig. 34 These spheres generally serve as the main areas of contact for the guests and the working areas of the personnel. Lamps with a light colour rendering index are essential so that the guests can see and evaluate the food. Thermal radiation must be restricted, however. Low-pressure discharge lamps are particularly apt in this context and can be deployed, with reflectors, in a compact form, yet very large in number, in the areas described.

Fig. 36: Examples of shop-window illumination

Fig. 37: The illumination of sales areas

Restaurant tables are to be illuminated to a far greater degree than in the surrounding areas. Generally speaking, illumination of this type is created with pendant lights installed at heights of 50 cm to 70 cm above the table top. Lamps with a high colour rendering index are used, so that the food, as well as the other people at the table, can be clearly identified. On the whole, halogen lamps are used, which generate a warm-white light colour.

The illumination of the sales rooms and presentation lighting

In the case of the illumination plans for the sales rooms, the presentation area of the window is generally the main focal point. It is not only the initial area of contact, but also the first source of information for customers. In this case, illumination strengths of more than 1,000 lx are required, as well as, lights with good colour-reproduction properties, which means using high-pressure and low-pressure discharge lamps. In general, ceiling lamps are employed which feature modifiable systems adapted to suit the changing displays. Apart from widely scattered light designed for general illumination, individual products can be greatly accentuated via spotlights and downlights. By choosing suitable glazing with a minimal reflection share, an unhindered view of the display can be assured day and night. > Fig. 36

The type of sales area – in conjunction with the products to be sold – determines the lighting plan. People generally associate a variety of intensive illumination and light colours with familiar scenarios. Hence, for instance, sales areas equipped with a high level of illumination favour associations with discount supermarkets and DIY stores. Radiators and individual lights are merely used to draw attention to their very high-grade product ranges. The frequently monotonous architecture and the apparent lack of decorative effort involved (hence, inconspicuous from a builder's point of view) and an economical approach to resources have been adopted, allowing companies to offer their customers the best sales prices. > Fig. 37 With low illumination densities, warm light colours accentuate of certain sub-domains, so customers unconsciously feel that the goods on display are of high quality and deserve special attention. In the same vein, counters displaying food in a wide range of colours suggest fresh quality by displaying, for example, white light with salads and vegetables, and red tones with meat products. As the greater part of the sales areas involves products that change every week or season, and are, therefore, repeatedly positioned anew, flexible illumination systems – especially where accent lighting is concerned – are advisable.   ■

The cash points, information counters and individual counters for customer enquiries (in a furniture store, for example) ought to be treated separately, since, on the one hand, the routes for the customers are clearly laid out whereas, on the other hand, guidelines for workplace illumination have to be followed, as the sales personnel largely remain in these fields.

> ■ **Tip:** Depending on the product, the type of illuminant and the light colour, the lamps, the luminous colour and the nature of the lamps, dazzling effects and reflections can be created or avoided. Items of clothing and furniture ought to be illuminable without such effects, whereas in the case of exhibited wares, such as jewellery and technical products, sparkle and reflection lend these products a more sophisticated and modern look.

WORKSTATIONS

The most common task in lighting design lies in the planning of workplaces. Whereas the overriding concern in lighting design for living spaces tends to involve the subjective feelings of the users and the design aspects, far-reaching and comprehensive demands and guidelines have to be demanded of workplaces, which have to be considered in the planning and are frequently stated as the planning goal. As a rule – and inasmuch as the stipulations and spatial orientation permit – a combination of daylight and artificial light will be used to achieve a constant level of brightness in the face of changing weather conditions.

In this field, visual tasks determine the nature and intensity of the required lighting. In the case of a one-person-office workstation, very different planning elements are required in order to make available the necessary illumination factors, which differ from those encountered in industrial factories and laboratories.

The office workstation   Office workstations are subject to norms and guidelines concerning illumination intensities. Hence, the illuminance level for artificial light is cited as 500 lx; in the particular case of a <u>daylight-oriented workstation</u>, it lies at 300 lx. In addition to the overall room illumination, a workspace/ workplace always has to be viewed separately and, if sufficient illumination cannot be obtained via the central room lighting, it will have to be equipped with additional lamps. The size and position of the windows provide the ideal zone for setting up a workstation in the office, because the high light densities typically required for visual tasks are reached next to the windows, whereas the deeper-lying zones are more suitable for storage space, cupboards and other uses involving less demanding visual tasks. Hence, the spread of light in an interior room can be determined via simple rules. Areas are considered bright when they lie within a 30° angle to the upper edge of the window or beneath an upper skylight. > Fig. 38 In order to make a room flexible and usable, a window's width has to occupy at least 55 % of the room's width and the window's surface area in the facade must account for at least 30 %. Other influences, such as trees, the construction of neighbouring buildings, and so on, must be taken into account here, since they can mean that light propagation is limited (in direction or intensity) in comparison with other equally oriented rooms.

The desired and largely necessary use of daylight for workplaces generally involves antiglare measures being taken on all window surfaces, and often involves carrying out additional solar protection measures too. Furthermore, blending, which arises from the direct or reflecting effects of lamps, must be avoided. The office workstation itself – which takes its orientation from the monitors and lamps – should be set up so that the

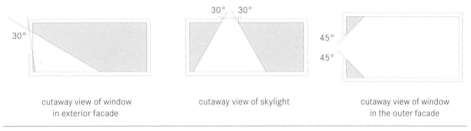

| cutaway view of window in exterior facade | cutaway view of skylight | cutaway view of window in the outer facade |

Fig. 38: The natural illumination of a workstation

Fig. 39: The illumination of an office workstation

direction of the user's gaze runs parallel to the windows. The working environment (i.e., the desk, the walls and the ceilings) should be equipped with light-coloured matte surfaces to ensure a high degree of reflection – but an absence of reflected glare. The main working area should also be equipped with its own individually adjustable lighting, as well as desk lamps and/or individually controllable standing lamps, because – alongside the generally regulated minimum standards – the user-requirements different greatly. In the case of office spaces alongside a workspace proper, which is devoted to more complex visual tasks such as writing, reading, and so on, additional lamps will be provided in order to generate the necessary amount of light.

Ideally, additional artificial lighting in the workplace should be regulated by a light control system tied to the presence of people in the room and light. By integrating sun protection measures into the control system, it would be possible to run an economical as well as an optimally tuned light concept designed for maximum comfort.

Fig. 40: The illumination of conference rooms

A special, planned case, which is becoming increasingly common, is that of the <u>daylight-oriented workplace</u>. This means that for at least 70 % of the working hours, daylight – without the addition of artificial light – provides sufficient illumination. This value is directly dependent on daylight factor D, since a higher daylight quotient already implies a lower degree of dependence on supplementary artificial illumination. It can be roughly estimated that with a daylight factor of more than 3 % per day, a high-quality daylight-oriented workplace can be created.

Conference room/ meetings

In conference rooms, the lighting design must ensure that all of the participants can be easily identified from each and every position. The conference table is usually placed in a central position vis-à-vis the ceiling or the pendant lamps. The luminaires must direct their light laterally, without creating any glare. > Fig. 40 Inside the room, care must be taken to avoid stark contrasts in brightness caused by the general lighting and the surface qualities, since contrasts of this nature can create fatigue among participants even when they are in a peripheral area.

Industrial factory halls

In <u>industrial halls</u> running production processes, lighting design depends on the nature of the visual tasks and the hall's geometry. In the case of a high room, powerful <u>lamps</u>, such as metal high-pressure steam lamps, high-pressure sodium lamps and fluorescent lamps, will be needed to generate a sufficient degree of illumination at the place of work. If the hall's ceiling is lower (less than 6.00 m), fluorescent lamps arranged in screens – or strip lighting/lights – will be ideal. If fluorescent lights are used, care must be taken to ensure they are aligned parallel to the working surface in order to avoid glare. Illumination intensities of 1,500 lx have to be reached in order to create a working ambience conducive to productivity and an environment that prevents accidents. Most industrial

Fig. 41: The illumination of industrial factory halls

workplaces have illumination intensities of 600 lx and neutral white colours. If emissions occur during indoor operation (e.g., from dust or similar pollution), steps must be taken to ensure that sufficient protection is taken when using lamps.

As it is normally impossible to rely on natural illumination via the facade openings in a factory hall, the daylight entering the skylights is generally used. > Fig. 41 Given the available daylight, a control is needed to lessen the economic burden caused by permanently using artificial light, which can represent a considerable cost-factor in a large business. Electronic ballast units can increase cost-effectiveness, especially in factories operating on a shift-work basis and high switch-on times.

When people are working in warehouses, lower illumination levels are needed than is the case in production sites and factories using industrial processes. The nature of the hall, as well as its use, determines the required lighting level. > Tab.10 Reflector luminaires are frequently used as strip lighting in combination with fluorescent lamps, which, along with

Tab. 10: The required illumination intensities of diverse packing rooms

Type of storage	Luminance level [lx]
Storage spaces for large stocks of the same item	50
Storage spaces for varied goods	100
Storage spaces with reading functions	200
Dispatch and packing room	300

Fig. 42: Examples of warehouse lighting

directed reflectors, adequately illuminate corridors, shelves and stored merchandise, and also offer protection against glare if looked at directly. Furthermore, a motion controller is advisable in storage areas that are not permanently used. Please note that in the desk area and other work-places involving visual tasks of greater complexity, supplementary illumi-nation must be provided that is similar to the office working space.

EMERGENCY AND SAFETY LIGHTING

To facilitate orientation in the case of a disruption to the main power supply, an emergency (or security) lighting source is necessary in spe-cific cases. This applies to public areas in which the identification and visibility of the emergency and escape routes must be secured perma-nently so that people can escape in situations of danger. As a rule, the emergency escape routes are identified by self-illuminating rescue signs. In battery mode, the escape routes are controlled by a special power cir-cuit designed to ensure that signage continues to function. Escape route signs/pictograms that are not supplied by electricity, but dispose of phos-phorescent surfaces, can be allowed if this is explained in the fire-pro-tection concept. > Fig. 43 In the case of escape-route lighting, a minimum illumination intensity of 1 lux must be ensured for a distance of 2.0 m. To ensure that escape is possible, a specified level must be reached – i.e., illuminance of 40 lux – along the course of the middle line of the escape route.

In the case of workstations with special requirements, where there is a danger of the illumination failing, the security illumination must be designed on such a scale that leaving the place of work and even ending a necessary job is possible.

Fig. 43: Examples of emergency and security illumination

THE ILLUMINATION OF PRIVATE SPACES

The illumination of private rooms is less structured than it is in the preceding scenarios. In this case, it is more the wishes and feelings of the inhabitants and users that determines the planning definitions. Furthermore, the way a room is used may differ from case to case. For example, the functions performed by a living room can vary greatly from one user to another.

The external impact of a building at dusk and night is shaped by the illumination of the facade, the garden and the entrance area. In addition to any design aspects, the illumination of the access routes and the entrance area serves as orientation and security. Diverse entrance situations can make various types of illuminants worthwhile. Hence, if there is a porch, lamps can be integrated above the house door, otherwise various wall lamps can be fitted in the facade. Access to building entrances and garages, as well as steps, pedestals and external stairs, should certainly be illuminated. Bollard luminaires and plinths, as well as lamps that have been integrated into the ground, are most qualified for this task. It is important to ensure that the pathway illumination avoids light-and-dark contrasts and clearly identifies obstacles. In this case, the distance between the lamps should be adjusted to match the selected height of the light source and the direction of the beam. In the case of light columns, a larger distance can be chosen than is the case with pendant luminaires. House numbers can also be designed as self-illuminating objects or beamed via a single lamp, if the customary illumination is otherwise not powerful enough, or if the number needs to be permanently emphasized.

> Fig. 44

Home illumination and garden illumination

Fig. 44 The illumination of the house and the facade

In contrast to a semi-public entrance area, a garden can display far greater contrasts in order to emphasize certain spots and objects. As a rule, a garden needs direct accentuation and focus rather than wide-scale general illumination. In this case, the desired atmosphere can be attained with light and dark areas. The general sense of security can be enhanced by motion-controlled lighting. In order to illuminate features such as trees and other solitary objects, such as sculptures, well-directed spotlights are ideally suited. The distance must be adapted to the size – or to the magnitude – of the object to be emphasized. The alignment of the illumination should be planned in a way that avoids glare.

As with the illumination of open public spaces, here, too, it is absolutely necessary to pay attention to the use of illuminants with an appropriate protection class.

When selecting an illuminant, the type of switch and the time of the switching are overriding factors. If a certain feature, such as a house door, is to be permanently illuminated, it is advisable to use economical LEDs or compact fluorescent lamps. To this end, twilight switches and time switches can be used, which automatically regulate the illumination. In the case of shorter switching cycles, as in the case of a motion detector or a push switch, halogen lamps and energy-saving lamps can be used. Please note that when using motion detectors on paths, illuminants should be used that release their full luminous flux immediately after the lighting has been switched on, and without a long interim phase, in order
■ to ensure their immediate accessibility.

The living room   Suitable lighting of a living room depends upon the room's geometry, the size of the windows, and the furnishings, as well as the specific uses of the room. Superordinate general lighting, combined with court-

Fig. 45: Living room illumination

yard lighting of the sofas and a lounge unit, as well as accentuation of other elements, calls for thorough planning. The visual axes must be defined to exclude glare and to clearly lay down the positioning of the luminaires. Reflections on objects such as televisions, pictures and so on, are to be avoided.

The overall illumination should be kept separate from the additional single lamps and be dimmable. The desired brightness should be emitted not via a single lamp but via several well-distributed lamps. Since these lamps can differ greatly from one another in the various areas, wall and ceiling lamps can be used just as well as spotlights on power rails and pendant luminaires. Particularly suitable here is lighting viewed as "comfortable", such as warm-white sources. The illumination of squares and outside areas can be supplemented by dimmable individual lamps, standard lamps and table lamps, allowing the user to adjust the brightness to his or her liking. Very often, uplights are used to enhance the level of the general illumination in certain parts of the room. Additional sources of accent lighting, aimed at highlighting features such as artworks, plants, furniture, as well as wall and ceiling surfaces, can be provided via downlights and spotlights. > Fig. 45

■ **Tip:** Light planning of the external domain of private buildings is to be undertaken and coordinated at an early stage of the planning, because many of the components required for electrical installations (cable routes, connections for a sub-distribution unit, etc.) have to be laid under plaster during an early stage of the construction work. Planning external installations and other jobs late in the day generally results in inconvenience and causes delays in subsequent installations.

Fig. 46: The illumination of the dining table

Dining room/ dining table

As in restaurants and cafés, the main focus of a dining room illumination is the dining table. Here, general illumination plays more of a subordinate role: it is, however, important to allow for a certain degree of orientation when the dining table is not being used, or rather: when the dining table illumination is not being used. In larger dining rooms, however, additional and general degrees of illumination must be provided – independently of the table lighting. The number and design of the table illuminations is to be adapted to the size, form and material of the table. Very often, pendant luminaires are used. In this case, they should be hung slightly above eye-level. As with diverse choices of dining room furniture, luminaires are supplied in almost all forms and materials. > Fig. 46

The kitchen

In the kitchen, there is a need to see clearly into cupboards and shelves. Thus, there is a need for more powerful illumination than is the case in other rooms. This applies to the general lighting as well as the illumination of the working surfaces. General lighting ought to be managed via a number of light sources, in order to ensure there is sufficient brightness in all parts of the kitchen. On the whole, the ceiling illumination will consist of an extension in the form of a surface-mounted luminaire or a fitted spotlight with warm-white lamps. In the working areas, the illumination will have to be even more powerful, to ensure a level of brightness appropriate for kitchen work. The same applies to the colour rendering index $R_a > 90$, so that the foodstuffs, including their state and quality, can be easily seen. The additional illuminated working surfaces can be organized via directed spotlights, downlights and individual spots, which can, for example, be arranged beneath the top kitchen cupboards. Their position must be chosen so that users don't create shadows when they are working on these surfaces. Nobody who is working in a kitchen should be distracted by the lighting. The area around the stove and oven also needs additional illumination, which can, in many cases, be integrated into an extractor hood. Owing to the occasionally intense presence of fat,

Fig. 47: Kitchen Illumination

liquids and so on, covers that are illuminated and easy-to-clean-and-dis-
mantle are ideal. Kitchen cupboards can always be cleaned separately,
so the illumination in these areas can be switched on and off via door
contact. The illumination of bars and dining tables in the kitchen domain
can be effected in much the same way as the dining table illumination.
> Fig. 47   O

In addition to illuminating the mirror surfaces and cosmetic areas, The bathroom
standard lighting with a high degree of illumination intensity and a good
colour rendering index (R_a > 90) is provided in the bathrooms. Depending on the materials used for the surfaces (gloss or matte tiles, the tile
colours, the number and size of the mirror surfaces), a great deal of
reflection may be caused by the illumination. For this reason, the number
of lamps, as well as their illumination intensity, will vary even in bathrooms with the same dimensions. In order to avoid glare, measures must
be taken to spread the light by choosing appropriate light covering.

O **Note:** In order to integrate illuminations into the
furnishings and fixtures — such as kitchen cupboards,
shelves and other items of furniture — it is essential
that the selected illuminations be provided with a
MM mark. To this end, these illuminations are defined
as devices with a limited surface temperature, thus
providing the necessary fire protection.

Fig. 48: Bathroom illumination and mirror luminaires

Fig. 49: The illumination of the stair flights and steps

For general lighting, primarily ceiling illumination should be used. It is, therefore, important to note where people stand or sit (in front of the washbasin or the bathtub, for example) in order to avoid undesirable shadows or glare. Additional illuminations with light-scattering properties should be planned above the mirrors, or on both sides of them. As these illuminations have to attain far greater illumination strengths than standard lighting, more economical illuminants — such as LEDs and energy-saving lamps — are recommended. > Fig. 48

As bathrooms are often damp or wet areas, special lamps providing adequate protection should be used. With respect to the electrical installations, it is essential that only approved materials be used. Furthermore, general illumination must render wet areas clearly in order to avoid accidents.

When planning the illumination of stairs, it is imperative to regard them as traffic routes and to be aware that failure to use a sufficient luminance level (100 lux) is impermissible. First and foremost, general and constant illumination is absolutely essential, and the additional development and accentuation of individual steps permissible. The overall illumination of a staircase should begin from above: via the walls and the ceiling luminaires. In order to achieve an equal distribution of light, a number of broadly radiating or light-diffusing lamps can be used. > Fig. 49

The position of the stairs also plays a key role in light planning, especially when it comes to switching the lighting on and off, because a staircase that is frequently used by many people is easier to regulate with individual switches, or with motion detectors using time-controlled switching. In this case, the safety of people using the stairs must be guaranteed. Lamps can be switched on or off in combination with the illumination of an adjacent room.

In conclusion

Successful lighting design calls for a rigorous debate on the planning tasks throughout every phase of the work. In addition to taking into consideration the wishes expressed by the client, the demands arising from the various guidelines and standards, as well as the lighting's location and use, it is essential, above all, to constantly re-examine and adapt the specific conditions of the project within the overall framework of light. Now that the design concept is completed and the specialized companies have been commissioned, care must be taken that during the course of construction the planned interaction between daylight and artificial light, as well as the interweaving of the individual planning elements, is realized as planned and in line with the standards for the varied elements' subsequent operation. The preparation of simulations during the design process serves to clarify the planned measures for the user, and ensures that the required standards of luminance are adhered to and that the structure is actually built as planned. However, it is always essential to allow for a certain degree of flexibility during the planning phase.

Appendix

Literature

ROOM CONDITIONING

Hazim B. Awbi: *Ventilation of Buildings,* Spon Press, London 2003

Sophia and Stefan Behling: *Solar Power,* 2nd ed., Prestel, Munich 2000

Klaus Daniels: *Advanced Building Systems,* Birkhäuser Verlag, Basel 2003

Klaus Daniels: *Low-Tech Light-Tech High-Tech,* Birkhäuser Verlag, Basel 1998

Baruch Givoni: *Climate Considerations in Building and Urban Design,* John Wiley & Sons, New York 1998

Baruch Givoni: *Passive and Low Energy Cooling of Buildings,* John Wiley & Sons, New York 1994

Gerhard Hausladen, Michael de Saldanha, Petra Liedl, Christina Sager: *Climate Design,* Birkhäuser Verlag, Basel 2005

Norbert Lechner: *Heating, Cooling, Lighting: Design Methods for Architects,* 4th ed., John Wiley & Sons, New York 2014

Christian Schittich (ed.): *Solar Architecture,* 2nd ed., Birkhäuser Verlag, Basel 2012

Steven V. Szokolay: *Environmental Science Handbook for Architects and Builders,* The construction press/Lancaster, London 1980

Steven V. Szokolay: *Introduction to Architectural Science: The Basis of Sustainable Design,* 3rd ed., Routledge, London 2014

WATER CYCLES

John Arundel: *Sewage and Industrial Effluent Treatment,* Blackwell Science, Oxford/Malden, MA, 2000

Tanja Brotrück: *Basics Roof Construction,* Birkhäuser, Basel 2007

Committee on Public Water Supply Distribution Systems, National Research Council of the National Academies: *Drinking Water Distribution Systems: Assessing and Reducing Risks,* National Academies Press, Washington, DC, 2006

Herbert Dreiseitl, Dieter Grau (eds.): *New Waterscapes—Planning, Building and Designing with Water,* Birkhäuser, Basel 2005

Herbert Dreiseitl, Dieter Grau (eds.): *Recent Waterscapes. Planning, Building and Designing with Water,* 3rd ed., Birkhäuser, Basel 2012

Herbert Dreiseitl, Dieter Grau, Karl Ludwig (eds.): *Waterscapes— Planning, Building and Designing with Water,* Birkhäuser, Basel 2001

Gary Grant: *Green Roofs and Facades,* IHS BRE Press, Bracknell 2006

Institute of Plumbing (ed.): *Plumbing Engineering Services. Design Guide,* Institute of Plumbing, Hornchurch 2002

Margrit Kennedy, Declan Kennedy (eds.): *Designing Ecological Settlements: Ecological Planning and Building,* Chap. Water, 2nd ed., Reimer Verlag, Berlin 2001

Heather Kinkade-Levario: *Design for Water: Rainwater Harvesting, Stormwater Catchment and Alternate Water Reuse,* New Society Publishers, Gabriola Island, BC, 2007

Axel Lohrer: *Basics Designing with Water,* Birkhäuser, Basel 2008

Celeste Allen Novak, Eddie Van Geisen, Kathy M. Debusk: *Designing Rainwater Harvesting Systems. Integrating Rainwater into Building Systems,* Wiley, New York 2014

Thomas Schröpfer: *Dense + Green. Innovative Building Types for Sustainable Urban Architecture,* Birkhäuser, Basel 2016

Frank R. Spellman: *Handbook of Water and Wastewater Treatment Plant Operations,* 2nd ed., CRC Press, Boca Raton, FL, 2008

Ruth F. Weiner, Robin A. Matthews: *Environmental Engineering,* 4th ed., Butterworth-Heinemann, Amsterdam/London 2003

Bridget Woods-Ballard et al.: *The SUDS Manual,* CIRIA, London 2007

ELECTRO-PLANNING

Bert Bielefeld: *Planning Architecture*, Birkhäuser, Basel 2016

Dirk Bohne: *Technischer Ausbau von Gebäuden*, Springer Vieweg, Wiesbaden 2014

Wolfgang Burmeister, André Croissant, and Matthias Kraner: *Das Baustellenhandbuch der Elektroinstallation*, Forum, Mering 2011

Andrea Deplazes: *Constructing Architecture*, Birkhäuser, 3rd expanded edition, Basel 2013

Georg Giebeler: *Refurbishment Manual*, Birkhäuser, Basel 2009

Gerhard Hausladen: *Interiors Construction Manual*, Birkhäuser, Basel 2010

Ismail Kasikci: *Elektrotechnik für Architekten, Bauingenieure und Gebäudetechniker. Grundlagen und Anwendung in der Gebäude-planung*, Springer Vieweg, Wiesbaden 2013

Jörn Krimmling (ed.), Uwe Deutschmann, André Preuß, and Eberhard Renner: *Atlas Gebäudetechnik. Grundlagen, Konstruktionen, Details,* 2. Auflage, Rudolf Müller, Cologne 2014

Thomas Laasch and Erhard Laasch: *Haustechnik. Grundlagen-Planung-Ausführung*, 13. Auflage, Springer Vieweg, Wiesbaden 2015

RWE: *Bau-Handbuch*, 15. Ausgabe, EW Medien und Kongresse, Essen 2014

LIGHTING DESIGN

Andreas Achilles, Diane Navratil: *Basics Glass Construction,* Birkhäuser Verlag, Basel 2008

Bert Bielefeld (ed.): Planning Architecture: *Dimensions and Typologies,* Birkhäuser Verlag, Basel 2016

Mohamed Boubekri: *Daylighting Design: Planning Strategies and Best Practice Solutions,* Birkhäuser Verlag, Basel 2014

Ulrike Brandi Licht: *Detail Practice: Lighting Design: Principles, Implementation, Case Studies,* Edition DETAIL, München 2006

Ulrike Brandi: *Light for Cities: Lighting Design for Urban Spaces. A Handbook,* Birkhäuser Verlag, Basel 2006

Ulrike Brandi, Christoph Geissmar-Brandi: *Lightbook: The Practice of Lighting Design,* Birkhäuser Verlag, Basel 2001

Hans-Georg Buschendorf (ed.): *Lexikon Licht- und Beleuchtungstechnik,* Verlag Technik, Berlin 1989

Andrea Deplazes (ed.): *Constructing Architecture,* 3rd edition, Birkhäuser Verlag, Basel 2013

Jill Entwistle: *Detail in Contemporary Lighting Design,* Laurence King Publishing, London 2012

Doris Haas-Arndt, Fred Ranft: *Tageslichttechnik in Gebäuden,* Hüthig Jehle Rehm, Heidelberg 2007

Gerhard Hausladen, Petra Liedl, Michael de Saldanha: *Building to Suit the Climate.* A Handbook, Birkhäuser Verlag, Basel 2012

Manfred Hegger e.a.: Aktivhaus. *The Reference Work,* Birkhäuser Verlag, Basel 2016

Roland Krippner, Florian Musso: *Basics Facade Apertures,* Birkhäuser Verlag, Basel 2007

Vincent Laganier, Jasmine van der Pol (eds.): *Light and Emotions. Exploring Lighting Cultures,* Birkhäuser Verlag, Basel 2011

Wolfram Pistohl, Christian Rechenauer, Birgit Scheuerer: *Handbuch der Gebäudetechnik,* Band 2: *Heizung | Lüftung | Beleuchtung | Energiesparen,* 8. Auflage, Werner Verlag, Cologne 2013

Alexander Reichel, Kerstin Schultz (eds.): *Scale: Open | Close. Windows, Doors, Gates, Loggias, Filters,* Birkhäuser Verlag, Basel 2009

Hans Rudolf Ris: *Beleuchtungstechnik für Praktiker,* VDE, Berlin 2015

Wolfgang M. Willems (ed.): *Lehrbuch der Bauphysik: Schall – Wärme – Feuchte – Licht – Brand – Klima,* 7. Auflage, Springer Vieweg, Wiesbaden 2013

Sage Russell: *The Architecture Of Light: A textbook of procedures and practices for the Architect, Interior Designer and Lighting Designer,* 2nd edition, Conceptnine 2012

Peter Tregenza, David Loe: *The Design of Lighting,* 2 edition, Routledge, London 2013

Peter Wotschke: *Basics Electro-Planning,* Birkhäuser Verlag, Basel 2017

Standards and Guidelines

ROOM CONDITIONING

DIN 1946	"Ventilation and air conditioning", Part 2 "Technical health requirements (VDI ventilation rules)", 1994-01 (withdrawn)
DIN EN 12831	"Heating systems in buildings – Method for calculation of the design heat load", Supp.1 "National Annex", 2008-07 with Corrigendum 2010-11
DIN EN 15251	"Indoor environmental input parameters for design and assessment of energy performance of buildings addressing indoor air quality, thermal environment, lighting and acoustics", 2012-12
DIN EN ISO 7730	"Ergonomics of the thermal environment – Analytical determination and interpretation of thermal comfort using calculation of the PMV and PPD indices and local thermal comfort criteria (ISO 7730:2005)", 2006-05 with Corrigendum 2007-06
DIN V 18599	"Energy efficiency of buildings – Calculation of the net, final and primary energy demand for heating, cooling, ventilation, domestic hot water and lighting", Part 1 "General balancing procedures, terms and definitions, zoning and evaluation of energy sources", 2011-12 with Corrigendum 2012-05
DIN EN 13779	"Ventilating non-residential buildings: the general conditions and requirements for ventilation and air-conditioning systems", 2007-09
VDI 2078	"The calculation of thermal loads and room temperatures (design of cooling loads and annual simulation)" 2015-06
VDI 2050 Blatt 1	"The challenges facing technical centers: the technical foundations for planning and execution" 2013-11

WATER CYCLES

EN 752	Drain and sewer systems outside buildings
EN 805	Water supply – Requirements for systems and components outside buildings
EN 806-2	Specifications for installations inside buildings conveying water for human consumption
EN 1717	Protection against pollution of potable water in water installations and general requirements of devices to prevent pollution by backflow
EN 12056	Gravity drainage systems inside buildings
EN 12255	Wastewater treatment plants, Part 5: Wastewater treatment plants. Lagooning process

ELECTRO-PLANNING

In order to minimize technical risks and to protect all parties involved in the handling of electrical components, in most countries electrical installations are standardized by extensive planning rules. While standards were mainly developed on a national level decades ago, initiatives are now being implemented centrally through the International Electrotechnical Commission (IEC) and subsequently transferred from regional to national standardization.

It is only if the IEC is not interested in processing a standard or if there is a time restriction that a draft design is processed regionally. If necessary, specific requirements of the building and plant operator (such as factory regulations) and the responsible distribution system operator (VNB) must also be observed and adhered to in the planning and construction of buildings.

An overview of the most important standards and standardization institutions is listed below in Tab. 10.

Tab. 10: Overview of standards and standardization institutions

Regional	America	Europe	Australasia	Asia	Africa
	PAS	CENELEC			
National	USA: ANSI	D: DIN VDE	AUS: SA	CN: SAC	SA: SABS
	CA: SCC	I: CEI	NZ: SNZ	IND: BIS	
	BR: COBEI	F: UTE	...	J: JISC	
	...	GB: BS		...	
		...			

ANSI	American National Standards Institute	JISC	Japanese Industrial Standards Committee
BIS	Bureau of Indian Standards		
BS	British Standards	PAS	Pacific Area Standards
CEI	Comitato Elettrotecnico Italiano	SA	Standards Australia
CENELEC	European Committee for Electrotechnical Standardization (fr: Comité Européen de Normalisation Electrotechnique)	SABS	South African Bureau of Standards
		SAC	Standardization Administration of China
COBEI	Comitê Brasileiro de Eletricidade, Eletrônica, Iluminação e Telecomunicações	SCC	Standards Council of Canada
		SNZ	Standards New Zealand
DIN VDE	Deutsche Industrie Norm Verband deutscher Elektrotechniker	UTE	Union Technique de l'Electricité et de la Communication
EN	European Norm		
IEC	International Electrotechnical Commission		

LIGHTING DESIGN

European Standards

BS EN 1838 "Emergency lighting"

BS EN 12464-1:2011-08 Title: "Light and lighting – Lighting of work places" – Part 1: Indoor work places; German Version EN 12464-1:2011

BS EN 12464-2:2014-05 Title: "Light and lighting – Lighting of work places" – Part 2: Outdoor work places; German version EN 12464-2:2014

BS EN 12665 "Light and lighting – Basic terms and criteria for specifying lighting requirements"

BS EN 13032 "Light and lighting – Measurement and presentation of photometric data of lamps and luminaires"

BS EN 13201 "Road lighting"

BS EN 60529:2014-09 "Degrees of protection provided by enclosures" (IP Code) (IEC 60529:1989 + A1:1999 + A2:2013); German version EN 60529:1991 + A1:2000 + A2:2013

BS EN 60598-1:2015-10; VDE 0711-1:2015-10; "Luminaires" – Part 1: General requirements and tests (IEC 60598-1:2014, modified); German version EN 60598-1:2015

German Standards

DIN 5034 "Daylight in interiors"

DIN 5035 "Artificial lighting"

Guidelines

VDI 6011 "Lighting technology – Optimisation of daylight use and artificial lighting – Fundamentals and basic requirements"

ASR A3.4 Lighting

Picture credits

ROOM CONDITIONING
Drawings
Barbara Raaff, Oliver Klein

WATER CYCLES
Photographs
All photographs by Doris Haas-Arndt

Drawings
Jenny Pottins
Simon Kassner
Helen Weber
Sebastian Bagsik
Indira Schädlich

ELECTRO-PLANNING
Figs. 9, 11, 12: Bert Bielefeld: Planning Architecture, Birkhauser, Basel 2016
Fig. 33: Busch-Jager Elektro, GmbH: Produktkatalog, Ludenscheid 2016
All other illustrations: the author

LIGHTING DESIGN
Fig. 6, left: Feans, flickr.com
Fig. 7, left: Roman Pfeiffer, flickr.com
Fig. 17: Sebastian Terfloth, User: Sese_Ingolstadt – Eigenes Werk, licensed by CC-SA-3.0 via Wikimedia Commons – https://commons.wikimedia.org/wiki/File:Lounge_ICE_3.jpg
Fig. 19, right, User Ozguy89, licensed by GNU Free Documentation License, transferred from en.wikipedia to Commons by User: Wdwd using CommonsHelper, – https://commons.wikimedia.org/wiki/File:150_Watt_Metal_Halide.jpg
Fig. 25, centre: Walter Schärer, flickr.com, processed
Fig. 33, left: C MB 166, flickr.com
Fig. 43, right: David Hollnack
The author thanks Bogdan Napieralski for helping with the preparation of the photographs for Figs. 4, centre; 22, right; 27; 28; 30 left+right

The Authors

ROOM CONDITIONING

Oliver Klein, Dipl.-Ing., is a freelance architect, energy consultant and energy efficiency expert (dena). He is also very involved in research and theory, and specializes in building technology as an integral aspect of energy-saving architecture.

Jörg Schlenger, Dr. Ing., is a senior project partner and team leader specializing in energy efficiency and sustainability consultancy at Drees & Sommer Advanced Building Technologies, as well as in energy design and management in Frankfurt am Main.

WATER CYCLES

Prof. Dr.-Ing. Doris Haas-Arndt, professor at the Fachhochschule des Mittelstands, Pulheim, specializes in the fields of energy-saving construction, building and environmental technology, building restoration and building construction.

ELECTRO-PLANNING

Prof. Dr. (ETH) Peter Wotschke teaches at the Berlin School of Economics and Law and is the Chairman of the Management Board of BMC Baumanagement & Controlling AG Berlin.

LIGHTING DESIGN

Dipl.-Ing. Architect Roman Skowranek is working as an architect in Dortmund.

Basics Timber Construction
Ludwig Steiger
ISBN 978-3-7643-8102-8

Available as a compendium:
Basics Building
Construction
Bert Bielefeld (ed.)
ISBN 978-3-0356-0372-9

Professional Practice
Basics Budgeting
Bert Bielefeld,
Roland Schneider
ISBN 978-3-03821-532-5

Basics Project Planning
Hartmut Klein
ISBN 978-3-7643-8469-2

Basics Site Management
Lars-Phillip Rusch
ISBN 978-3-7643-8104-2

Basics Tendering
Tim Brandt,
Sebastian Franssen
ISBN 978-3-7643-8110-3

Basics Time Management
Bert Bielefeld
ISBN 978-3-7643-8873-7

Available as a compendium:
Basics Project Management
Architecture
Bert Bielefeld (ed.)
ISBN 978-3-03821-462-5

Urbanism
Basics Urban Analysis
Gerrit Schwalbach
ISBN 978-3-7643-8938-3

Basics Urban Building Blocks
Thorsten Bürklin,
Michael Peterek
ISBN 978-3-7643-8460-9

Building Services/
Building Physics
Basics Electro-Planning
Peter Wotschke
ISBN 978-3-0356-0932-5

Basics Lighting Design
Roman Skowranek
ISBN 978-3-0356-0930-1

Basics Room Conditioning
Oliver Klein, Jörg Schlenger
ISBN 978-3-7643-8664-1

Basics Water Cycles
Doris Haas-Arndt
ISBN 978-3-7643-8854-6

Landscape Architecture
Basics Designing with Plants
Regine Ellen Wöhrle,
Hans-Jörg Wöhrle
ISBN 978-3-7643-8659-7

Basics Designing with Water
Axel Lohrer, Cornelia Bott
ISBN 978-3-7643-8662-7

Available at your bookshop or at
www.birkhauser.com

Series editor: Bert Bielefeld
Concept: Bert Bielefeld, Annette Gref
Project management: Silke Martini, Lisa Schulze
Production: Heike Strempel
Layout and cover design: Andreas Hidber
Typesetting: Sven Schrape
Translation from German into English:
Foreword: Anna Roos
Basics Room Conditioning: Raymond D. Peat
Basics Water Cycles: Raymond D. Peat
Basics Electro-Planning: Anna Roos
Basics Lighting Design: Robin Benson

Library of Congress Cataloging-in-Publication data
A CIP catalog record for this book has been applied for at the Library of Congress.

Bibliographic information published by the German National Library
The German National Library lists this publication in the Deutsche Nationalbibliografie; detailed bibliographic data are available on the Internet at http://dnb.dnb.de.

This publication is also available in a German language edition (ISBN 978-3-0356-0927-1).

© 2017 Birkhäuser Verlag GmbH, Basel
P.O. Box 44, 4009 Basel, Switzerland
Part of Walter de Gruyter GmbH, Berlin/Boston

Printed on acid-free paper produced from chlorine-free pulp. TCF ∞

Printed in Germany

ISBN 978-3-0356-0928-8

9 8 7 6 5 4 3 2 1

www.birkhauser.com